Conrad's Rebels
The Psychology of Revolution in the Novels from *Nostromo* to *Victory*

Studies in Modern Literature, No. 42

A. Walton Litz, General Series Editor
Professor of English
Princeton University

Thomas C. Moser
Consulting Editor for Titles on Joseph Conrad
Professor of English
Stanford University

Daniel Mark Fogel
Consulting Editor for Titles on Henry James
Professor of English
Louisiana State University
Editor, The Henry James Review

Other Titles in This Series

No. 39	*Conrad's Endings: A Study of the Five Major Novels*	Arnold E. Davidson
No. 40	*Theories of Action in Conrad*	Francis A. Hubbard
No. 41	*The Ludic Imagination: A Reading of Joseph Conrad*	Kenneth Simons
No. 43	*Conrad's Heroism: A Paradise Lost*	Michael P. Jones
No. 46	*The Making of* Romance	Raymond Brebach
No. 47	*The* Nouvelle *of Henry James in Theory and Practice*	Lauren T. Cowdery
No. 48	*Women of Grace: James's Plays and the Comedy of Manners*	Susan Carlson
No. 49	*Henry James and the Problem of Audience: An International Act*	Anne T. Margolis

Conrad's Rebels
The Psychology of Revolution in the Novels from *Nostromo* to *Victory*

by
Helen Funk Rieselbach
Assistant Professor, Honors Division
Indiana University
Bloomington, Indiana

UMI RESEARCH PRESS
Ann Arbor, Michigan

Copyright © 1985, 1980
Helen Funk Rieselbach
All rights reserved

Produced and distributed by
UMI Research Press
an imprint of
University Microfilms International
A Xerox Information Resources Company
Ann Arbor, Michigan 48106

Library of Congress Cataloging in Publication Data

Rieselbach, Helen Funk, 1935-
Conrad's rebels.

(Studies in modern literature ; no. 42)
Revision of thesis (Ph.D.)—Indiana University, 1980.
Bibliography: p.
Includes index.
1. Conrad, Joseph, 1857-1924—Characters—
Revolutionists. 2. Conrad, Joseph, 1857-1924—
Knowledge—Psychology. 3. Conrad, Joseph, 1857-1924—
Political and social views. 4. Revolutionists in
literature. 5. Revolutions in literature.
6. Psychology in literature. I. Title. II. Series.

PR6005.04Z7875   1984   823'.912   84-23917
ISBN 0-8357-1600-7 (alk. paper)

To my mother

Contents

Acknowledgements *ix*

1 Introduction *1*

2 *Nostromo* *9*

3 *The Secret Agent* *37*

4 *Under Western Eyes* *59*

5 *Chance* *87*

6 *Victory* *113*

Notes *135*

Bibliography *145*

Index *151*

Acknowledgments

I owe a tremendous debt of gratitude to Mary Burgan, without whose kind and generous encouragement this study might never have been completed. I wish also to thank Breon Mitchell, James Naremore, Lee Sterrenburg, and Thomas Moser, all of whom made helpful comments on the manuscript.

I am grateful to Albert Guerard, with whom I first read Conrad as an undergraduate at Radcliffe College, and to Alan Hollingsworth and Robert G. Kelly, in whose stimulating graduate seminars many of these ideas were germinated.

My deepest gratitude, however, belongs to my husband. His patience and faith in this project were unwavering, and he buoyed me up many times when I was about to sink under its weight. Lastly, I thank my children, Erik, Kurt, Alice, and Karen, for their acute critical comments and for being such good company.

1
Introduction

The novels *Nostromo*, *The Secret Agent*, *Under Western Eyes*, *Chance*, and *Victory*, published in the years between 1904 and 1915, have been described as constituting Joseph Conrad's "magic mountain," his vision of the breakdown of Western civilization.[1] Conrad's earlier works, although undeniably pessimistic in their emphasis on human beings' capacity for self-deception and betrayal, still predicated a code of behavior that provided a standard by which men and women could measure their own and others' actions. When, in *Lord Jim*, the hero fails his test, he knows he has violated a clear moral imperative—the seaman's duty to remain at his post—at the same time that he has betrayed himself. Beginning with *Nostromo*, however, these external standards of behavior seem to have much less force, or to contain ambiguities, or to cease to exist altogether. Nostromo, in stealing the silver, betrays himself (like Jim), but what else can he be said to have betrayed? The silver itself is merely a symbol of the corruption that pervades the social fabric. In *Under Western Eyes*, Razumov must choose between betraying a revolutionary movement in which he does not believe and betraying a social order he sees as autocratic and repressive. Unable to put his faith in any creed (the novel also condemns Western liberalism as Rousseauean sentimentality), Razumov is fated to remain perpetually outcast: "I am independent—and therefore perdition is my lot," he cries near the end of the book. Razumov's *"non serviam!"* is seen, in the novel's terms, as the only possible rational response to the idiocies of political ideology.

Caught between the demands of society and the emotional claims of family, neither Razumov nor Nostromo can decide where duty lies. In the third of Conrad's "political" novels, *The Secret Agent*, however, no social *or* family loyalties exert much influence on the novel's central figure, Verloc. Verloc is a complete opportunist, devoted only to his own well-being; ideological or humanitarian considerations are not features of his moral landscape. This is true not only of Verloc, but also of most of the subsidiary characters. The world of *The Secret Agent* is a world almost totally without morality, where ethical standards and personal loyalties are absent.

Although *Nostromo* and *Under Western Eyes* deal with revolutionaries (of quite different sorts), and *The Secret Agent* with anarchists (ludicrously ineffectual), their main concerns are with the breakdown of human relationships—sexual and familial—rather than with a threatened social order. Conrad evinces an extreme skepticism about the possibilities of political action—as the child of failed revolutionaries, he had reason to know first-hand the unforeseen consequences of that action—and he seems never to have entertained the belief that revolution could bring about a real amelioration of the human condition. Politics are essentially a backdrop in these novels, as we see more clearly when we look at the two novels that followed: *Chance* and *Victory*. These novels detail attempts to leave the social world behind entirely—in life aboard ship or on an isolated island—but the attempts to change one's personal fate by avoiding the contagion of society are doomed as surely as were the efforts to change society itself. In the politics of personal relationships, as in the politics of revolution, it becomes increasingly clear that it is impossible to understand others' motives or to predict the outcome of one's own actions, and that to commit oneself to another is to risk death. The progressive narrowing of focus these novels exhibit, moving from *Nostromo*, with its proliferation of characters and incidents, to *Victory*, with its almost claustrophobic sense of isolation, serves to emphasize Conrad's growing conviction of the limited possibilities of human actions and of the increasing difficulties of human relationships.

Relationships between friends, lovers, parents and children are all doomed to failure, and—in these five novels—that failure is often made inevitable by the protagonists' commitments to ideologies of one sort or another. Ideologues tend to be blind to the real feelings and needs of others and to misinterpret their own motives and emotions. These ideologues include, in *Nostromo*, the Christian imperialist Holroyd; Charles Gould, who adopts his surrogate father Holroyd's faith as a justification for his own will to power (which he has inherited from his biological father); old Viola the garibaldino; the Nostromo of the last part of the novel, who has adopted the politics of *his* surrogate father, Viola; the elitist political philosopher, Avellanos, whose daughter Antonia is also committed to his cause; and Avellanos's brother-in-law, the fanatical priest Corbelan. These true believers are contrasted with the faithless skeptics, Decoud, Monygham, and the prelapsarian Nostromo, who are clear-sighted about their own and others' motives, but whose attempts at action end in defeat.

In *The Secret Agent*, Stevie is caught between conflicting ideologies: the Candide-like optimism his sister Winnie tries to inculcate, and the sense of pervasive social injustice he has picked up from Verloc's cronies. Hopelessly confused, the simple-minded Stevie vacillates, we are told, between immoderate compassion and pitiless rage: a parody, for Conrad, of the revolutionary. *Under Western Eyes* also explores ideological confusion as Razumov, who wants only to avoid all political controversy, is caught between the Czarist regime, represented by his natural father, Prince K., and the revolutionaries, represented by another surrogate father, Peter Ivanovitch.

All these novels emphasize the fact that devotion to an ideology deforms by impairing the ability to form close personal relationships; they also make clear that ideology is most often inherited. It is parents who are ultimately responsible for their children's psychic wounds. (Although there are virtually no real children in evidence in Conrad's works, the adult protagonists are emphatically their parents' children.) In *Chance*, for instance, Mrs. Fyne and her brother, Roderick Anthony, each embody different aspects of their father's personality: Anthony, his romanticism (although in the father's case this romantic idealism was only a pose), and Mrs. Fyne, his emotional coldness (like her father, too, she is a writer). *Victory* offers perhaps the most thorough anatomization of parental influence. Here, Axel Heyst tries consciously to live according to his father's precepts ("Look on—make no sound," his father has counseled), whereas Anthony and his sister are not consciously aware that they display their father's traits.

In the case of Heyst, Anthony, and Mrs. Fyne, fatherly influence reaches out from the grave; Charles Gould's father also exerts his influence posthumously. There are very few living fathers (especially of sons) in these novels, and those few exert a generally baleful effect. Razumov's father not only refuses to acknowledge his son, he causes Razumov's destruction when he agrees that Razumov be inducted as police spy, just as Verloc, in *The Secret Agent*, destroys his surrogate son, Stevie. Fathers of daughters are sexually possessive and murderously jealous of potential suitors, as in the cases of Viola and deBarral, or themselves need to be taken care of like children: Avellanos, Lena's father, and again Viola.

If fathers, dead or alive, are inevitably culpable, mothers are also found wanting. Many mothers have "abandoned" their children by dying: motherless characters include Charles Gould and his wife Emilia, Nostromo, Antonia, the Viola girls (in the last part of *Nostromo*), Razumov, Anthony, Mrs. Fyne, Flora, Heyst, and Lena.[2] Surrogate mothers Signora Viola and Winnie Verloc fail their "sons": the former when her deathbed curse precipitates Nostromo's identity crisis and eventual self-destruction; the latter when her misreading of Verloc's character leads to Stevie's sacrifice at his "father's" hands.

But Signora Viola and Winnie are only mother figures to male children; with the exception of Mrs. Haldin, whose son is already dead when we meet her, all the "real" mothers in these novels are mothers of daughters: Mrs. Haldin's living child is a daughter; Signora Viola's biological children are daughters, as are Mrs. Fyne's children. Although Winnie Verloc's aged mother is also the mother of a son, Stevie, it is Winnie who is head of the household and who acts as Stevie's protector. Like the fathers mentioned above, the old lady has declined into a child-like state, and although Winnie and her mother are totally devoted to each other, each totally misunderstands the other's motives. Mother-daughter relationships are as flawed as other parent-child relations. Mrs. Haldin torments her daughter with her distrust, while Mrs. Fyne is emotionally disengaged from her daughters. She reminds Marlow of a governess.

But if relations between parents and children are problematic, love relationships betwen adult men and women are fraught with danger. Women are seen as threatening presences or as predestined victims; sometimes, as in the case of Natalia Haldin, they are both. The heroes, on the other hand, often seem cases of arrested development. (For Stevie, this is literally true.) Nostromo is perhaps the most striking example of the child-like hero, innocent and naive about the ways of the world in spite of his great reputation, but Razumov, Anthony, and Heyst also seem immature, sexually diffident and guileless as preadolescents. With the exception of Stevie, all these heroes are motherless, and all have had difficult relationships with their fathers. Products of loveless childhoods, they cannot enter into adult sexual relationships.

Furthermore, as Bernard Meyer has noted, traditional sex roles are often reversed in these novels.[3] The heroes are often passive and easily intimidated by women. Even the great leader of men, Nostromo, is shy with women: he lacks the courage to declare openly his preference for Giselle, and he allows his "native" sweetheart symbolically to unman him when she cuts the silver buttons from his coat. (At one point, he confides to Decoud that he only courts women because his public expects it!) Decoud also is in awe of his beloved Antonia, and just before he dies has a vision of her as fearsome and threatening. In *The Secret Agent*, the indolent and obtuse Verloc is not merely threatened by his wife; he is actually murdered. In *Under Western Eyes* the male revolutionaries are mostly full of idle talk, while the women we see (Tekla and Sophia Antonovna) are ruthlessly committed to action. In fact, Sophia Antonovna denounces men as over-delicate—a view further amplified in *Chance*, where Marlow argues that men are inhibited by their code of honor from being as brutally unscrupulous as women. (The misogynistic Marlowe also frequently invokes the old saw that, although women may appear powerless, they really—in some mysterious way—have the upper hand.)

In *Chance*, it is Flora who initiates sexual contact (as Lena does in *Victory*), thus resolving the rather ridiculous misunderstanding on which the plot hinges. Other sexually dominant women in *Chance* are Mrs. Fyne and Flora's terrifying governess. But Lena is perhaps the most striking example of sexual role reversal, as she physically bests the armed and "desperate" Ricardo, and makes an active effort to save Heyst's life, while he remains immobilized by self-doubt. Nevertheless, Lena is presented somewhat ambiguously: Heyst cannot bring himself to trust her completely, and there is a suggestion that like Ricardo, whom she so easily captivates, she is an outlaw. Even the most "idealized" heroine is potentially threatening.

But if women constitute a threat to men, they are also, paradoxically, men's victims. It is the heroines' helplessness—or seeming helplessness—that makes them attractive. This is true not only of Flora and Lena, but also of Miss Haldin, Winnie, and even Mrs. Gould, who is a penniless orphan at the time of her marriage. This ambivalence is reflected also in Conrad's treatment of feminism, used in *Under Western Eyes* as a symbol of revolutionary humbug and hypocrisy, and in *Chance* as emblematic of general wrong-headedness. Yet the novels, especially *Chance* and *Victory*, make clear that women do have legitimate social grievances, and Conrad himself supported the movement for women's suffrage.[4]

Women are not the only victims in these novels, of course. From *Nostromo* to *Victory*, there is a growing sense that everyone is a potential victim—even of another's careless word. In fact, anyone can intrude on one's life merely by commenting on it! Razumov, Anthony, and Heyst are helpless victims of others' misapprehensions of their motives and characters, as are Verloc (in his relations with Vladimir as well as with Winnie), and Nostromo. (Unlike the others, Nostromo determines to capitalize—in both senses of the word—on misapprehension.) Even a careless word can wreak disaster: Winnie unwittingly suggests Stevie to Verloc's purpose, and Verloc brings about his own murder by saying precisely the wrong thing. In *Under Western Eyes*, the revolutionary students' stated belief in Razumov's good character causes his downfall—and Haldin's. In *Chance*, Anthony's overreaction to Fyne's charge that he is "tak[ing] advantage of a girl's distress" leads to a great deal of unnecessary suffering, and Heyst's intense, and somewhat irrational, dismay at the news he is an object of gossip paralyzes him, and ultimately brings about the wholesale carnage that ends *Victory*.

But it is not only the spoken word that can destroy. The written word also can exert pernicious influence. Journalistic propaganda is condemned in *Nostromo*, where Decoud, like Heyst (in his brief career as coal company manager), must preach a gospel in which he does not believe.[5] Avellanos's political history of Costaguana, *Fifty Years of Misrule*, provides the philosophic justification for revolution, but ends up being used for wadding for the blancos' rifles. Both Mrs. Fyne's and Peter Ivanovitch's writings on feminism are seen as dangerous nonsense, as is Heyst's father's nihilistic philosphy, which has hopelessly distorted his son's life, just as Charles Gould's father's letters have warped Charles. Writings that do not have an actively evil influence may have no influence at all, like Ossipon's political pamphlets; or may be destined to go forever unread, like Michaelis's endless autobiography, which is merely a form of self-communication; or may be written to deceive the world about the writer's true character, as in the case of Carleon Anthony. In any case, writers in these novels—and each novel features at least one—are invariably self-deluded and egotistical.

In *Nostromo* and *The Secret Agent*, talkers and actors are generally opposed. In the former novel, for example, strong, silent men of action like Nostromo and Charles Gould are set against the skeptical onlookers, Decoud and Monygham, and against impotent theorists like Avellanos, while in *The Secret Agent*, the Assistant Commissioner and the Professor embody activity, in contrast to the general windy lassitude of the anarchists. Beginning with *Under Western Eyes*, however, the central characters exhibit a tendency towards silence *and* inactivity: Razumov, Anthony, and Heyst are all silent men who attempt to withdraw from the world to avoid the demands of others. Each is moved to action at the behest of a human being in need (even Razumov originally intends to aid Haldin's escape), and each discovers that action has unintended consequences. On the other hand, passivity can also prove dangerous, even fatal, as Decoud and Heyst both discover.

Although many of the novels' characters seek silence and solitude, they are often intensely concerned with others' *opinions*. From the simple man of action, Nostromo, to the involuted and withdrawn Heyst, the heroes (and heroines, in the cases of Flora and Lena) are very aware of their reputations. In *Nostromo*, Dr. Monygham, who cannot bear to be well thought of because of his strong sense of self-condemnation, is a mirror image of Nostromo, who cannot bear the lack of admiration: both are hypersensitive to opinion. Others concerned with reputation include Charles Gould (whose vanity is parodied in various subsidiary characters like General Barrios, just as Heyst's exaggerated self-consciousness is parodied in Jones, Ricardo, and Schomberg); Verloc, Vladimir, and the professor in *The Secret Agent*; Razumov, Peter Ivanovitch, and Nikita in *Under Western Eyes*; and virtually all the characters in *Chance* and *Victory*.

This concern for reputation sometimes seems to imply that we exist *only* as others define us: Lena asserts that if Heyst were to cease to think of her she would cease to exist, and Nostromo and Decoud both feel they have become insubstantial and ghostly presences when they are forced to remain solitary. Heyst and Marlow are even tempted to reassess their own characters to accord with other people's bad opinion; both men begin to doubt themselves, and to suspect that they may, in truth, be as base as others judge them! Interestingly, the narrative method of *Chance* reenacts the activity so strongly condemned in that novel and in *Victory*: gossip.

In the other novels as well, form is intimately related to subject, and I have tried to focus on each work's structure to underscore this relationship. In *Nostromo*, for example, the deliberately confused chronology presents us with the fall of the Ribiera government before we see its establishment—effectively jaundicing our view from the beginning—and shows us the strains in the Goulds' marriage before we see the idealism apparent in their courtship. Nostromo and Heyst are initially presented through others' eyes: we have their reputation before their reality. In *The Secret Agent*, on the other hand, we first see Verloc as he sees himself, as a much put upon husband and employee, and as a faithful protector of the status quo: only later do we apprehend the sordid reality of his life. The first part of *Under Western Eyes* presents Razumov and his dilemma directly, while the rest of the novel shows events as filtered through the consciousness of the narrator, the teacher of languages; there is a considerable stylistic contrast between the two parts, but the switch to an obtuse narrator serves to emphasize—and to generalize—the theme of misunderstanding, which is a central concern.

A narrator, of course, is a useful distancing device, one Conrad often employs, and in the novels that follow *Lord Jim* the reader is always kept at a carefully controlled distance from the action. No longer are we invited to enter into the hero's dilemma, to share the hero's suffering, or to make the hero's choices. The Marlow who narrates *Chance* is not intimately involved with the protagonists of the tale as he is in *Heart of Darkness* or *Lord Jim*. *Chance* is a prolonged speculation on the part of Marlow and the shadowy primary narrator on the meaning of events in which they have no personal stake, and their conjectures often seem merely an exercise in idle curiosity.

Lord Jim explores the conflict between an ideal conception of oneself and the reality of one's actions, which often do not correspond to that ideal. In that novel, Stein recommends that one should try to live one's dream, to enact the ideal. The novels that follow show the results of such attempts. While each of these novels attempts to formulate a possible escape from the general human condition as the characters seek a way "to be," as Stein puts it, each details a more crushing failure than the last. Thus, at the conclusion of *Nostromo*, Mrs. Gould survives as a positive moral force: she has understanding, even though she has no power. *The Secret Agent* ends with the destruction of the Verloc family—a purposeless destruction. No improvement is brought about in society at large; even the Assistant Commissioner does not entirely achieve his aim. Yet the state itself, in all its inefficiency, survives as a positive force, capable of withstanding the idiocies of anarchists, foreign subversives, and even of its own bureaucrats and policemen! In *Under Western Eyes*, Razumov finally escapes the nightmare world in which he is plunged. He casts off the hated demands of the state and of human society, retiring to a hermit-like existence, where his deafness serves as a symbol of his total disengagement. His freedom is won, however, at the cost of terrible physical suffering for himself and of mental anguish for Natalia. In *Chance*, Marlow's emphasis on the catastrophic results of attempted samaritanism, and on the impenetrability of others' motives, leads to the conclusion that attempts at amelioration are doomed on the personal level, just as on the political. Although the misunderstanding between Anthony and Flora is finally resolved, their happiness is brief; Flora is soon widowed. At the end of the novel we are promised another wedding, but what we are left with is the ashy taste of Marlow's cynicism. *Victory* offers the bleakest vision of all. Not only are all the central characters dead by the end of the book, murdered or suicides, Lena's "victory" is an illusion. She has not won Heyst's love—or even his trust. While, in *Chance*, it is the presence of Flora's father that inhibits the lovers and impedes the resolution of their misunderstanding, in *Victory*, Heyst's dead father's influence prevents Heyst from loving Lena. Even before the arrival of the outside world in the persons of the villains, Heyst and Lena are unable to establish the Eden they have envisioned; even in a world of two there is room for misinterpretation and mistrust. In these novels, Conrad's speculations on the possibilities of human action and of commitment to others move in ever narrowing circles—from politics, to the influence of the family, to sexual love—and the vision grows ever darker: "The sedge has withered from the Lake/ And no birds sing!"

2

Nostromo

> "...to will is to stir up paradoxes."
> —Albert Camus

As Albert Guerard has noted, the reader of *Nostromo* is like Captain Mitchell's captive listener, "stunned and as it were annihilated mentally by a sudden surfeit of sights, sounds, names, facts, and complicated information imperfectly apprehended...."[1] The difficulties the novel presents—with its deliberately confused chronology, its immense cast of characters, and its incredible wealth of detail—mirror one of the novel's central concerns: the unpredictable outcome of human action. In *Nostromo*, virtually every action has unexpected or ambiguous results, and the actors, although they believe they are making history, are in reality history's slaves. As Conrad explained, in a letter to Ernst Bendz: "Silver is the pivot of the moral and material events, affecting the lives of everybody in the tale."[2]

The novel is, in fact, a strong condemnation of imperialism and a cautionary tale on the corrupting effect of wealth; but perhaps the deepest impression the novel leaves is of the futility of political action. This is partly a result of the confused chronology, since, as Jocelyn Baines remarks, "The elimination of progression from one event to another...has the effect of implying that nothing is ever achieved."[3] Because political action is seen as futile, a game for the self-interested or the self-deluded, and because most of the great events of the Sulacan revolution occur off stage, finally the "political" story seems a mere backdrop for the stories of failed human relationships.

We see very little action at first hand. There is a sense of immediacy only at the end of the novel, in the story of Nostromo's love for Giselle; most of the novel is insistently retrospective. Conrad is interested here in the *results* of action. Thus we see the failed conclusions of undertakings before we see their hopeful inceptions (we have Ribiera's fall before his rise, and the strains in the Goulds' marriage before the idealism of their engagement), or we have juxtaposed contrary interpretations of the same event (as Mitchell's account of the benefits the mine has brought is juxtaposed with Monygham's denunciation of its evil influence).⁴ Indeed, *all* action seems doomed to failure here. The collapse of the Ribiera government in a sense stands for the inevitable failure of all political institutions in Costaguana; the rift between the Goulds suggests the impossibility of enduring commitments between men and women: "love was only a short moment of forgetfulness, an short intoxication, whose delight one remembered with a sense of sadness, as if it had been a deep grief lived through," Mrs. Gould concludes at the end of the novel.⁵

The novel details the failure of other human relationships. Nostromo fails his surrogate parents, Giogio and Teresa Viola, by refusing to adopt Giorgio's political precepts (although when he finally does so he is destroyed) and by refusing to fetch a priest for the dying Teresa. He further betrays them by seducing Giselle while he is betrothed to her sister Linda. Martin Decoud also betrays a "father," Senor Avellanos, by allowing the old man to think him a true believer, and by trying to persuade Antonia to adandon the political struggle—and her father. Decoud becomes involved in politics only as a way of courting Antonia. His love for Antonia proves too weak to save him from despair, however. When he experiences isolation, he feels he has gone out of existence, and he commits suicide.

The novel is also radically pessimistic about political ideology, condemning not only Charles Gould's faith in imperialistic capitalism, and Avellanos's faith in oligarchic "liberalism," but also Giorgio Viola's faith in the ultimate triumph of a people's democracy; Nostromo, once politically enlightened, is led immediately to personal corruption. *Nostromo* further questions the notions of "progress," in the satire directed at Captain Mitchell; of heroism, in Monygham's experience, as well as in Nostromo's career; of fidelity (as we have noted, betrayal is pervasive here, but even the standard Conradian value of fidelity to the task at hand is scrutinized critically, as Nostromo comes to recognize that he has been merely a tool of the rich); and of religion (there are three priests important in the novel: one a torturer, one a fanatic, and one good-hearted but stupid; the Protestantism of Holroyd is seen as a heartless attempt to justify exploitation).

The narrative technique repeatedly reminds the reader to cast a cold eye on the characters, events, and political and social ideals the novel presents. Even the novel's three part structure emphasizes the movement from illusion to disillusion. In terms of the time scheme, Part I represents the past; Part II, the present (it centers around the book's pivotal event, the riot, and its immediate aftermath), and Part III, the future (detailing the results of the struggle to establish a separate Sulacan state). The story of Charles and Emilia Goulds' establishment of the silver mine dominates Part I; the emphasis is on their youthful love and idealism, on their hopes for establishing a just and stable political order and for bettering the lives of the natives. But our view of them is qualified throughout: first, as noted earlier, by the fact that we see at the outset the Ribiera government's collapse, a government the Gould Concession has put in power; second, through the account we are given of the various small disagreements between Charles and Emilia (it is clear that Charles is somewhat self-deceived about his own motives, as is emphasized further in Part II); and third, by the very complexity of the narrative (its jumbled chronology and multiple points of view prevent us from recognizing the Goulds as centers of interest until we are many pages into Part I).

Part II centers on the actual events of the Sulacan revolution, and Martin Decoud's is the controlling point of view. Decoud is intensely skeptical both about the "foreigners'" (with whom he brackets Charles Gould) real interest in Costaguanan politics, and about the Costaguanans' own capacity for honest and rational government. In Part II we tend to lose interest in Charles Gould and, in moving away from him, to judge him more harshly, and to accept Decoud's view of things as "true." In Part III, however, Decoud disappears; the omniscient narrator condemns him as a "trifler," and pronounces irony and skepticism to be "affectations" (556). Decoud is replaced as controlling consciousness by the equally skeptical Dr. Monygham, whose view of Charles Gould is even harsher than Decoud's, since Monygham loves Emilia and is aware of how deeply she suffers from her husband's neglect. Nevertheless, Monygham's chief target is Nostromo. Tortured by his own sense of unworthiness, Monygham resents Nostromo's reputation as "incorruptible." As our center of interest in Part III is Nostromo, Monygham's point of view serves to keep us at a proper distance, just as Decoud's point of view kept us at a distance from Gould.

Like Decoud, Nostromo has been seduced into action, fighting for a cause in which he has no real belief: Decoud acts at the behest of Antonia; Nostromo, out of vanity, to enhance his own reputation. However, Nostromo has an emotional commitment to the enterprise of saving the silver that Decoud lacks, since Nostromo's vanity is stronger than Decoud's love! This is made clear when Nostromo chooses his "mission" over his filial duty to Teresa Viola, who is on her deathbed. In fact, all three of the novel's "heroes," seem somewhat schizophrenic: each has a hidden side. For the hero to recognize this darker side is to risk destruction. Gould is idealist and bandit—he does acknowledge his kinship with the outlaw Hernandez, and that knowledge, together with his necessary involvement with the corrupt political officials of the capital, drives him to withdraw from others, even from his wife; Decoud is both lover and philosophic nihilist—no human commitment can withstand his conviction that nothing has any real importance; Nostromo is incorruptible and a thief—he is also both a defender of the status quo and a revolutionary, like Charles Gould.

Gould and Nostromo share other characteristics. Both are overwhelmingly vain, and both are slaves to the silver. Although each man thinks to use the silver for his own purpose—Gould wishes to make a success of the mine to "redeem the time," to give meaning to his father's suffering, and to prove that he can do what his father could not, while Nostromo hopes the silver will make him a rich and important man—the silver, which seems almost a supernatural force, has them in thrall. The silver, symbol of material interests, finally destoys everything and everyone. It blights Nostromo's relationship with the Violas. It causes the disintegration of the Goulds' marriage. Finally, it is both the ultimate cause and the means of Decoud's death—he goes to the bottom of the sea weighted with the silver bars.

The evil influence of material interests pervades the entire social fabric, from the humblest *indio* to the highest official. With the coming of the steam engine, Sulaco, previously inaccessible, has been opened to conquest and exploitation, and the imperialists' belief that every virgin territory must contain a hidden treasure is satirized in the Sulacans' conviction that the rocky peninsula, Azuera, which is uninhabited and totally without vegetation, contains a store of gold. The barren Azuera is believed to be "blighted by a curse," as Nostromo's life will be blighted by Teresa's curse, and as Mrs. Gould's marriage is made barren, literally and metaphorically, by the curse of the silver. The natives also believe the cursed treasure is guarded by two gringo ghosts, whose "souls cannot tear themselves away from their bodies mounting guard over the discovered treasure" (5). These "impious adventurers" will become Nostromo's particular spectres, but they are also emblematic of all the foreign speculators in Costaguana.

The landscape itself has an illusory, almost supernatural, aspect: "The Cordillera [a mountain range] is gone from you as if it had dissolved itself into great piles of gray and black vapors that travel out slowly to seaward and vanish into thin air all along the front before the blazing heat of the day" (6). Things (and people) in *Nostromo* appear and disappear mysteriously. We cannot always trust our perceptions, nor can we put complete faith in continuity or predictability. Nostromo himself often materializes out of nowhere. We are presented initially with only short glimpses of him, or we hear him spoken of. In this way we see his outward shell, his reputation, before we see his real character (Heyst is presented similarly, in *Victory*), but Nostromo's unexpected brief appearances, in Part I, serve also to make him seem larger than life, to give him an almost mythic stature.

While Nostromo habitually appears unexpectedly, Charles Gould most often *disappears*. We glimpse him going out the door, or we hear the jingle of his spurs dying out in the distance, or we see the backside of his horse! This oblique presentation of both Gould and Nostromo has the effect of adding a certain verisimilitude; we learn about the central characters gradually, almost as we learn about people in real life. But it also has the effect of distancing us from the "heroes," since we are never permitted to share their points of view uncritically—nor are we certain these characters will prove *to be* important, after we have been given so many false leads in the early chapters.

The opening chapter gives us the physical background for the story Conrad is about to tell, and even indicates the moral of the tale in the legend of the gringo ghosts; the second chapter hints at the attitude we are to take toward the story with Captain Mitchell's capsule history of Costaguanan politics:

> The political atmosphere of the republic was generally stormy in these days. The fugitive patriots of the defeated party had the knack of turning up again on the coast with half a steamer's load of small arms and ammunition. Such resourcefulness Captain Mitchell considered as perfectly wonderful, in view of their utter destitution at the time of flight. He had observed that "they never seemed to have enough change about them to pay for their passage-ticket out of the country." And he could speak with knowledge; for on a memorable occasion he had been called upon to save to life of a dictator, together with the lives of a few Sulaco officials—the political chief, the director of the customs, and the head of police—belonging to an overturned government. Poor Senor Ribiera (such was the dictator's name) had come pelting eighty miles over mountain-tracks after the lost battle of Socorro, in the hope of out-distancing the fatal news—which, of course, he could not manage to do on a lame mule. The animal, moreover, expired under him at the end of the Alameda, where the military band plays sometimes in the evenings between the revolutions. "Sir," Captain Mitchell would pursue with portentous gravity, "the ill-timed end of that mule attracted attention to the unfortunate rider. His features were recognized by several deserters from the Dictatorial army among the rascally mob already engaged in smashing the windows of the Intendencia." (12)

Here, as often in the novel, the important detail is buried among other details and impressions. Beginning with a general statement about Costaguanan politics, in which revolution is a constantly recurring phenomenon, Mitchell moves to a particular moment in history, that "memorable occasion" that is to be a touchstone for the reader's apprehension of the entire action of the novel: from this event, Ribiera's ignominious arrival in Sulaco after the collapse of his government, one must work backwards and forwards to reconstruct the time scheme and the order in which events occur.

Mitchell's account emphasizes the comic-opera quality of South American politics (to use Decoud's phrase), in details like the military band that "plays sometimes in the evenings between the revolutions," and especially in the attention paid the miserable mule, whose "ill-timed" expiration precipitates a two-day riot. The passage manages to convey a comic view of Ribiera (who has come "pelting" over the mountains), and of Costaguanan politics in general while making it clear that Mitchell himself viewed the incident with "portentous gravity."

Mitchell is, in fact, a pompous ass, one of those Conradian simple souls whose innate bravery is qualified by lack of imagination—like MacWhirr in *Typhoon.* Perhaps the fact that it is the obtuse Mitchell who introduces Nostromo—"a man absolutely above reproach"—should alert us to the possibility that the title character will prove to be something other than the universal factotum Mitchell describes. It is Nostromo who has saved Ribiera's life, and Mitchell basks in the reflected glory of his "discovery." But Mitchell's is not the only perspective we have on Nostromo. The narrative switches abruptly from Mitchell's historical account to the scene of the riot itself; suddenly we are in its midst, and we see Nostromo briefly through the eyes of the cargadores he leads: "And behold! there he was that day, at their head, condescending to make jocular remarks to this man or the other" (15).

Chapters 3 and 4 offer another perspective on the riot and on Nostromo, as the scene changes to Giorgio Viola's inn. The old Garibaldino's abode appropriately stands "alone half-way between the harbor and the town," for Viola is an outsider, who looks with scorn on both the proletarians of the dock and the aristocrats of the Alameda. (One of the aristocrats is, however, a close friend of the Viola family—Mrs. Gould, who herself has grown up in Italy.) Viola's idealistic commitment to the "old, abstract revolutions," contrasts with the greedy self-interest of the Costaguana revolutionaries. Viola is, nevertheless, a faintly ridiculous figure, "pottering about the 'casa' in his slippers, muttering angrily to himself his contempt of the non-political nature of the riot, and shrugging his shoulders" (17).[6]

The Viola family has informally adopted Nostromo, and at Viola's urging, Nostromo has become Mitchell's capataz. Like Mitchell, Giorgio and Teresa Viola feel a proprietary interest in their "son." Teresa particularly resents Nostromo's success with "the English," and on the day of the riot she feels he has abandoned her. When Giorgio points out that Nostromo is only doing his duty, Teresa argues that his first duty is to protect his family. Devotion to duty is the central tenet of Giorgio's life; "duty" is the last word he pronounces before his death. But where does duty lie, and what are the consequences of doing one's duty? Giorgio will kill Nostromo while performing his duty: a father's duty to protect his daughter. There are no unambiguous codes of conduct here; nothing is predictable; anyone can be made to betray a best-loved person or a fondest hope, as Dr. Monygham has learned so painfully.

Nostromo is fated to betray the expectations of both Giorgio and Teresa. Giorgio takes pride in Nostromo's prodigious reputation; he hopes Nostromo will use his talent for leadership to serve the people. But it is only after the sinking of the lighter, when Nostromo realizes he has risked his life for nothing, that he gives emotional assent to Giorgio's political doctrines. But Giorgio's doctrines have a curious effect on Nostromo: instead of inspiring him to political action, they lead him to cynicism. Once Nostromo sees that he has been a pawn in the class struggle, "a dog of the rich," he determines to live only for himself and to use the hidden silver to become rich. Giorgio, on the other hand, despises wealth.

Nostromo also fails Teresa when at her deathbed he refuses her request that he fetch a priest, choosing instead to take the silver out to sea. But he disappoints her most grievously by his failure to return her love. Although she scolds him and belittles his achievements, her anger arises from jealousy:

> He was escaping from her, she feared.... She railed at his poverty, his exploits, his adventures, his loves and his reputation; but in her heart she had never given him up, as though, indeed, he had been her son. (282)

Nostromo appears incapable of returning the affection both Giorgio and Teresa have for him, however. He comes to see them as very demanding "parents." When he finally chooses Giselle over Linda, it is because of the latter's resemblance to her mother and father:

> Linda, with her intense, passionately pale face, energetic, all fire and words, touched with gloom and scorn, a chip of the old block, true daughter of the austere republican, but with Teresa's voice, inspired him with a deep-seated mistrust. (586)

Giselle, on the other hand, is "pliable, silent, fond of excitement under her quiet indolence"—like Nostromo.

Our introduction to the Violas in the early pages of the novel prepares the ground for Nostromo's destruction; Nostromo's relationship with the Viola family functions almost as a frame story. The tragic misunderstanding that brings about Nostromo's death is presaged here, as we first see Giorgio sitting "sternly in the middle of the darkened cafe with an old gun on his knees"(17)—the gun that will kill Nostromo.

Like Nostromo, Charles Gould is first seen through the eyes of others—or rather, heard about, for we learn of his reputation before we meet him. Nostromo and Gould share a number of characteristics: both are proud, even vain, men with a habit of silence, and both seem when one has penetrated behind the reputation, hollow men, empty vessels. (Decoud also proves "hollow at the core" when he is deprived of his social role.) Gould and Nostromo are also alike in that both choose silver over love. Mrs. Gould makes the connection explicit when she tells Giselle, after Nostromo's death:

> "Console yourself, child. Very soon he would have forgotten you for his treasure."
> "Senora, he loved me. He loved me," Giselle whispered, despairingly. "He loved me as no one had ever been loved before."
> "I have been loved too," Mrs. Gould said, in a severe tone. (626)

The story of the failure of the Goulds' marriage and the corollary failure of the mine to work its magic, to bring about social order and to transform the lives of the poor, is a central concern, but we get at that story in an extremely oblique way. Chapter 5 suddenly switches from the riot and the Violas' inn to another "historic occasion," an official lunch on board the *Juno,* one of Mitchell's boats, eighteen months before the riot we have just witnessed. The lunch is a celebration of the turning of the first sod for the railway, which we have seen in operation at the time of the riot, and the guest of honor is Senor

Ribiera, the dictator of Costaguana, at the height of his glory. We see this occasion through the eyes of Sir John, the chairman of the railway board, who has come from England to negotiate the purchase of land for the construction of the railway, and who proves to be of very peripheral importance as a character. It is his expressed curiosity about the Goulds that leads us into the account of the history of the mine and of the Goulds' courtship and marriage. After our first view of Sir John on the *Juno* we have another flashback: an account of his journey over the mountains from the capital to Sulaco, in the course of which he meets the chief engineer of the railway. During their conversation, Charles Gould's name is mentioned, and Sir John asks, "What sort of a man is he?"[7] Thus the main center of interest in Part I is introduced. It is hard to conceive of a more circuitous route to the heart of the matter.

Charles Gould, we learn, is a third-generation "Costaguanero," a descendant of "liberators, explorers, coffee-planters, merchants, revolutionists," whose grandfather fought with Bolivar, and whose uncle had served as president of the Sulacan province. But in spite of his hereditary ties to the country, Charles Gould seems an outsider. Educated in England, Gould has adopted an aloof inscrutability to cover his awareness of the contradictions between his upbringing and the realities of life in Costaguana, with its pervasive political corruption and perpetual social unrest:

> His mind preserved its steady poise as if sheltered in the passionless stability of private and public decencies at home in Europe. He accepted with a like calm the shocking manner in which the Sulaco ladies smothered their faces with pearl-powder till they looked like white plaster casts with beautiful living eyes, the peculiar gossip of the town, and the continuous political changes, the constant saving of the country, which to his wife seemed a puerile and blood-thirsty game of murder and rapine played with terrible earnestness by depraved children. (54)

Here the yoking together of such incongruities as the Sulaco ladies'"shocking" use of cosmetics and "murder and rapine" indicates the novel's heavily ironic attitude toward politics. This passage further indicates that the Goulds' views on "Costaguana life" are not in complete accord. Mrs. Gould is

> not...able to take the public affairs of the country as seriously as the incidental atrocity of methods deserved. She saw in them a comedy of naive pretences, but hardly anything genuine except her own appalled indignation. Charles, very quiet and twisting his long mustaches, would decline to discuss them at all. Once, however, he observed to her very gently:
> "My dear, you seem to forget that I was born here." (54)

Later we discover that Gould avoids discussing political affairs because he is maddened by the necessity for bribing corrupt officials and for taking their pretensions seriously. At this point, early in the marriage, Charles Gould has already begun to move away from his wife and to change his self-image. Gould's statement here—"you seem to forget that I was born here"—is in sharp contrast to a statement he makes during his courtship (the account of which is, characteristically, given later in the novel). Charles has explained to Emilia his father's difficulties with the mine.

> And when she wondered frankly that a man of character should devote his energies to plotting and intrigues, Charles would remark, with a gentle concern that understood her wonder, "You must not forget that he was born there."...
> "Well, and you? You were born there, too."
> He knew his answer.
> "That's different. I've been away ten years." (66, 67)

Charles assures Emilia—and himself—that he is very different from his father: it is this difference that will ensure his success where his father has failed, he believes. It is something of a rite of passage for Charles to take over the mine, in defiance of his father's wishes, and make it pay, but in supplanting his father, Charles in a sense *becomes* his father, devoted in his turn to "plotting and intrigues."

Although Charles Gould rationalizes his decision to disobey his father and return to Costaguana as an attempt to redeem his father's suffering, it is clear that the elder Gould's obsession with the mine has been mysteriously passed on to his son:

> [B]y the time he was twenty Charles Gould had, in his turn, fallen under the spell of the San Tome mine. But it was another form of enchantment, more suitable to his youth, into whose magic formula there entered hope, vigor, and self-confidence, instead of weary indignation and despair. (64)

The crisis of identity Charles undergoes when his father dies "fill[s] his breast with a mournful and angry desire for action." The omniscient narrator remarks:

> In this his instinct was unerring. Action is consolatory. It is the enemy of thought and the friend of flattering illusions. Only in the conduct of our action can we find the sense of mastery over the Fates. (72)

Charles is consummately the man of action; he is also the victim of "flattering illusions," as Decoud will point out. Moreover, the "sense of mastery over the Fates" that action provides is only an illusion: the Fates can never be mastered. The outcome of action is always unpredictable, as Mrs. Gould discovers, late in the novel.

> There was something inherent in the necessities of successful action which carried with it the moral degradation of the idea. She saw the San Tome mountain hanging over the Campo, over the whole land, feared, hated, wealthy, more soulless than any tyrant, more pitiless and autocratic than the worst government, ready to crush innumerable lives in the expansion of its greatness. He [Charles] did not see it. He could not see it. (583)

This then is the end result of Charles's "consolatory" action. The mine has become a Frankenstein's monster, inhuman but with a life of its own, "soulless" and destructive.

Charles, from the beginning, sees the mine as part of a vast historical abstraction. Defending the American capitalist Holroyd, who has become almost a second father to him, against his wife's observation that Holroyd preaches "the religion of silver and iron," Charles observes that even the powerful Holroyd serves something greater, and that were Holroyd "to die tomorrow... the great silver and iron interest shall survive, and someday shall get hold of Costaguana along with the rest of the world" (91). And Charles goes on to offer a justification for "material interests":

> Only let the material interests once get a firm footing, and they are bound to impose the conditions on which alone they can continue to exist. That's how your money-making is justified here in the face of lawlessness and disorder. It is justified because the security which it demands must be shared with an oppressed people. A better justice will come afterwards. That's your ray of hope. (93)

Emilia is persuaded by this argument (the conversation takes place about a year after their marriage); she believes her husband "competent because he ha[s] no illusions." But this notion that the mine has a redemptive power *is* an illusion, and Decoud later points out that Charles "cannot act or exist without idealizing every simple feeling, desire, or achievement" (237).

Emilia does not recognize that her husband is in the grip of an illusion, nor does she see his self-deception as to his own motives. We are told that she was attracted to Charles "from the first by his unsentimentalism, by that very quietude of mind which she had erected in her thought for a sign of perfect competency in the business of living" (54). Again, Decoud sees Charles otherwise, describing him as "that sentimental Englishman." He adds:

> I won't speak of his wife. She may have been sentimental once. The San Tome mine stands now between those two people. (264)

Decoud sees that Gould's "sentiments" are engaged by the mine as they could not be by any human being, even by Emilia; he also speculates, correctly, that Emilia shared her husband's idealized conception of the mine at the beginning of the marriage. The narrator explains:

> A vague idea of rehabilitation had entered the plan of their life. That it was so vague as to elude the support of argument made it only the stronger. It had presented itself to them at the instant when the woman's instinct of devotion and the man's instinct of activity receive from the strongest of illusions their most powerful impulse. The very prohibition imposed the necessity of success. (82)

This implies that the whole project of reclaiming the mine was, from the outset, an illusion, "part of some fairy-tale," undertaken under the stimulus of "the strongest of illusions"—love. Moreover, Charles and Emilia are driven by a certain sense of guilt. They have disobeyed Charles's father's injunction, and there is also a hint that Charles may feel guilty about marrying Emilia, about becoming an adult and thus supplanting his father. He has, after all, determined on immediate marriage to Emilia only on learning of his father's death. Charles rationalizes that his father commanded him to have nothing to do with the mine because he did not recognize Charles's strength of character:

> Poor father did not understand. He was afraid I would hang on to the ruinous thing [the mine]...and waste my life miserably. That was the true sense of his prohibition, which we have deliberately set aside. (80)

To implement his plan of disobedience, Charles has recourse to another "father," Holroyd, without whose advice and money Charles would be powerless. Holroyd represents Capital in the abstract—the growth of "material interests" which will eventually choke out everything human and good—but Holroyd is himself an upright Christian man, who takes a genuine fatherly interest in Charles. Holroyd is also a believer in America's manifest destiny:

> Time itself has got to wait on the greatest country in the whole of God's universe. We shall be giving the word for everything—industry, trade, law, journalism, art, politics, and religion.... We shall run the world's business whether the world likes it or not. The world can't help it—and neither can we, I guess. (84, 45)

Charles feels he can use Holroyd's help without bothering about the financier's ideas: "What's it to me whether his talk is the voice of destiny or simply a bit of clap-trap eloquence?" (91). Charles, a man of few words, distrusts "eloquence." As he tells Emilia, the windy declamations of Avellanos make him impatient, and serve to remind him that his "poor father could be eloquent, too" (92).

Giorgio Viola's rhetoric, like the rhetoric of Holroyd, Avellanos, and Gould Sr., is also denigrated, as in the vignette of the Sulaco policemen who, riding away from the inn, feel "the drone of old Giorgio's declamatory narrative seem[ing] to sink behind them into the plain" (36). All these "eloquent" father figures are not only slightly ridiculous, but also ultimately death-dealing to their "sons." As we have seen, Nostromo is both physically and spiritually destroyed by his association with Viola; Decoud perishes when he takes on the role Avellanos assigns him; Gould inherits his fatal obsession with the mine, and his other "father," Hoyroyd, as representative of soulless material interests, ultimately brings about the destruction of Gould's dream for a redemptive captialist enterprise—and the destruction of Charles and Emilia's happiness as well.

Charles's violation of his father's command is the root of the curse that finally blights all the characters' lives; as in a fairy tale, a disregarded prohibition brings destruction. By entering into competition with his father Charles determines his doom, for the reclamation of the mine demands that he act in opposition to his own conscience and principles, that he

> fight for life with such weapons as could be found at once in the mire of a corruption that was so universal as to almost lose its significance. He was prepared to stoop for his weapons. For a moment he felt as if the silver-mine, which had killed his father, had decoyed him farther than he meant to go; and with the roundabout logic of emotions, he felt that the worthiness of his life was bound up with success. There was no going back. (93-94)

And Charles does "stoop for his weapons"; he is forced to bribe officials, to ally himself with bandits, and to engage in revolutionary activities he finds contemptible.

Nevertheless, the mine does bring a measure of peace and prosperity for a time. The concluding chapter of Part I shows us the mine at its most successful, during the brief reign of Ribiera—Charles Gould has helped to finance the revolution that brought him to power. But there are hints that the poor are not appreciably better off than before. The dock workers, for instance, live in huts "like cow-byres, like dog-kennels," and Nostromo uses physical force to get them to work. The common people are still subject to impressment in the army—the San Tome miners wear uniforms so as to avoid being kidnapped by army recruiters.

This chapter also offers some retrospective glimpses of the mine. We have the Goulds' first sight of the mine, set in a beautiful landscape, where "the thread of a slender waterfall flashed bright and glassy through the dark green of the heavy fronds of the tree-ferns," and we have Don Pepe's ambiguous comment: "Behold the very paradise of snakes, senora" (116). Now, however, this verdant landscape has become a wasteland:

> The waterfall existed no longer. The tree-ferns that had luxuriated in its spray had dried around the dried-up pool, and the high ravine was only a big trench half filled up with the refuse of excavations and tailings. (117)

This scene of desiccation suggests the withering of Charles and Emilia's love, which will become, like the waterfall, only a memory.

Emilia has watched the production of the very first silver ingots, which seems to her a miracle—a birth:

> On the occasion when the fires under the first set of retorts in their shed had glowed far into the night she did not retire to rest... till she had seen the first spungy lump of silver yielded to the hazards of the world by the dark depths of the Gould Concession; she had laid her unmercenary hands, with an eagerness that made them tremble, upon the first silver ingot turned out still warm from the mould; and by her imaginative estimate of its power she endowed that lump of metal with a justificative conception, as though it were not a mere fact, but someting far-reaching and impalpable, like the true expression of an emotion or the emergence of a principle. (118)

We are reminded here again of the idealistic, "unmercenary" impulse that led the Goulds to regenerate the mine. Ironically, the silver will be the only product of the Goulds' marriage, and it—Mrs. Gould's only child—does not fulfill its promise; instead, it devours its progenitors.

At the end of Part I, the narrative has circled back to the day of the celebration on the *Juno*—the dictator Ribiera's finest hour. The omniscient narrator's remark: "No wonder, then, that Sir John, coming from Europe to smooth the path for his railway, had been meeting the name (and even the nickname) of Charles Gould at every turn in Costaguana"(129), serves to close the parenthesis begun on page 46 ("Sir John had heard much of Charles Gould in Sta. Marta, and wanted to know more"). A measure of the degree of concentration *Nostromo* requires of the reader!

Sir John's thoughts here (Good faith, order, honesty, peace, were badly wanted for this great development of material interests") echo Charles Gould's earlier justification for money making, but this exalted sentiment is deflated by General Montero, the unwelcome spectre at the feast, who proposes a toast to Sir John, saying: "I drink to the health of the man who brings us a million and a half of pounds" (133). This bald statement of economic reality effectively undercuts Sir John's (and implicitly, Charles's) moral posturing. Ribiera's speech also deals in "simple watchwords of honesty, peace, respect for law, political good faith abroad and at home" (132), while, to Mrs. Gould, the dictator appears "more pathetic than promising." And, at the very end of Part I, the omniscient narrator takes us back to the scene Mitchell began by describing:

> Next time when the "Hope of honest men" was to come that way, a year and a half later, it was unofficially over the mountain tracks, fleeing after a defeat on a lame mule, to be only just saved by Nostromo from an ignominious death at the hands of a mob. (144)

The circularity of the narrative, along with the multiple changes in chronology and in point of view, which finally create the impression that characters and events are virtually interchangeable, underscore the novel's deeply pessimistic view of history and of human nature.

Just before Part I concludes, however, we are offered one more glimpse of Nostromo, who as the center of attention for the celebrants at the feast honoring Ribiera's visit (the day of the party on the *Juno*), is shown teasing one of his lovers rather cruelly.

> "Querido," [The Morenita] murmured, caressingly, "why do you pretend not to see me when I pass?"
>
> "Because I don't love thee any more," said Nostromo, deliberately, after a moment of reflective silence.
>
> . . .
>
> "Has it come, then, ever-beloved of my heart?" she whispered. "Is it true?"
>
> "No," said Nostromo, looking away carelessly. "It was a lie. I love thee as much as ever."
> (142)

The woman then asks him for a present, and when he refuses she exclaims: "Juan, . . . I could stab thee to the heart." Nostromo calls for a knife, and in what the narrator describes as a "witty freak," invites her to cut all the silver buttons off his coat. The whole scene suggest the intimate association of love and death pervasive in Conrad's fiction; in this novel it is particularly apparent in the relationship between Decoud and Antonia, as well as in Nostromo's love affair with Giselle. Here, while we expect that Nostromo will offer to let the Morenita kill him, he does in fact allow himself to be symbolically unmanned. Furthermore, it is implied that Nostromo really has no romantic interest in the woman. His ambiguous statement, "I love thee as much as ever," suggests the addendum: that is, not at all. His flirtation is merely part of his role as "capataz." Later he tells Decoud: "as to those girls that boast of having opened their doors to my knock, you know I wouldn't look at any one of them twice except for what the people would say" (33). Nostromo values the illusion of reputation over the reality of human commitment.

Part I focuses on the Goulds and their idealistic hopes for the mine, and shows, too, the forces of darkness arrayed against them in the form of habitual political chaos and social corruption inherent in Costaguana. Part II gives us the reaction of important people of Sulaco to Montero's revolt against the Ribiera regime. Here Martin Decoud is the central figure, and his denunciations serve to emphasize the extent to which Sulaco is, and has been historically, under foreign domination. We see Charles Gould, also an agent of foreign imperialists, through Decoud's critical eyes.

Unlike Charles Gould and Nostromo, Decoud has a living family. He is "an only son, spoiled by his adoring family" (197), and is often characterized by the epithet "the son Decoud." He is like Gould, however, in that he is deceived about his own true feelings and motives. He has adopted a pose of cynicism that insulates him from any deep involvement: "He had pushed the habit of universal raillery to a point where it blinded him to the genuine impulses of his own nature" (169). Decoud has lived most of his life in Paris, where as an outsider, it is implied, he plays the fool to gain acceptance. Indeed, Conrad condemns him in quite strong terms:

> As a matter of fact, he was an idle boulevardier, in touch with some smart journalists, made free of a few newspaper offices, and welcomed in the pleasure haunts of pressmen. This life, whose dreary superficiality is covered by the glitter of universal blague, like the stupid clowning of a harlequin by the spangles of a motley costume, induced in him a Frenchified—but most un-French—cosmopolitanism, in reality a mere barren indifferentism posing as intellectual superiority. (168)

The less than felicitous phrasing here may indicate that Conrad was not entirely comfortable with this characterization, for Decoud's skeptical attitude is very like Conrad's, as many readers have noted.[8] In fact, Decoud's declaration "Of course, government in general, any government anywhere, is a thing of exquisite comicality to a discerning mind; but really we Spanish-Americans do overstep the bound," puts the novel's political theme in a nutshell.

On returning to Costaguana, with a shipment of rifles he has procured at the behest of his godfather, Avellanos, Decoud is affected by "the absolute change of atmosphere," and is "moved in spite of himself by that note of passion and sorrow unknown on the more refined stage of European politics" (173). Furthermore, Avellanos's effusive praise makes it too awkward for Decoud to confess he intended to return immediately to Europe; he stays and takes on the role Avellanos assigns him: "the brilliant defender of the country's regeneration, the worthy expounder of the party's political faith before the world!" And although Decoud says he acts this assigned role only for Antonia's sake, many of his words suggest that he is more emotionally involved in the political struggle than he cares to admit. He is enough of a patriot to become incensed when a young English railway engineer remarks that he hopes the revolution will not interfere with the building of the railroad—and with the progress of his own career. Decoud bursts out:

> The natural treasures of Costaguana are of importance to the progressive Europe represented by this youth, just as three hundred years ago the wealth of our Spanish fathers was a serious object to the rest of Europe—as represented by the bold buccaneers. There is a curse of futility upon our character: Don Quixote and Sancho Panza, chivalry and materialism, high-sounding sentiments and a supine morality, violent efforts for an idea and a sullen acquiescence in every form of corruption. (189)

Decoud himself will be a victim of that "curse of futility"; his discovery that all activity is meaningless will drive him to suicide. Still, he is more clear-sighted about the realities of the situation than are Avellanos and the other habitues of

Casa Gould. Decoud knows that the foreign saviors of Costaguana—including Charles Gould—are motivated by self-interest.

Even the ignorant and drunken General Barrios perceives this. He tells the English who have gathered at the harbor to watch the troop embarkation:

> Senores, have no apprehension. Go on quietly making your ferrocarril—your railways, your telegraphs, your—There's enough wealth in Costaguana to pay for everything—or else you would not be here. Ha! ha!... Fear nothing; develop the country; work, work. (182)

Barrios's speech, a parody of Avellanos's ideals, serves as a commentary on those ideals, and on Avellanos, who has tied his country's fate too closely to Europe.

Avellanos is presented somewhat ambiguously.[9] In our first brief glimpses of him he seems a bit ridiculous; Charles Gould finds him a bore. Once we see his suffering while imprisoned, however, he appears a heroic figure. But although he has the highest principles, and has devoted his whole life to his country, Avellanos (like Giorgio Viola) represents a European political tradition that does not translate to Costaguana. In practical terms, the Ribiera government depends entirely on European and North American financing and is operated for the benefit of the foreigners. Moreover, Avellanos is frail and impotent. Broken in health by his imprisonment, he is cared for by his daughter, Antonia, who "devote[s] herself to 'poor papa'"—the adjective recalls Charles Gould's "poor old boy." Avellanos does not recognize the extent of Antonia's self-sacrifice: "He accepted [Antonia's devotion] in the benighted way of men, who, though made in God's image, are like stone idols without sense before the smoke of certain burnt offerings" (155).

Antonia is caught between her father and Decoud. She realizes that Decoud's attacks on the foreign investors are also attacks on her father's policies. Because he believes his country is fated to be continually exploited, Decoud cannot take its politics seriously: "his disdain grew like a reaction of his skepticism against the action into which he was forced by his infatuation for Antonia. He soothed himself by saying he was not a patriot, but a lover" (194). But Decoud is a rather strange lover. For Decoud, Antonia seems to represent something of a threat.

> "You know you were a very terrible person, a sort of Charlotte Corday in a school-girl's dress; a ferocious patriot. I suppose you would have stuck a knife into Guzman Bento?"
> She interrupted him. "You do me too much honor."
> "At any rate," he said, changing suddenly to a tone of bitter levity, "You would have sent me to stab him without compunction." (198, 199)

And Decoud goes on to reproach her with "keep[ing] me here writing deadly nonsense," and with risking his life for nothing. Decoud conceives his plan to separate Sulaco from the rest of Costaguana out of desperation when Antonia refuses to join him in fleeing the country. As he tells Mrs. Gould: "I cannot part with Antonia, therefore the one and indivisible republic of Costaguana must be made to part with its western province" (238).

Still, Decoud seems to feel ambiguously about Antonia:

> [S]he fascinated him, and sometimes the sheer sagacity of a phrase would break the charm, replace the fascination by a sudden unwilling thrill of interest. Some women hovered, as it were, on the theshold of genius, he reflected. They did not want to know, or think, or understand. Passion stood for all that, and he was ready to believe that some startlingly profound remark, some appreciation of character, or a judgment upon an event, bordered on the miraculous. (202, 203)

Decoud does not want to be persuaded by Antonia's arguments, and he does not want to take her seriously as a thinker—in fact he does not believe women capable of logical thought. Antonia's sagacity borders "on the miraculous." Moreover, the very austerity that has attracted the dilettante Decoud is often a source of annoyance.

> Decoud had often felt his familiar habit of ironic thought fall shattered against Antonia's gravity. She irritated him as if she, too, had suffered from that inexplicable feminine obtuseness which stands so often between a man and a woman of the more ordinary sort.

This denigrating reference seems somewhat gratuitous, since Antonia is far from obtuse—she is merely a serious person—but this low opinion of women's intelligence is no doubt Conrad's, as well as Decoud's. The omniscient narrator says, earlier in the novel, that Mrs. Gould has "an eager intelligence," but:

> It must not be supposed that Mrs. Gould's mind was masculine. A woman with a masculine mind is not a being of superior efficiency; she is simply a phenomenon of imperfect differentiation—interestingly barren and without importance. (73)

In any case, Decoud's devotion to Antonia seems masochistic. It is notable that Decoud's irony is describes as "shattered against Antonia's gravity," for later, when Decoud is alone on the island, he has a vision of her as "gigantic and lovely like an allegorical statue, looking on with scornful eyes at his weakness" (556). Decoud feels that Antonia has coerced him into playing a false role, and he seems to feel from the beginning that it will cost him his life. He has already given up hope of having her before he leaves Sulaco, for he writes his sister: "whether I escaped or stayed to die, there was for us no coming together, no future. And that being so, I had no pity to waste upon the passing moments of her sorrow" (265). There is even an implication that his love for Antonia was, from the beginning, something of a pose. When Decoud and Nostromo are on the lighter with the silver, Decoud is suddenly overcome by an impression of futility.

> All his active sensations and feelings, from as far back as he could remember, seemed to him the maddest of dreams. Even his passionate devotion to Antonia, into which he had worked himself up out of the depths of his skepticism, had lost all appearance of reality. (296)

The birth of Decoud's new state is to coincide with Don Jose Avellanos's death; the shock of the collapse of Ribiera's government is too much for the old man, who has also seen the pages of his *magnum opus,* a history of Costaguana called *Fifty Years of Misrule,* "littering the Plaza, floating in the gutters, fired out as wads for trabucos loaded with handfuls of type, blown in the wind, trampled in the mud... floating upon the very waters of the harbor" (261). Before Avellanos dies, however, Decoud obtains his blessing on the scheme of separation, although this is counter to the doctrine Avellanos has always espoused. Decoud writes his sister:

> I bent my ear to his withered lips, and made out his whisper, something like "In God's name, then, Martin, my son!" I don't know exactly. There was the name of God in it, I am certain. It seems to me I have caught his last breath—the breath of his departing soul on his lips...with that whisper urging me to attempt what no doubt his soul, wrapped up in the sanctity of diplomatic treaties and solemn declarations, must have abhorred. (262)

When Decoud tells Antonia, "Your father told me to go on in God's name," she responds, "He has?... Then, indeed, I fear he will never speak again" (265). Antonia realizes that her father has conceded defeat for his ideals in allowing Decoud to pursue his plan of separation. At the end of the novel, Antonia and her uncle, the fanatical priest, Corbelan, are planning yet another revolution: this one to reannex the rest of Costaguana to Sulaco, which Antonia now asserts, she is convinced "was from the first poor Martin's intention" (569). Dr. Monygham pronounces her "incorrigible."

Avellanos's "blessing" seems itself a bit ambiguous—Decoud is not certain just what the old man said! He interprets it as he wishes, just as Charles Gould has reinterpreted his father's last command. But Decoud recognizes no similarities between himself and Gould; for Decoud, Gould is "of another blood." While Decoud is skeptical, he is also voluble, using words in which he does not believe; he is able to spout revolutionary rhetoric at will, but he remains personally detached. Charles Gould, on the other hand, is idealistic and silent, and his silence, although it drives a wedge between Gould and his wife, has been "assumed with a purpose" (406), as a defense against the irrationality and corruption surrounding him:

> Unlike Decoud, Charles Gould could not play lightly a part in a tragic farce. It was tragic enough for him, in all conscience, but he could see no farcical element. (405)

Yet there are similarities. Gould's statement,

> The words one knows so well have a nightmarish meaning in this country. Liberty—democracy—patriotism—government. All of them have a flavor of folly and murder. (453)

might have been made by Decoud. And both have been unwittingly seduced into political action. Gould comes to realize that the mine itself has "corrupted his judgment," involving him in a course of action, and in political commitments, he would never have chosen freely. He realizes, too, that his commitment is irrevocable; although he now sees he was wrong to back Ribiera, he must go on with his involvement in the new revolution to establish Sulaco as an independent state. Charles also realizes that he has deceived himself about his own character and heritage. When courting Emilia, he assures her: "In Costaguana we Goulds are no adventurers" (70). Later, he sees the truth:

> After all, with his English parentage and English up-bringing, he perceived that he was an adventurer in Costaguana, the descendant of adventurers enlisted in a foreign legion, of men who had sought fortune in a revolutionary war, who had planned revolutions, who had believed in revolutions. For all the uprightness of his character, he had something of an adventurer's easy morality, which takes count of personal risk in the ethical appraising of his action. He was prepared, if need be, to blow up the whole San Tome mountain sky-high out of the territory of the republic. This resolution expressed the tenacity of his character, the remorse of that subtle conjugal infidelity through which his wife was no longer the sole mistress of his thoughts, something of his father's imaginative weakness, and something, too, of the spirit of a buccaneer throwing a lighted match into the magazine rather than surrender his ship. (406, 407)

Behind Charles Gould's facade of moral rectitude lies the soul of a pirate. Although Charles has tried to pretend that the Goulds were above politics (he has told Emilia that his uncle Harry, the president of an earlier Sulacan republic, was "no politician"), he now recognizes the depth of their involvement. He is associated with these adventurers, as he is associated with the bandit Hernandez, who is "master of the Campo" as Gould is "master of the mine": "They were equals before the lawlessness of the land. It was impossible to disentangle one's activity from its debasing contacts" (401). Charles Gould's family heritage, his association with Holroyd, and his obsession with the mine all place him squarely in the company of the exploiters Decoud has denounced. But the recognition that he is, indeed, an "adventurer," and that his idealism is hopelessly tainted by its "debasing contacts" does not free Charles from his enslavement; he is condemned to go on as before.

Like Charles Gould, Decoud and Nostromo each experience painful moments of self-recognition. Like Gould also, they are described as adventurers, involved in a perilous enterprise—the attempt to save the silver—

that has a different significance for each man: "There was no bond of conviction, of common idea; they were merely two adventurers pursuing each his own adventure, involved in the same imminence of deadly peril" (328). The two men could hardly be more different. Decoud is an aristocrat, a pampered only son with important social position, and an intellectual; Nostromo, an orphan, living in a country not his own, without wealth, except for the treasure of his reputation. Perhaps the only attitude they share is anti-clericalism, but Nostromo has a superstitious dread of Teresa's dying prophesy: "Your folly shall betray you into poverty, misery, starvation" (285). In refusing to fetch a priest, he has chosen the silver over Teresa. He tells Decoud that he was unwilling even to see Teresa because, "I felt already this cursed silver growing heavy upon my back, and I was afraid that, knowing herself to be dying, she would ask me to ride off again for a priest" (297). Nostromo's concern for the silver already seems almost as great as Charles Gould's; Gould is prepared to blow up the entire mountain rather than surrender his mine, while Nostromo vows to "let the sea have the treasure rather than give it up to any stranger" (296). Nevertheless, Nostromo has pangs of conscience.

> "Senor, I refused to fetch a priest for a dying woman..."
> Decoud was heard to stir.
> "You did, capataz!" he exclaimed. His tone changed. "Well, you know—it was rather fine."
> You do not believe in priests, Don Martin? Neither do I. What was the use of wasting time? But she—she believes in them. The thing sticks in my throat. She may be dead already, and here we are floating helpless with no wind at all. Curse on all superstition. She died thinking I deprived her of paradise, I suppose. It shall be the most desperate affair of my life." (297)

Nostromo implies here that their helpless predicament is somehow a consequence of Teresa's prophesy, and indeed the silver and Teresa's death remain closely associated in his mind. Bernard Meyer has suggested that "among its other meanings the silver of *Nostromo* symbolizes the dead and buried mother... who bars the way to love for all who are involved with the treasure...." He quotes in support of this the passage near the end of the novel where the silver is personified, as Nostromo realizes the silver is more powerful than his love for Giselle. "The spectre of the unlawful treasure arose, standing by her side like a figure of silver, pitiless and secret with a finger upon its pale lips."[10] Perhaps the strongest support for this identification occurs in a passage Meyer does not cite. Giselle asks Nostromo:

> "But what could stand between you and me?..."
> "Your dead mother," he said, very low.
> "Ah!... Poor mother! She has always.... She is a saint in heaven now, and I cannot give you up to her." (602)

Nostromo believes that in some mysterious way Teresa's curse has brought on his enslavement to the silver; he also knows that he has violated her wishes by choosing Giselle over Linda.

Nostromo's abandonment of Teresa prefigures his abandonment of Decoud. Both these acts of betrayal are committed in the name of a higher duty. Nostromo, of course, could not have anticipated Decoud's precipitious mental collapse. Decoud already feels under the shadow of death when he writes the letter to his sister before setting out with Nostromo. He has come from the dying Avellanos to the dying Teresa, and he writes:

> "I...don't really know whether to count myself with the living or with the dead....But no!...all this is life, must be life, since it is so much like a dream." (276)

This confusion between death and life, sleeping and waking, continues. In the stygian darkness and silence of the placid gulf, Decoud feels under the spell of "a powerful drug. He didn't even know at times whether he were asleep or awake" (290). A bit later, he "imagine[s] the lighter sinking to the bottom with an extrordinary shudder of delight" (295). When the lighter is struck by the transport ship and the stowaway Hirsch is carried off, the aftermath of the collision seems to Decoud like waking "up in your bed in a dark room from a bizarre and agitated dream" (325). Left on the island with the buried silver, he is "solitary... like a man in a dream" (335). But Decoud will do no dreaming on the island; he remains sleepless, as the silence of the placid gulf is perpetuated day after day. Decoud dies from solitude. With all his social roles stripped away, he comes to doubt his very existence.

> The brilliant "Son Decoud," the spoiled darling of the family, the lover of Antonia and journalist of Sulaco, was not fit to grapple with himself single-handed.... After three days of waiting for the sight of some human face, Decoud caught himself entertaining a doubt of his own individuality. It had merged into the world of cloud and water, of natural forces and forms of nature. In our activity alone do we find the sustaining illusion of an independent existence as against the whole scheme of things of which we form a helpless part. (556)

That human beings are independent and that their actions have meaning is only an illusion, but it is a necessary illusion. The novel makes this point frequently. Yet, as we have noted, action, however well-intended, invariably brings disaster for someone. Nostromo saves the silver at the cost of Teresa's peace of mind, as, by fetching Barrios, he saves Sulaco itself at the cost of Decoud's life. Even Decoud's efforts on behalf of the revolution finally serve to perpetuate his country's exploitation by foreign capitalists, setting the stage for the cataclysmic revolt about to break forth at the novel's end. In deceiving Sotillo, Monygham succeeds in preventing his joining forces with Montero, but is responsible for the torture and murder of Hirsch. And, as noted earlier, the Goulds' efforts to establish the mine as a stabilizing social force bring about revolution and repression. Furthermore, much of this "heroic" action is an exercise in futility—as, for example, when Nostromo is told by Monygham that taking the silver out to sea, "the most desperate affair of [Nostromo's] life," for which he has "deprived [Teresa] of paradise" (297), was a fool's errand, and that the silver was really of no importance!

Part II ends with Decoud left alone on the Great Isabel. Part III begins with a switch in focus, back to the Violas' inn, where Charles Gould, Monygham, and the chief engineer discuss strategy. Monygham believes sending the silver out to sea was a mistake—it would have been better to have it on hand for bribes. We discover also that Nostromo has flattered himself that being chosen to pilot the boat was a great honor. The chief engineer remarks:

> Gould, Decoud, and myself judged that it didn't matter in the least who went. Any boatman would have done just as well. (356)

Monygham sees that Nostromo has been treated cavalierly and asserts that Nostromo could have been a political power in his own right, instead of merely a servant of "you good people of the railway and the harbor... I don't know why the devil he should be faithful to you, Gould, Mitchell, or anybody else," Monygham adds, concluding: "I think that Nostromo is a fool" (357).

Nostromo himself will come to the same conclusion. Waking up "in solitude but for [a] watchful vulture" (462), Nostromo, like Decoud, is overpowered by a feeling of unreality and futility. Deprived of his social role, without the support of his admiring public, Nostromo suddenly sees that he is only a pawn, and accepts the truth of Viola's assertion that the rich and powerful keep the people as they keep dogs, "to fight and hunt for their service" (463).

Nostromo has a vision of "universal dissolution," including the destruction of his own personality, since he has "no intellectual existence or moral strain to carry on his individuality, unscathed, over the abyss left by the collapse of his vanity" (466). By the time Nostromo realizes the truth of Giorgio and Teresa's pronouncements and the value of their advice, the comfort they might give has been snatched away. Teresa no longer lives, and Giorgio is too stunned by grief to help Nostromo. Nostromo is orphaned again.

Decoud will be left to his fate because Nostromo has no one he can trust with the knowledge of the silver's location. Fatally, the first person Nostromo meets on his return to Sulaco is Dr. Monygham, of whom Nostromo has a superstitious dread—and who, in turn, dislikes Nostromo. Meeting by accident at the Custom House, the two men discover the body of Hirsch, who has been tortured and shot. Nostromo receives a further blow to his vanity when Monygham tells him the Europeans now consider sending the silver out to sea a mistake, and he is angered by Monygham's lack of interest in the details of the "desperate affair." But most of all he is shocked by Hirsch's fate, for which he holds Monygham responsible. Monygham, hoping to keep Sotillo too busy looking for the silver to join forces with the other Monterists, has attempted to confirm Sotillo's belief that Hirsch's claim the silver is sunk is a lie. "You are a dangerous man," Nostromo tells Monygham; and, in fact, the doctor's fanatical devotion to Mrs. Gould has "left his heart steeled against remorse and pity" (491).

Initially presented rather unsympathetically, as a man with a shady past whom no one but Mrs. Gould likes or trusts, Monygham's real history is finally revealed. He, like Avellanos, has been a prisoner of Guzman Bento, and under torture has betrayed his friends. He has lived ever since with his guilt and with his shattered self image. The reader, privy to this information as Nostromo is not, judges Monygham less harshly than does the capataz, but there are a number of indications that the doctor's devotion to Mrs. Gould is a fixed idea that may indeed, as Nostromo declares, make him a dangerous man. As the narrator has earlier observed with regard to Gould, "A man haunted by a fixed idea is insane. He is dangerous even if that idea is an idea of justice..." (422). And like Gould, Monygham (on this occasion) exhibits the "adventurer's easy morality, which takes count of personal risk in the ethical appraising of [an] action" (407). Monygham feels that risking his own life justifies the sacrifice of Hirsch:

> ...the risk, deadly enough, to which he exposed himself had a sustaining and comforting effect. To that spiritual state the fate of Hirsch presented itself as part of the general atrocity of things. (491)

Hirsch's corpse broods over the scene between Nostromo and the doctor—a momento mori further confirming Nostromo's distrust of Monygham, whom Nostromo now believes capable of consigning him to a fate like Hirsch's. In denouncing Monygham, Nostromo identifies himself with Hirsch, despised and outcast.[11]

> You fine people are all alike. All dangerous. All betrayers of the poor who are your dogs.
> ...
> I say that you do not care for those who serve you. Look at me! After all these years, suddenly, here I find myself like one of these curs that bark outside the walls—without a kennel or a dry bone for my teeth... I am nothing! Suddenly—... Nothing to anyone. (508, 509)

Class consciousness has emerged from Nostromo's wounded vanity. Returning to Giorgio Viola's inn, Nostromo tries to make the old man understand that he, Nostromo, has finally seen the truth of Giorgio's "message":

> ...Nostromo saw clearly that the old man understood nothing of the words. There was no one to understand; no one he could take into the confidence of Decoud's fate, of his own, into the secret of the silver (525).

As Nostromo has expected, Giogio is too stunned by Teresa's death to respond. Nostromo is haunted by Teresa's curse.

> And what a curse it was, that which her words had laid upon him! He had been orphaned so young that he could remember no other woman whom he called mother. Henceforth there would be no enterprise in which he would not fail. The spell was working already. (526)

Although Nostromo has lost all illusions about his real value to the *hombres finos,* he agrees to make a last heroic effort on their behalf and ride to Cayta to bring back General Barrios. He does this partly to fulfill Teresa's last command, to "save the children," even though he fears "it [may be] only a part of the curse to lure me on," and even though it involves saving "all the Blancos together" (527).[12]

Teresa's curse and the curse the silver represents become increasingly associated in Nostromo's mind. He feels his guilty actions in abandoning both Decoud and Teresa, have in a sense earned him the right to the silver: "It was paid for by a soul lost and by a vanished life" (561). Furthermore, he feels *forced* to take possession of the silver—since neither the missing four ingots nor Decoud's disappearance can be explained.[13] Nostromo's concern for reputation would make even a suspicion that he were a thief or murderer intolerable, just as his conception of himself as "incorruptible" makes his concealment and use of the silver seem a curse. The missing ingots seem to Nostromo a further betrayal by Decoud, who first betrayed Nostromo by embroiling him in the affairs of the "fine people."

> And four ingots! Did he take them in revenge, to cast a spell, like the angry woman who had prophesied remorse and failure, and yet had laid upon him the task of saving the children. (561)

On his deathbed, Nostromo explains to Mrs. Gould:

> Decoud took four. Four ingots. Why? Picardia! To betray me? How could I give back the treasure with four ingots missing? They would have said I had purloined them. The doctor would have said that.
>
> ...
>
> [Decoud] went away! He betrayed me. And you think I have killed him! You are all alike, you fine people. (623, 624)

Nostromo is both betrayer and betrayed. Although he comes to adopt Giorgio's view of the class struggle, Nostromo has become a capitalist instead of a revolutionary. His role as a leader in the "secret societies" that conspire, along with Antonia and her uncle Corbelan, to foment a new revolution must be assumed to be merely window dressing, since his real aim is to amass enough wealth to leave the country with Giselle. Nostromo has constructed a new identity, as Captain Fidanza, "the unquestioned oracle of secret societies, a republican like old Giorgio, and a revolutionist at heart (but in another manner)" (587). As Avrom Fleishman has noted, that "other manner" is Nostromo's theft of the silver.[14] This gesture of revolt violates not only Nostromo's idea of his own character (incorruptible), but also Giorgio's highest principle: his disdain for money. Even as he adopts Viola's rhetoric, Nostromo betrays Viola's ideals, as he betrays Viola personally by courting Giselle while betrothed to Linda.[15]

Nostromo's courtship, like his possession of the silver, is illicit and secret. Nostromo hopes Giselle's love will free him from his enslavement to the treasure, that it will "cast a spell stronger than the accursed spell of the treasure...[and change] his weary subjection to that dead thing into an exulting conviction of his power" (604). But love and the treasure are closely associated—the novel's very last words refer, ironically, to Nostromo's "conquests of treasure and love"—and both are aspects of the forbidden, part of the spell, the fate that beckons Nostromo towards death. Nostromo's love is not strong enough to free him. Giselle says: "Your love is to me like your treasure to you. It is there, but I can never get enough of it" (610). This statement might also have been made by Mrs. Gould, with whom Giselle, "who would have followed a thief to the end of the world," is associated, and Mrs. Gould recognizes the similarity in their situations as she makes the bitter remark, quoted earlier: "Very soon he would have forgotten you for his treasure." At the end of the novel, Mrs. Gould foresees that the mine will bring death to Charles; death will triumph over the Goulds' love as it has over Decoud and Antonia and over Nostromo and Giselle. Defeated by "material interests," she will be left, like Antonia and Giselle, to live out her life alone.

> [S]he saw clearly the San Tome mine possessing, consuming, burning up the life of the last of the Costaguana Goulds; mastering the energetic spirit of the son as it had mastered the lamentable weakness of the father. A terrible success for the last of the Goulds. The last! She had helped for a long, long time, that perhaps—But no! There were to be no more. An immense desolation, the dread of her own continued life, descended upon the first lady of Sulaco. With a prophetic vision she saw herself surviving alone the degradation of her young ideal of life, of love, of work—all alone in the Treasure House of the World. (583)

The "lost" silver shipment has come to symbolize, for Mrs. Gould, all the destructive power of the mine; it recalls for her the one instance in which she has deceived her husband, conspiring with Decoud to keep from Gould the news of the imminent arrival of the Monterists. Even the "incorruptible" Mrs. Gould

(Nostromo whose habitual epithet it is, applies the word to Mrs. Gould when on his deathbed) "had been corrupted by her fears at that time, and she had never forgiven herself" (621). Her one direct involvement in political action has had terrible unforeseen consequences: Nostromo's ruin, the deaths of Hirsch and Decoud, and the near death of Monygham. Unlike Monygham, who never admits his culpability in Hirsch's death, Mrs. Gould recognizes these consequences, and now "hate[s] the mere mention of that silver." When Monygham summons her to Nostromo's deathbed, suggesting: "He wants perhaps to tell you something concerning that silver which—" she answers:

> Oh no! No!... Isn't it lost and done with? Isn't there enough treasure without it to make everybody in the world miserable? (621)

Mrs. Gould, "monastically hooded," performing the priestly function earlier denied Teresa, hears Nostromo's confession but refuses his final secret: the whereabouts of the treasure. Mrs. Gould refuses to hear the secret because she too believes the silver is a curse, because she sees it would cause Nostromo pain to tell her, even now, and because she wants to protect Nostromo's reputation, which is his real treasure.

A number of years after the novel's publication, Conrad discussed Nostromo's character, in a letter to Edmund Gosse:

> But Nostromo is not a thief. He is a strong man succumbing to a temptation of which mere greed is the smallest possible ingredient.... In the very hour of death he is reluctant to disclose his secret to Mrs. Gould. Perhaps it is only then that Nostromo secures that recognition of his character for which he had been thirsting all his life, when Mrs. Gould, the perfectly sympathetic woman, is obscurely moved to refuse the confession (which she sees it costs him so much to make)...[16]

But here, as in the author's prefaces to the various novels, Conrad's explanation seems a bit misleading. Mrs. Gould's refusal of the secret has ambiguous results: it spares Nostromo immediate emotional pain, but it perpetuates his enslavement to the treasure. Might not a full confession have freed Nostromo from the spell? In a sense, Nostromo dies unshriven, like Teresa, having been prevented from making a complete confession.

It is a tragic irony that Nostromo dies at the hand of Giorgio. In the novel's three love stories, the fathers or father figures not only come between the lovers but also are ultimately the cause of the heroes' deaths. Charles Gould's inherited obsession with the mine destroys his marriage; by the end of the novel, Mrs. Gould sees that it is killing Charles—that she will soon be a widow. Avellanos's exalted (but futile) principles, which Antonia shares, prevent Antonia from fleeing the country with Decoud, and thus condemn Decoud to death. Nostromo's theft of the silver (initiating his self-destruction) is partly motivated by Nostromo's belief in Giorgio's rhetorical imprecations against the rich, while Giorgio shoots Nostromo because he represents a threat to Giorgio's daughter—to his honor—although, of course, it is a case of mistaken identity. For Nostromo, and by implication for the novel's other heroes, the silver represents forbidden sexuality. The details of the landscape where the treasure is hidden suggest femininity, as does the name of the hiding place, the Great Isabel, and as noted earlier, Nostromo himself often associates his treasure and his love. When Giselle finds him dying and asks why he has come in spite of her warning:

> the voice of the resourceful capataz de cargadores, master and slave of the San Tome treasure, who had been caught unawares by old Giorgio while stealing across the open towards the ravine to get some more silver, answered, careless and cool, but sounding startlingly weak from the ground:
> "It seemed as though I could not live through the night without seeing thee once more—my star, my little flower." (618)[17]

The "crime" of love elicits Giogio's revenge; Nostromo has stolen Giselle as well as the silver.

Beginning in the turmoil of a political uprising, involving many characters, *Nostromo* ends with a focus on the title character's ill-fated love affair and destruction at the hands of his "father," just as the five novels under consideration move from the social and political to the private spheres, and if the domestic and political spheres seem imperfectly meshed in the love story that ends *Nostromo,* they are most successfully intertwined in the novel that follows—*The Secret Agent.*

3

The Secret Agent

"The passions rise higher at domestic rather than at imperial tragedies."
—Samuel Johnson

In *Nostromo*, political involvement proves destructive of personal relationships; history intrudes on the lives of individuals and, ultimately, crushes them. *The Secret Agent*, on the other hand, explores the effect seemingly insignificant domestic dilemmas can have on the wider political scene, as Verloc's attempt to preserve his domestic tranquility leads him to perpetrate a social "outrage," while the Assistant Commissioner's parallel desire to preserve marital harmony leads him to take extraordinary, and unorthodox, measures to solve the crime. In *The Secret Agent*, marriage is the cradle of anarchy, and while the novel satirizes many social institutions—the law, the police, science, bureaucracy, journalism—it is marriage that is satirized most savagely. The Verlocs' marriage, like the Goulds', is marked by a lack of communication, but in this case *both* partners cultivate the habit of silence. In contrast to the Goulds, however, Winnie and Verloc misunderstand one another from the beginning. Their marriage is not entered into in the spirit of a youthfully idealistic adventure, moreover; it is a commercial transaction, the terms of which the participants are completely ignorant.

This novel, like *Nostromo*, describes the destruction of a "son" by his "father," and again ideology is instrumental in this destruction, as Verloc convinces the simple-minded Stevie of the moral rightness of bomb-throwing. Frederick Karl finds the novel "a perverse shattering of the family situation," and argues that, in view of the fact *The Secret Agent* was written while Jessie Conrad was pregnant with her second son, "In a figurative sense, Conrad the novelist has eliminated *his* family, which consisted of a much younger wife (as Winnie is with Verloc) and their young child."[1] In this Karl follows Bernard Meyer, who sees in the novel Conrad's sublimation of "infanticidal impulses."[2] Of course Stevie is not really a child. He must be at least twenty-one years old, since his brief employment as office-boy occurred when he was fourteen and antedated Winnie's marriage, and Winnie and Verloc have been married for seven years. Nevertheless, Stevie does seem much younger; his speech is that of a very small child, and his mental deficiency renders him defenseless. He is always referred to as a "boy," and his rather gratuitous destruction has a poignancy (especially in its effect on Winnie) that only Conrad's masterful irony keeps from being overwhelming. Whether or not the novel reflects Conrad's own anxieties about fatherhood, it does exhibit a heightened concern with the dangers inherent in "the family situation."

The book's opening paragraph emphasizes the fact that Verloc is a family man—in fact, it gives us the Verlocs' domestic situation encapsulated:

> Mr. Verloc, going out in the morning, left his shop nominally in charge of his brother-in-law. It could be done, because there was very little business at any time, and practically none at all before the evening. Mr. Verloc cared but little about his ostensible business. And, moreover, his wife was in charge of his brother-in-law.[3]

Verloc is a man with a shop, a brother-in-law, and a wife—all accoutrements of his life to which he is accustomed to give little thought. (Later we are told that "Mr. Verloc loved his wife as a wife should be loved—that is, maritally, with the regard one has for one's chief possession" [179].) This initial mention of Stevie is of course comically misleading, since Stevie is incapable of being "in charge" of anything; also misleading is the description of Verloc as businessman.

Verloc's business is pornography, although he also sells political pamphlets—obscenities merely of different variety for Conrad. Among the items for sale are "photographs of more or less undressed dancing girls," and "now and then it happened that one of the faded, yellow dancing girls would get sold to an amateur, as though she had been alive and young"(5).[4] Winnie, who is introduced in the next sentence and significantly described as young, is associated with these "dancing girls." She has sold herself to an "amateur" Verloc, in exchange for security for Stevie and her mother, although Verloc is blind to this fact, believing he is "loved for himself." Verloc, while engaging in a variety of secret and illegal occupations, remains "thoroughly domesticated," we are told. His various social roles are enumerated:

> Mr. Verloc carried on his business of a seller of shady wares, exercised his vocation of a protector of society and cultivated his domestic virtues. These last were pronounced. He was thoroughly domesticated. Neither his spiritual, nor his mental, nor his physical needs were of the kind to take him much abroad. He found at home the ease of his body and the peace of his conscience, together with Mrs. Verloc's wifely attentions and Mrs. Verloc's mother's deferential regard. (6)

The passage points up the comic incongruities in Verloc's character. A pretended revolutionary, he is at heart a conservative, and fancies himself a "protector of society"; a spy for the police, his "cover" is dealing in pornography; a denizen of the wilds of international espionage, a frequent foreign traveler, and a man of mixed nationality, he is really a homebody, unwilling to stir far from his own hearth—although his habit of wearing his hat and overcoat indoors gives the impression he is always about to depart the premises.

Like Verloc, Winnie is not what she seems; her husband finds her "a mystery" (180), and she is repeatedly described as "unfathomable." (She has an "air of unfathomable indifference" [5] and "unfathomable reserve [6].)[5] The indolent Verloc makes no effort to ascertain Winnie's true nature, of course; all the members of the Verloc household misunderstand each other completely. But Winnie's stolid exterior hides a passionate heart. When confronted with injustice or pain, she responds just as Stevie does, with rage. Winnie describes to Verloc Stevie's agitation after reading one of the shop's political pamphlets:

> [T]here was a story in it of a German soldier officer tearing half-off the ear of a recruit, and nothing was done to him for it.
>
> . . .
>
> I had to take the carving knife from the boy...He was shouting and stamping and sobbing. He can't stand the notion of any cruelty. He would have stuck that officer like a pig if he had seen him then. It's true, too! Some people don't deserve much mercy. (60)

Like Stevie, Winnie does not see the irony in expressing one's hatred of cruelty by sticking the offender "like a pig." The passage prepares for the climactic murder of the pig-like Verloc, with its reference to the fatal carving knife, and especially with Winnie's concluding moral pronouncement: "Some people don't deserve much mercy."

Stevie and Winnie are the novel's real anarchists, ready to avenge injustice even by murder, while the pitiful, self-deluded theorists who gather at Verloc's do nothing but talk. In contrast to his anarchistic family, however, Verloc is a deep-dyed conservative, who sees himself as the protector of the established order:

> He surveyed through the park railings the evidences of the town's opulence and luxury with an approving eye. All these people had to be protected. Protection is the first necessity of opulence and luxury.... the whole social order favourable to their hygienic idleness had to be protected against the shallow enviousness of unhygienic labor. (12)

The social criticism implicit in the heavily ironic tone here is not shared by Mr. Verloc, of course. Committed by his vocation as police informer to the preservation of the status quo, Verloc does not personally believe in the possibility of anarchy: "at the notion of a menaced social order he would perhaps have winked to himself if there had not been an effort to make in that sign of skepticism." Verloc knows revolutionaries too well to take them seriously, but he also has a deep faith in the impregnability of the social order. Comically enough, Verloc, although his "respectability" is a sham, although he is engaged in criminal activities, is at heart the quintessential middle-class man. In his complacent conservatism, in his domesticity, in his characteristic reluctance to look deeply into the motives and feelings of others, Verloc personifies the values of the society he "protects."

In fact, Verloc is closely associated with Chief Inspector Heat, who represents those other protectors of society, the police.[6] Throughout the novel, the police are seen not only as tainted by their necessary contact with criminals ("the mind and the instincts of a burglar are of the same kind as the mind and the instincts of a police officer"), but also by their role as instruments of the rich. Many details emphasize this. During Verloc's interview with Vladimir, the former glances out the window, noting "a policeman watching idly the gorgeous perambulator of a wealthy baby being wheeled in state across the Square." Later in the novel, in a key passage, Stevie, whose "sense of indignation and horror" has been aroused by the plight of the cabman and his wretched horse, attains a philosophic insight: "Bad world for poor people." When Winnie answers, "Nobody can help that," Stevie suggests the police:

> "The police aren't for that," observed Mrs. Verloc cursorily....
>
> . . .
>
> "What are they for then, Winn? What are they for? Tell me."
>
> Guiltless of all irony, she answered yet in a form which was not perhaps unnatural in the wife of Mr. Verloc, Delegate of the Central Red Committee, personal friend of certain anarchists, and a votary of the social revolution.
>
> "Don't you know what the police are for, Stevie? They are there so that them as have nothing shouldn't take anything away from them who have."
>
> . . .
>
> "What?" he asked at once, anxiously. "Not even if they were hungry? Mustn't they?"
>
> . . .
>
> "Not if they were ever so," said Mrs. Verloc.... (172, 173)

As Conrad says in the novel's preface, "I have no doubt... that there had been moments during the writing of the book when I was an extreme revolutionist...."

But although the police are satirized—even condemned as oppressors of the poor—the English faith in law and due process remains a stabilizing force, perhaps the only stabilizing force, in this dark and degenerate world.[7] The upholders of the law may be as self-deceived or as self-interested as those seeking to subvert it, but they represent the social norm of the novel—a norm menaced from the left by the Professor, who unlike the "anarchists" who congregate in Verloc's shop is actively engaged in destruction, and from the right by Vladimir, the First Secretary of the (presumably) Russian embassy, who rails against the English political complacency:

> This country is absurd with its sentimental regard for individual liberty.... The imbecile bourgeoisie of this country make themselves the accomplices of the very people whose aim is to drive them out of their houses to starve in ditches. (29)
>
> The sensibilities of the class you are attacking are soon blunted. Property seems to them an indestructible thing. You can't count upon their emotions either of pity or fear for very long. (32)

Vladimir's aim is truly anarchistic. He plans "an act of destructive ferocity so absurd as to be incomprehensible, inexplicable, almost unthinkable." He puts his faith not in reason, but in madness: "Madness alone is truly terrifying, inasmuch as you cannot placate it either by threats, persuasion, or bribes"(33)[8]

Like Vladimir, the Professor is committed to destruction, and his appraisal of the English echoes Vladimir's:

> [T]his country... is dangerous, with her idealistic conception of legality. The social spirit of this people is wrapped up in scrupulous prejudices, and that is fatal to our work. (73)

Theorists of the destructive potential, Vladimir and the Professor in effect collaborate to bring about Verloc's—and Stevie's—destruction. Vladimir supplies the impetus for the "outrage"; the Professor supplies the explosive. It is up to Verloc to find the detonator (the Professor's prime aim is the invention of "a really intelligent detonator"). Verloc settles on Stevie, who does not precisely fit the Professor's specification. Like Vladimir, the Professor fears the masses may prove impervious even to the horror of madness. He uses Vladimir's very words when, late in the novel, he confesses to Ossipon:

> Ah! that multitude, too stupid to feel either pity ot fear. Sometimes I think they have everything on their side. Everything—even death—my own weapon. (304)

Nostromo shows a society in perpetual revolution; *The Secret Agent* offers an England *impervious* to revolution. Verloc's anarchist cronies do not really menace society; none has ever "raised personally as much as [a] little finger against the social ediface." Furthermore, they are condemned to fail at revolution, the Professor asserts, because they play by society's rules. Like the criminal class, the revolutionaries are part of the game.

> You revolutionists, [the Professor tells Ossipon]... are slaves of the social convention, which is afraid of you; slaves of it as much as the very police that stands up in the defense of that convention. (68)

Unlike the revolutionaries, the Professor is free of social restraints; he is not a slave of "the social convention," since he has deliberately cut himself off from human ties. He is devoted solely to destruction. Freedom, as the novel defines it, can only be obtained by going outside the social order, by becoming an outlaw—as the Assistant Commissioner does when he decides to circumvent Inspector Heat and solve the crime himself, and as Winnie does, most radically, by murdering Verloc, thus ending her domestic slavery.

Winnie has originally denied the possibility that anyone could be a slave in England. "We aren't German slaves here," she asserts, reacting to the horror story of the assaulted German recruit. Later, after the explosion, when Verloc tells her they will have to leave the country, she replies:

> I should like to know who's to make you. You ain't a slave. No one need be a slave in this country—and don't you make yourself one. (194)

And she repeats this sentiment to Heat when he asks her what she thinks about the bombing: "I call it silly," she pronounced, slowly. She paused. "We ain't downtrodden slaves here" (205). After discovering the true facts of the case, Winnie realizes she herself is a slave—sold to Verloc: "Now he had murdered Stevie he would never let her go. He would want to keep her for nothing" (256). Murdering Verloc, she becomes "a free woman," but that freedom is quickly surrendered as she throws herself on Ossipon's mercy.

Many of the men in the novel have fastened parasitically on women. All Verloc's anarchist friends depend on women for their very existence: Karl Yundt, "nursed by a blear-eyed old woman"; Michaelis, "annexed by his wealthy old lady"; and Ossipon, who will "want for nothing as long as there [are] silly girls with savings-bank books in the world" (52,53). Winnie and her mother have devoted their lives to caring for Stevie, while incidentally ministering to the needs of their gentlemen lodgers, and have suffered physical abuse from the "licensed victualler." Even Mrs. Neale, the charwoman, is described as "[v]ictim of her marriage with a debauched joiner [and] oppressed by the needs of many infant children" (180). At the opposite end of the social scale, The Great Lady, patron of Michaelis, is seen by the Assistant Commissioner as "the specially choice incarnation of the feminine, wherein is recruited the tender, ingenuous, and fierce bodyguard for all sorts of men who talk under the influence of emotion, true or fraudulent; for preachers, seers, prophets, or reformers" (112). The rather incongruous adjectives that describe the lady— "tender, ingenuous, and fierce"—are equally applicable to Winnie, "bodyguard" to Stevie.

All these female caretakers of men are, in a sense, victimized by their attachment. The lady, who feels "a deep, calm, convinced infatuation" (110) for Michaelis, is really his dupe, since she misunderstands the practical consequences the implementation of Michaelis's brave new world would have. In a richly satiric passage, we have the lady's view of Michaelis's socialism:

> It would do away with all the multitude of the "parvenus."... With the annihilation of all capital they would vanish, too; but universal ruin (providing it was universal, as it was revealed to Michaelis) would leave the social values untouched. The disappearance of the last piece of money could not affect people of position. She could not conceive how it could affect her position. (110,111)

The lady's acceptance of the prospect of "universal ruin" in order to rid the world of "parvenus," ill accords with the characterization of her, by the Assistant Commissioner, as "kindness personified," and "practically wise." But he adds a misogynistic caveat: "both her kindness and her wisdom were of unreasonable complexion, distinctly feminine, and difficult to deal with"(112). The combination of top lofty snobbism and stupidity the lady exhibits is typical of all high society, the novel implies. It is not only "the imbecile bourgeoisie...[who] make themselves the accomplices of the very people whose aim is to drive them out of their houses to starve in ditches," the rich have clasped to their bosoms Michaelis, who represents a threat from the left, and Vladimir, a threat from the right.

Vladimir himself is a secret agent in more than one sense. Working secretly to subvert the English legal system, he also takes care to keep his true character well hidden from the society ladies whose company he enjoys—for he too is a ladies' man and frequents the great lady's salon. In reality, Vladimir is a cruel bully. The contrast between his private manners and his public mask is made ironically when, on being introduced to the hapless Verloc, Vladimir remarks to his aide:

> "You are quite right, mon cher. He's fat—the animal."
> Mr. Vladimir, First Secretary, had a drawing-room reputation as an agreeable and entertaining man. He was something of a favorite in society. (19)

While Vladimir attacks Verloc's appearance ("You—a member of a starving proletariat—never!"), and charges him with incompetence ("You wouldn't deceive an idiot"—which will prove untrue), we are repeatedly reminded that Vladimir's social manner is quite different: "The features of Mr. Vladimir, as well known in the best society by their humorous urbanity, beamed with cynical self-satisfaction, which would have astonished the intelligent women his wit entertained so exquisitely" (35).

But virtually all the novel's characters have such a hidden side. The Assistant Commissioner dislikes his administrative job and longs for his former colonial position, to which his wife will not allow him to return. He has married for money and social position—his wife is a favorite of the great lady—but his wife is an unpleasant person, "devoured by all sorts of small selfishnesses, small envies, small jealousies" (112). There is also an implication that the marriage is sexually unfullfilling; his wife is "exceptionally sensitive in the matter of colonial climate, besides other limitations testifying to the delicacy of her nature—and her tastes" (113).[9] Thus, the Assistant Commissioner's marital situation has certain resemblances to the Verlocs'—Winnie finds Verloc's lovemaking distasteful, and like the Assistant Commissioner's wife, refuses to go abroad; and both Winnie and the Assistant Commissioner view marriage as a bargain, a transaction that involves giving something up in order to gain a presumably higher good. Verloc, however, would be shocked at this cynical view of marriage; he believes he is loved for himself. Thus the Assistant Commissioner has a hidden motive for marriage and a hidden dissatisfaction with his wife and with his job. He also hides from Inspector Heat his intention to pursue Verloc on his own; Heat, in turn, has made his career out of his secret connection with Verloc.

But the profoundest secrecy obtains in the Verloc household, whose members are completely ignorant of one another's true character and motives. (Winnie does not even know what Verloc's real profession is, although she knows it has something to do with politics.) This ignorance, we are told, is the result of laziness, of congenital incuriosity, and most of all of Verloc and Winnie's shared habit of silence. Although Verloc is most often silent because he is brooding about the impossible task Vladimir has assigned him, and Winnie is silent because she believes "things do not stand much looking into," both are capable of using silence more aggressively. Verloc's morose silence upsets Winnie's habitual equanimity and "affect[s] her nerves" (177). Winnie herself uses silence more consciously as a weapon. Winnie's mother fears her daughter, "whose displeasure was made redoubtable by a diversity of dreadful silences" (152, 153). Verloc, just before he is killed, reflects that:

> If she would go on sulking in that dreadful overcharged silence—why then she must. She was a master in that domestic art. (259)

Stevie, too, is given to moping, although he is also subject to "fits of loquacity."

Both Winnie and her mother are obtuse about each other's motives. Winnie's mother has no idea Winnie married Verloc in a spirit of self-sacrifice, as Winnie cannot recognize the old woman's self-sacrifice in moving to the charity home, but both women are solely concerned with Stevie's welfare. Winnie feels that Verloc's sexual interest in her ensures Stevie's future. When her mother expresses concern that "Mr. Verloc is getting tired of seeing Stevie about," Winnie replies "with a rather grim pertness: 'He'll have to get tired of me first'" (40). And, late in the novel, in the scene leading up to Verloc's murder, Conrad repeatedly emphasizes Winnie's (misplaced) confidence in "the power of her charms" to provide for Stevie's security. When Veloc suggests that they may have to leave the country, Winnie argues, "You've a comfortable home.... And you are not tired of me" (194, 195). Winnie then gives Verloc a glance, half arch, half cruel, out of her large eyes—a glance of which the Winnie of the Belgravian mansion days would have been incapable, because of her respectability and her ignorance. But the man was her husband now, and she was no longer ignorant. (195)

Although Winnie uses sexual wiles to get around Verloc, the assertion here that she would have been incapable of such behavior before her marriage contradicts R. W. Stallman's assumption that the young Winnie has been little better than a prostitute. Stallman says:

> The life of Winnie's mother has consisted in running what Conrad politely calls "business houses" where "queer gentlemen" boarded. One conjunctures that Winnie, being a dutiful daughter to her "impotent" mother, contributed certain accommodations to these queer gentlemen.[10]

Stallman's "conjuncture" is further contradicted when, after murdering Verloc, Winnie is begging Ossipon to help her leave the country:

> in the depths of the loneliness made round her by an insignificant thread of blood trickling off the handle of a knife, she found a dreadful inspiration to her—who had been the respectable girl of the Belgravian mansion, the loyal, respectable wife of Mr. Verloc. "I won't ask you to marry me," she breathed out in shamefaced accents. (289)

The irony is that loyal, respectable Winnie should be driven to murder, and that the mysterious secret agent Verloc is really an ordinary bourgeois husband, who values his "domestic ease" above everything.

Oddly enough, a number of critics have denied that Verloc loves Winnie. Thomas Moser asserts: "Mr. Verloc resembles early lovers like Willems and Mr. Hervey in having so soon lost his physical passion for his wife."[11] No doubt Moser is thinking of Verloc's extreme passivity in the two bedroom scenes in the novel, but we are told several times that Verloc *does* have a "physical passion" for Winnie—and that she finds his lovemaking repugnant. Verloc's ambiguous reaction to Winnie's coquetry—"[it was] uncertain whether he meant to strangle or to embrace his wife" (196)—suggests the character of Verloc's passion. Winnie later tells Ossipon:

> Seven years—seven years a good wife to him, the kind, the good, the generous, the—and he loved me. Oh, yes. He loved me till I sometimes wished myself—Seven years. (276)

"Kind," "good," and "generous" are the adjectives Winnie and her mother use habitually in describing Mr. Verloc to Stevie, and the women do see Verloc this way, but the physical side of the marriage has obviously been a trial for Winnie. Verloc's devotion to Winnie is noted also by the Assistant Commissioner, who tells Sir Ethelred that Verloc has:

> A genuine wife and a genuinely, respectably, marital relation. He told me that after his interview at the Embassy [with Vladimir] he would have thrown everything up, would have tried to sell his shop, and leave the country, only he felt certain that his wife would not even hear of going abroad. Nothing could be more characteristic of the respectable bond than that, went on, with a touch of grimness, the Assistant Commissioner, whose own wife, too, had refused to hear of going abroad. (221)

But Stallman, like Moser, denies that Verloc feels affection for Winnie, arguing that Verloc marries for reasons of calculated self-interest:

> It wasn't out of love for Winnie that he transported her and her impotent mother and imbecile brother from their Belgravian house to Soho, where he set up the shop with money supplied by Winnie. He gathered that trio and their furniture "to his broad, good-natured breast" so as to provide himself thereby a protective mask. It's a shock to Verloc to be told off by Mr. Vladimir that anarchists don't marry and that he has discredited himself in his world by his marriage.[12]

The implication the Verloc married for financial gain is surely wrong. Winnie and her mother and Stevie have nothing but the lodging house and the furniture. Winnie has had to give up the young butcher she loves because he cannot afford to support the rest of the family. Winnie marries Verloc out of financial necessity ("What is a girl to do? Could I've gone on the streets?" she asks Ossipon), but Verloc marries Winnie because he is physically attracted to her. We are told early in the novel that he is susceptible to women— in fact he has served a prison sentence after being betrayed by a woman. Moreover, we are told explicitly that Verloc is aware that his family represents an economic burden. After the anarchists have left the meeting at his house, Verloc muses on the fact that they are all supported by women.

> A shade of envy crept into his thoughts. Loafing was all very well for these fellows, who knew not Mr. Vladimir, and had women to fall back upon; whereas he had a woman to provide for—. (53, 54)

A few moments later, Verloc encounters Stevie, who is unexpectedly still awake, having been terrified by Yundt's harrowing rhetoric.

> Mr. Verloc perceived with some surprise that he did not really know what to say to Stevie.... And this appeared very queer to Mr. Verloc in view of the fact, borne upon him suddenly, that he had to provide for this fellow, too. He had never given a moment's thought till then to that aspect of Stevie's existence. (55)

And, as he ascends the stairs, he hears his mother-in-law snoring. "Another one to provide for, he thought—."

There is also no evidence in Stallman's assertion that Verloc is shocked when Vladimir tells him anarchists don't marry. Verloc knows a good deal more about anarchists than Vladimir, who displays "an amount of ignorance as to the real aims, thoughts, and methods of the revolutionary world which filled the silent Mr. Verloc with inward consternation" (29, 30). Verloc's revolutionary associates see nothing unusual in his marriage. In fact, they are too self-absorbed to waste much speculation on others' motives or actions.

As suggested earlier, critics who assume Verloc is not a loving husband are probably thinking of the two bedroom scenes between Winnie and Verloc, in which Verloc is passive—actually, recumbent, a reminder of his posture while courting Winnie—and physically weak: in the first, he complains of feeling ill; in the second, he is so exhausted he can hardly move, and his arms are described as "rest[ing] on the outside of the counterpane like dropped weapons, like discarded tools" (179). Each of these scenes ends with Verloc telling his wife to put out the light, an ironic echo of *Othello* that hints at the murder to come.[13] (After the murder, Winnie pleads with Ossipon to put out the light in the parlor.)

Each of these scenes also emphasizes the lack of communication between husband and wife. Verloc remains almost totally silent, preoccupied with Vladimir's warning, and Winnie, as usual, is only interested in talking about Stevie. In the first scene, Winnie is explaining the cause of Stevie's agitation; Verloc, however, is not listening:

> Mr. Verloc's anxieties had prevented him from attaching any sense to what his wife was saying. It was as if her voice was talking on the other side of a very thick wall. (58, 59)

Verloc is on the verge of telling Winnie about his encounter with Vladimir, but her cross-preoccupation prevents it. Verloc says:

> "I haven't been feeling well for the last few days."
> He might have meant this as an opening to a complete confidence; but Mrs. Verloc laid her head on the pillow again, and staring upward, went on:
> "That boy hears too much of what is talked about here." (59)

The pattern is repeated in the second bedroom scene, at the end of chapter 8. Verloc is here "within a hair's breadth of making a clean breast of it all to his wife." But:

> [H]e forbore. Mr. Verloc loved his wife as a wife should be loved—that is, maritally, with the regard one has for one's chief possession. This head arranged for the night, those ample shoulders, had an aspect of familiar sacredness—the sacredness of domestic peace.... She was mysterious, with the mysteriousness of living being.... [Verloc] was not the man to break into such mysteries. (179, 180)[14]

Both Winnie and Verloc decide not to risk making a confidence and thus tragedy becomes inevitable. Because Verloc does not really listen to his wife, he is unaware how deeply she feels about Stevie; Verloc believes he himself is the focus for Winnie's love. After Stevie's death, Verloc attempts to console his wife by saying: "Do be reasonable, Winnie. What would it have been if you had lost me?" (234).

The Verlocs' inability to communicate is shared by the anarchists, who not only espouse contradictory doctrines—Michaelis preaches a sort of evolutionary socialism; Yundt, nihilism; and Ossipon, the triumph of science—but speak in such a way as to be virtually incomprehensible to one another. The fierce Karl Yundt has been an actor in his youth, but now "[h]is enunciation would have been almost totally unintelligible to a stranger" (42). Michaelis, because of his long solitary confinement in prison, is unable to carry on a conversation: "the mere fact of hearing another voice disconcerted him painfully" (45).

Ossipon, whose obsession with classifying everyone according to the dictates of Lombroso clouds his view of reality, cannot communicate with nonbelievers in his "favourite saint."[15] Ossipon takes a "scientific" interest in Stevie—"Very good type, too, altogether, of that sort of degenerate. It's enough to glance at the lobes of his ears" (46, 47)—yet while Ossipon's perceptions of reality are distorted by his propensity to theorize, as is true also of Michaelis and Yundt, Stevie trusts only to experience. Because he himself has felt pain, Stevie can sympathize with the suffering of others. He overhears Yundt's denunciation of Lombroso:

> Teeth and ears mark the criminal? Do they? And what about the law that marks him still better—the pretty branding instrument invented by the overfed to protect themselves against the hungry? Red-hot applications on their vile skins—hey? Can't you smell and hear from the thick hide of the people burn and sizzle? (47, 48)

Stevie takes the metaphor literally:

> Stevie knew very well that hot iron applied to one's skin would hurt very much. His scared eyes blazed with indignation: it would hurt terribly. (49)

It is Stevie's capacity for sympathy, for moral indignation, for "pity and fear" that fates him to become a victim. Michaelis's faith in the eventual triumph of a benign human nature and the Professor's raging impetus towards destruction are both satirized in Stevie, who inevitably moves from one extreme to the other:[16]

> In the face of anything which affected directly or indirectly his morbid dread of pain, Stevie ended by turning vicious.... The tenderness of his universal charity had two phases as indissolubly joined and connected as the reverse and obverse sides of a medal. The anguish of immoderate compassion was succeeded by the pain of an innocent but pitiless rage. (169)

Participating in an act of senseless destruction while motivated by the tenderest concern for humanity, Stevie is a parody revolutionary.

Stevie is also a parody humanitarian, since his faith in human goodness—specifically in Mr. Verloc's goodness—will prove his undoing.

> Mr. Verloc was *good*. His mother and sister had established that ethical fact on an unshakable foundation. They had established, erected, consecrated it behind Mr. Verloc's back, for reasons that had nothing to do with abstract morality. And Mr. Verloc was not aware of it. It is but bare justice to him to say that he had no notion of appearing good to Stevie. (175)

Although Stevie's attitude towards Verloc is "reverential," Verloc is barely aware of Stevie's existence.

Winnie is, of course, unaware that Verloc thinks so little of Stevie. She believes she has created a family:

> She watched the two figures down the squalid street, one tall and burly, the other slight and short, with a thin neck, and the peaked shoulders raised slightly under the large semi-transparent ears. The material of their overcoats was the same, their hats were black and round in shape. Inspired by the similarity of wearing apparel, Mrs. Verloc gave rein to her fancy.
> "Might be father and son," she said to herself. She thought also that Mr. Verloc was as much of a father as poor Stevie ever had in his life. She was aware also that it was her work. (186, 187)

Verloc, in turn, is totally unaware that Winnie has married him only to provide for Stevie's security, just as he is unaware of the depth of Winnie's feeling for her brother. Verloc believes he "is loved for himself." Winnie, however, has made a bargain with fate, a bargain that required such self-sacrifice she cannot imagine it not being kept. The Verlocs' life together has been founded on this mutual misunderstanding—on reticent silences and tactful omissions.

When, after Winnie has learned of Stevie's death, Verloc tries to explain matters, he realizes that "Mrs. Verloc's philosophical, almost disdainful incuriosity, the foundation of their accord in domestic life, made it extremely difficult to get into contact with her now this tragic necessity had arisen"(237). He has no idea how to communicate with her; he has no idea what she is really like. Because he is completely ignorant of Winnie's true feelings, Verloc says precisely the wrong thing at each point in the long scene that leads to his murder, and so effectively brings about his own death.[17] This scene is rendered from Verloc's point of view, and his misperceptions are underscored with heavy irony. Verloc is determined to be magnanimous, "not to overwhelm his wife with bitter reproaches" (for having sewn Stevie's address in his coat). He tries to explain himself to Winnie, but remembering his encounter with the dreadful Vladimir serves to enrage Verloc, and he is lead to a fatal burst of angry rhetoric that offers us—and Winnie—a new view of the good-natured, placid, indolent secret agent.

> "You don't know what a brute I had to deal with."
>
> ...
>
> "A silly, jeering, dangerous brute, with no more sense than—After all these years! A man like me! And I have been playing my head at that game. You didn't know. Quite right, too. What was the good of telling you that I stood the risk of having a knife stuck into me any time these seven years we've been married?"
>
> ...
>
> "There isn't a murdering plot for the last eleven years that I hadn't my finger in at the risk of my life. There's scores of these revolutionists I've sent off, with their bombs in their blamed pockets, to get themselves caught on the frontier." (237, 238)

Since Winnie has no idea to whom Verloc refers, she probably thinks the "brute, with no more sense than—" is Stevie. Verloc, on the other hand, does not realize that the "risk of having a knife stuck into [him] any time these seven years" was right at his own fireside. His phraseology here may even plant the idea in Winnie's mind. But Verloc remains confident of Winnie's love.

For the reader, it is also rather startling to learn that Verloc is capable of positive evil, as well as of such intemperate rage. He has seemed too lazy to be dangerous, but here we catch a glimpse of his victims—"revolutionists... with their bombs in their blamed pockets." As a secret agent, Verloc's business is betrayal, but he betrays in his domestic life as well, and Winnie, "maternal and violent," feels the "rage and dismay of a betrayed woman," as like a drowning person she sees the significant moments of her life with Stevie pass before her eyes. She remembers especially protecting Stevie from the wrath of their father, and giving up the young man she loved to marry Verloc, who would be Stevie's protector.[18] Finally, she remembers:

> the vision of her husband and poor Stevie walking up Brett Street side by side away from the shop. It was the last scene of *an existence created by Mrs. Verloc's genius*;... it wrung from Mrs. Verloc an anguished and faint murmur, reproducing the supreme illusion of her life, an appalled murmur that died out on her blanched lips.
> "Might have been father and son." (243, 244, emphasis added.)

Winnie's "supreme illusion" is that she had created a family.

But while Winnie is tortured by her memories of sacrifices made in Stevie's name, Verloc goes on ranting savagely.

> "The Embassy," Mr. Verloc began again, after a preliminary grimace which bared his teeth wolfishly. "I wish I could get loose in there with a cudgel for half-an-hour. I would keep on hitting till there wasn't a single unbroken bone left amongst the whole lot.... All the world shall know what I've done for them. Everything'll come out. Every damned thing. Let them look out!"

> In these terms did Mr. Verloc declare his thirst for revenge. It was a very appropriate revenge. *It was in harmony with the promptings of Mr. Verloc's genius.* It had also the advantage of being within the range of his powers and of adjusting itself easily to the practice of his life, which had consisted precisely in betraying the secret and unlawful proceedings of his fellow-men. (244, 245, emphasis added.)

Mrs. Verloc's genius is self-sacrifice; her husband's is betrayal.

Although Verloc believes he is explaining to Winnie how the tragedy came to occur, his ranting, which becomes progressively more and more aggressive, is largely incomprehensible to his wife. As Verloc expresses his furious anger at Vladimir, Winnie has no idea to whom he refers:

> I would have taken him by the throat. As true as I stand here, if I hadn't thought of you then I would have choked the life out of the brute.... (240)

Again, Winnie probably assumes Verloc is describing his hostile intentions towards Stevie. In any case, Verloc's angry words have the effect of enflaming Winnie, just as Karl Yundt's words enflamed Stevie. She has a new vision: "This man took the boy to murder him" (246).

The enormity of her betrayal becomes ever more evident to Winnie as Verloc goes on talking. Winnie feels she has "loyally paid for" the seven years of security her marriage has represented, and she had trusted Verloc to maintain his part of the bargain. Now, seeing how misplaced was her trust, she blames herself: "She had watched him, without raising a hand, take the boy away. And she had let him go, like—like a fool—a blind fool" (246). Faced with the reality of Stevie's death Winnie realizes that her bargain is at an end; she is "released from all earthly ties"; she is a "free woman."

> There was no need for her now to stay there, in that kitchen, in that house, with that man—since the boy was gone forever. No need whatever. (251)

She does "not exactly know what use to make of her freedom" (254), but in the moment before the murder, Winnie becomes "scrupulously aware of something wanting on her part for the formal closing of the transaction" (259). Verloc, acting always from the wildly mistaken notion that Winnie loves him, goads her to murder by reminding her over and over how much he cares for her—while Winnie is filled with repugnance at Verloc's very aspect, and is in the grip of an "excessive fear of being approached and touched by [him]" (252). But when Verloc voices Winnie's own thoughts, when he accuses her of being an accomplice in Stevie's murder, he seals his doom: "if you will have it that I killed the boy, then you've killed him as much as I." The authorial voice comments:

> In sincerity of feeling and openness of statement, these words went far beyond anything that had ever been said in this home, kept upon the wages of a secret industry eked out by the sale of more or less secret wares: the poor expedients devised by a mediocre mankind for preserving an imperfect society from the dangers of moral and physical corruption, both secret, too, of their kind." (258)

Here the connections between the domestic life and the private spheres are made explicit: the secrets of the Verlocs' marriage are mirrored in Verloc's two occupations—spying and selling pornography—which in turn mirror larger social concerns, being "poor expedients...[to preserve] an imperfect society from the dangers of moral and physical corruption...." With these injudicious words ("you've killed him as much as I") Verloc rips the veil of secrecy from the marriage, as he has ripped the veil from Winnie's face.[19] "Sincerity of feeling and openness of statement" have no place in the Verloc household; the introduction of these "virtues" can only lead to murder.

Mrs. Verloc has a final vision—of Stevie's dreadful death:

> A park—smashed branches, torn leaves, gravel, bits of brotherly flesh and bone, all spouting up together in the manner of a firework. They had to gather him up with the shovel. Trembling all over with irrepressible shudders, she saw before her the very implement with its ghastly load scraped up from the ground. Mrs. Verloc closed her eyes desperately, throwing upon that vision the night of her eyelids, where after a rain-like fall of mangled limbs the decapitated head of Stevie lingered suspended alone, and fading out slowly like the last star of a pyrotechnic display. (260)

This grisly picture is not without its comic touches, as Stevie's severed head hangs over the scene for a moment when all the other details have disappeared, "fading out slowly like the last star of a pyrotechnic display," calling to mind the Cheshire Cat's smile. Conrad's balancing of comedy, horror, and genuine poignance throughout the chapter is awesome.

Winnie's vision of her brother's terrible end leads to her determination to kill Verloc. The marital contract has been broken and Winnie's "doubts as to the end of the bargain no longer existed." She is a "free woman," for the first time responsible for her own life:

> [S]he felt herself to be in an almost preternaturally perfect control of every fibre of her body. It was all her own, because the bargain was at an end. (261)

Verloc, of course, does not realize the bargain is ended—or even that a bargain existed. He addresses Winnie "with an accent of marital authority":

> "Come here," he said in a peculiar tone, which might have been the tone of brutality, but was intimately known to Mrs. Verloc as the note of wooing.
> She started forward at once, as if she were still a loyal woman bound to that man by an unbroken contract. (262)

Verloc has sounded precisely the wrong note; Winnie has become convinced that he will want to "keep her for nothing" now. Later Winnie tells Ossipon of the effect Verloc's words had on her:

> ... he says to me like this: "Come here," after telling me I had helped to kill the boy. You hear, Tom? He says like this: "Come here," after taking my very heart out of me along with the boy to smash in the dirt.
> I had been looking at the knife, and I thought I would come then if he wanted me so much. Oh, yes! I came—for the last time... With the knife. (289, 290)

Verloc is depersonalized for Winnie throughout the chapter. From the moment she learns of Stevie's death, Winnie sees Verloc not as her husband but as "that man." And at the moment of Verloc's murder, chillingly rendered from his point of view, Winnie is also depersonalized, becoming, for Verloc, "that armed lunatic," or simply, "the woman." Thus the murder seems but an episode in the ongoing archetypal battle of the sexes.

The murder represents, for Winnie, the "formal closing of the transaction"; the marriage contract is ended with the plunge of a knife. She is free now of all ties, but she is free only for death:

> She had become a free woman with a perfection of freedom which left her nothing to desire and absolutely nothing to do, since Stevie's urgent claim on her devotion no longer existed.... She did not move, she did not think. (263)

Winnie is as motionless and as insensate as the dead Verloc. That silence that has been the foundation of their marital harmony is continued after death.

> Except for the fact that Mrs. Verloc breathed these two [Winnie and Verloc] would have been perfectly in accord: that accord of prudent reserve without superfluous words, and sparing of signs, which had been the foundation of their respectable home life. For it had been respectable, covering by a decent reticence the problems that may arise in the practice of a secret profession and the commerce of shady wares. (263, 264)

The ironic emphasis on the Verlocs' "respectability," and on the fact that their "accord" was founded on silence and on utter ignorance of each other's thoughts and feelings (described here as "prudent reserve" and "decent reticence") implies that *all* outwardly respectable and seemingly harmonious households are founded on mutual understanding, and that respectability inevitably covers "a secret profession and the commerce of shady wares." Later, Winnie makes a comic confirmation that respectability and love are mutually exclusive. When Ossipon says of Verloc, "You seemed to live so happily with him.... You seemed to love him." Winnie bursts out:

> "Love him!" Mrs. Verloc cried out in a whisper full of scorn and rage. "Love him! I was a good wife to him. I am a respectable woman. You thought I loved him!" (275)

The sense of freedom Winnie gains after striking the blow is short-lived; she is immediately overcome with terror at the prospect of being hanged: "With her eyes staring on the floor, her nostrils quivering with anguish and shame, she imagined herself all alone amongst a lot of strange gentlemen in silk hats who were calmly proceeding about the business of hanging her by the neck"—a scene that might almost have come from one of the Verlocs' pornographic pamphlets! Stumbling about in the street, unable to find her way to the river, where she wishes to drown herself, Winnie meets the other entrepreneur of sex, Comrade Ossipon. Their comedy of mutual misunderstanding parallels the preceeding scene, with the sexual roles reversed. As Verloc thought he was explaining his actions to the uncomprehending Winnie, Winnie now assumes she is explaining her reasons for killing Verloc. But Ossipon has no idea of the real situation, believing Verloc was killed in the Greenwich explosion. He has come to console the grieving widow, hoping to get a share of Verloc's inheritance. But when Winnie immediately responds to his advances, Ossipon is "a little shocked at his success. Verloc had been a good fellow, and certainly a very decent husband as far as one could see" (274). Ossipon is further surprised at Winnie's denunciation of Verloc as "a devil." Ossipon wonders "what sort of atrocities Verloc could have practised under the sleepy, placid appearances of his married life" (276).

> He even began to wonder whether the hidden causes of that Greenwich Park affair did not lie deep in the unhappy circumstances of the Verlocs' married life. (277)

Unwittingly, Ossipon has hit upon the true cause of the Greenwich Park outrage.

Planning to make use of Winnie "in a specially practical way" (278), Ossipon is terrified when he discovers she is a murderer and is intending to use *him* to help make her escape. Winnie, who has actually been sexually attracted to this "Apollo" all along, sees him as her only hope and believes in his protestations of love; she does not realize Ossipon has no idea of what has truly happened:

> [S]he had imagined her incoherence to be clearness itself. She had no conception of how little she had audibly said in the disjointed phrases completed only in her thought. She had felt the relief of a full confession, and she gave a special meaning to every sentence spoken by Comrade Ossipon, whose knowledge did not in the least resemble her own. (282)

Winnie, habitually silent, is not accustomed to making explanations. It is only when Ossipon discovers Verloc's body that he realizes the true situation. At first he suspects Verloc is only "simulating sleep"; Ossipon fears he is about to "be murdered for mysterious reasons by the couple Verloc" (285)—then he sees the knife in Verloc's breast. Ossipon is accustomed to view women as weak, malleable, and easily victimized; he is shocked to find Winnie capable of murder. She even physically overpowers him, in a parody of sexual embrace. Winnie and Ossipon are hiding from a policeman in the shop when Ossipon feels "his arms pinned to his side by a convulsive hug."

> He ceased to struggle; she never let him go. Her hands had locked themselves with an inseparable twist of fingers on his robust back. While the footsteps approached, they breathed quickly, breast to breast, with hard, laboured breaths.... (286)

Winnie finally seems "death itself" (291). Ossipon believes his very life is at stake. He foresees himself "living in abject terror in some obscure hamlet in Spain or Italy; till some fine morning they found him dead, too, with a knife in his breast—like Mr. Verloc" (291, 191). Winnie, however, has put all her trust in Ossipon, her "saviour." She is "no longer a free woman," and in giving over her freedom she condemns herself to another betrayal—and to the death she fears so much. Ossipon represents a terrible fatality for Winnie, as Conrad notes with heavy irony:

> She lamented aloud her love of life.... And, as often happens in the lament of poor humanity rich in suffering but indigent in words, the truth—the very cry of truth—was found in a worn and artificial shape picked up somewhere among the phrases of sham sentiment.
> "How could I be so afraid of death! Tom, I tried. But I am afraid. I tried to do away with myself. And I couldn't. Am I hard? I suppose the cup of horrors was not full enough for such as me. Then when you came...." (298)

Ossipon is left to live with the consequences of his act. He is tortured by remorse—although this seems not entirely consistent with his character—and haunted by the phrase from the newspaper article reporting Winnie's suicide: "This act of madness or despair." The phrase associates Winnie's will to destruction with the Professor's. "What do you know of madness and despair?" Ossipon asks the Professor, who replies: "Madness and despair! Give me that for a lever, and I'll move the world" (309). Madness and despair have tremendous destructive potential, and as we are often reminded, these destructive impulses can have their origin in such tender emotions as sympathy—as Stevie's "anguish of immoderate compassion was succeeded by the pain of an innocent but pitiless rage." When Inspector Heat gazes with horror at Stevie's remains—"an accumulation of raw material for a cannibal feast"—Conrad asserts that Heat is overcome "by the force of sympathy, which is a form of fear" (88).[20] The capacity for sympathy grows out of self-interest, just as much does the capacity for envy, and sympathy, compassion, pity lead inevitably, in *The Secret Agent*, to destruction. Michaelis, for example, has suffered his inhumanly cruel punishment as the result of the public's "outburst of furious indignation, of a raging, implacable pity for the victim" (196) of the politically motivated rescue attempt in which Michaelis was, peripherally, involved as a young idealist. Just as in the case of Winnie and Stevie, the sentiment of pity leads to a desire to vent one's spleen, to make "someone suffer for it." Thus, pity is a form of sentimentalism more dangerous in its way than the conscious, but selfless, will to destruction the Professor embodies.

But even the Professor is not so disinterested as he pretends. He is possessed of a totally unwarranted sense of his own merit and importance. The frustration of his overweening ambition leads the Professor to adopt, in a form of Satanic rebellion, an ethic of universal destruction. Life has treated him with "revolting injustice." Conrad remarks:

> The way of even the most justifiable revolutions is prepared by personal impulses disguised into creeds. The Professor's indignation found in itself a final cause that absolved him from the sin of turning to destruction as the agent of his ambition. (81)

That revolutionary movements have their origin in "personal impulses disguised into creeds" is an insight shared by Decoud and Monygham in *Nostromo* and by the narrarator in *Under Western Eyes* (although in the latter novel this judgment is called into question, as are other assumptions about politics inherent in *Nostromo* and *The Secret Agent*).

For Ossipon, Winnie embodies a destructive potential like the Professor's, and indeed Winnie, like her brother, is capable of savage indignation. Winnie and the Professor are associated in Ossipon's insights about their similar power to arouse terror.

> Ossipon had a vision of [the Professor's] round black-rimmed spectacles progressing along the streets on the top of an omnibus, their self-confident glitter falling here and there on the walls of houses or lowered upon the heads of the unconscious stream of people on the pavements. The ghost of a sickly smile altered the set of Ossipon's thick lips at the thought of the walls nodding, of people running for life at the sight of those spectacles. If they had only known! What a panic! (63)

Later, when Ossipon escorts Winnie to the train station after the murder, he observes: "She passed close to a little group of men who were laughing, but whose laughter could have been struck dead by a single word" (295).[21] Although the political terrorist and the domestic terrorist share the capacity for destruction, terror has an effect only in the domestic realm; the larger social world remains impervious. The explosion generated in the Verloc household, which was, ironically enough, intended to ward off the threat to Mr. Verloc's "repose and ... security," has caused the destruction of their small family, but has left the political fabric intact. The situation at the novel's end is much as it was at the beginning. Michaelis is still being cared for by the great lady; Yundt is still on the verge of being "extinguished"; Heat has lost his secret agent, but has not been forced to confront the Professor and his secret industry; the Assistant Commissioner has missed out on nailing Vladimir, but has preserved his social standing; and, of course, the Professor remains—the embodiment of the potential for disorder in an ordered, law-abiding society.

4
Under Western Eyes

> "History... is a nightmare from which I am trying to awake."
> —James Joyce, *Ulysses*

If *Nostromo* is largely concerned with the dangers inherent in action and *The Secret Agent* with the terrible destructive potential of sentiment, *Under Western Eyes* examines the murderous effect of words. The possible consequences of speech and of silence are pervasive themes in all three novels, of course: the habit of silence is as strong in the Gould household as in the Verloc. In *Under Western Eyes,* however, silence appears to have paradoxical consequences: on one hand, it offers an oasis of peace amid the continual hubbub of revolutionary jargon; on the other hand, it leads, as in *The Secret Agent,* to misunderstanding, betrayal, and death. The taciturnity of the aloof and solitary Razumov causes his fellow students to assume he is a deep thinker, a strong character, and politically committed, while in reality, Razumov is a blank page on which others project their hopes and desires and emotions.

The Secret Agent showed the effect of petty domestic matters on the wider political sphere; *Under Western Eyes,* like *Nostromo,* shows history intruding on the individual. However, *Under Western Eyes* shares *The Secret Agent*'s emphasis on victimization, but with a new twist—here victims seem *fated* for their roles. Verloc, Winnie, and even Stevie are victims because of their own misapprehensions of reality, but the suffering characters of *Under Western Eyes* are victims of cruel chance. This novel further offers an intensification of the earlier novels' terrible insight: to trust someone is to misunderstand him. Razumov, like Nostromo, inspires confidence in everyone, but is fated—also like Nostromo—to betray that confidence.

Conrad was always fascinated by the act of betrayal—the psychological motivations behind it and its consequences—but *Under Western Eyes* offers perhaps his most extended treatment of this theme. The central character, Razumov, is both a betrayer and a victim—a victim of Russian despotism; of his father, Prince K., who supports Razumov (meagerly) but refuses to acknowledge paternity; of the historical process; and of his own limitations. Solitary and utterly self-absorbed, Razumov's character is the opposite of Winnie Verloc's, whose existence was predicated on self-sacrifice and maternal devotion. Razumov is "nobody's child." And, "no home influences had shaped his opinions or his feelings. He was as lonely in the world as a man swimming in the deep sea."[1] Without family connections, even his name is "the mere label of a solitary individuality." Razumov bends all his efforts toward a single goal: a successful academic career. He wishes to "convert the label Razumov into an honoured name," since (as the narrator remarks) "A man's real life is that accorded to him in the thoughts of other men by reason of respect or natural love" (14). This observation proves highly ironic, as it turns out, for Razumov, like Nostromo, is condemned to destruction *because* he exists "in the thoughts of other men."

Razumov's secure, if straitened, existence is shattered when a fellow student, Haldin, who has just succeeded in assassinating a hated government official, comes to Razumov's room for aid. Razumov hardly knows Haldin, and has no idea why Haldin has turned to him. Haldin explains his choice with one word, "confidence." It is typical of the characters in this novel that they snatch at single words to explain complex phenomena: later, Haldin defines the divine element in the Russian soul as "resignation," and the book's narrator distills the essence of things Russian in the word "cynicism."

This narrator, an elderly Englishman who teaches languages, occasions quite a few technical problems for Conrad, but Conrad probably found him a necessity to provide psychic distance in dealing with a subject with so many painful autobiographical associations.[2] The narrator often denies any real connection with or understanding of the events and emotions he describes, as in the novel's opening sentence:

> To begin with I wish to disclaim the possession of those high gifts of imagination and expression which would have enabled my pen to create for the reader the personality of the man who called himself, after the Russian custom, Cyril, son of Isiodr—Kirylo Sidorovitch—Razumov.

He goes on to assure us that he "could not have observed Mr. Razumov or guessed at his reality by the force of insight, much less have imagined him as he was" (3). He also asserts that he has "no comprehension of the Russian character" (4). Although his profession is teaching languages, he has no faith in words, which are, for him, "the great foes of reality" (3). Razumov will come to share this conviction. For the narrator, the most striking feature of the Russian national character is loquacity, and it is Razumov's habit of silence that sets him apart and causes his fellow students to consider him "a strong nature—an altogether trustworthy man" (6), a man to whom Haldin unhesitatingly entrusts his life.

Haldin, who has misinterpreted Razumov's character and degree of political commitment, is self-deceived on other matters as well. Haldin describes the peasant Ziemianitch, whose team of horses he plans to use for his escape, as a "bright spirit," but when Razumov goes to fetch him, Ziemianitch is dead drunk. The other inhabitants of the inn where Ziemianitch resides, apostrophized by Haldin as the hope of the future, appear animal-like to Razumov. One customer is a "horrible, nondescript, shaggy being with a black face like the muzzle of a bear"; the owner has a "brown, cunning little face"; the slavey who does the washing up is a "wet and bedraggled creature, a sort of sexless and shivering scarecrow": Ziemianitch is a "pig," and a "pigeon"; while the inn itself is described as a "den," "a hive of human vermin," and a "byre."

Haldin romanticizes not only the peasants, but also his own historical role. He believes he has been divinely ordained for his revolutionary task.[3] "Men like me are necessary to make room for self-contained, thinking men like you"(19), Haldin tells Razumov—unconsciously turning the knife in the wound with the claim that he has acted for Razumov's benefit! Haldin even predicts his own immortality in several passages that perhaps derive from Conrad's original idea for the plot, in which Razumov was to marry Haldin's sister Natalia and they were to have a child who strongly resembled Haldin.[4] "My spirit shall go on warring in some Russian body till all falsehood is swept out of the world" (22), Haldin asserts; and once Russia has thrown off the yoke of tyranny, she will lead the rest of the world to a higher truth.

While Haldin expatiates on the future of Russia, Razumov is tormented by visions of his own future, now that he has been compromised by Haldin's arrival. Like the hero of *Lord Jim,* Razumov is afflicted with a too-vivid imagination.[5] Razumov's first thought, on learning of Haldin's crime, is: "There goes my silver medal" (16)! Razumov, in ironic counterpoint to Haldin's exalted explanation of his heroic mission, has a series of visions of what his own life is to become:

> Razumov saw himself shut up in a fortress.... He saw himself deported by an administrative order, his life broken, ruined, and robbed of all hope. He saw himself—at best—leading a miserable existence under police supervision, in some small, far-away provincial town....
>
> He saw his youth pass away from him in misery and half starvation—his strength give way, his mind become an abject thing. He saw himself creeping, broken down and shabby, about the streets—dying unattended in some filthy hole of a room....(21)

Meanwhile, Haldin has become dehumanized for Razumov, as Verloc was for Winnie in the moments before she murdered him. Razumov no longer thinks of Haldin as a person with an identity, a name: Haldin has become "this man," or "the man" (20, 21). Razumov has already unconsciously determined to betray Haldin. His experience with Haldin's "bright Russian soul," Ziemianitch, pushes him to the final decision.

As he walks through the snow on his mission to contact Ziemianitch, Razumov has a series of nightmarish visions. Passersby seem like terrible specters: "They came upon him suddenly, looming up black in the snowflakes close by, then vanishing all at once—without footfalls" (26). The very streets are maze-like and "interminable." And when Razumov, finding Ziemianitch drunk and totally insensible, takes out his frustration by beating the peasant with a stable fork, the scene is also nightmarish:

> ...the rain of blows fell in the stillness and shadows of the cellar-like stable. Razumov belaboured Ziemianitch with an insatiable fury, in great volleys of sounding thwacks. Except for the violent movements of Razumov nothing stirred, neither the beaten man nor the spoke-like shadows on the walls. And only the sound of blows was heard. (30)

The beating prefigures Razumov's own brutal beating by the revolutionaries at the end of the novel. Razumov's fate is closely entwined with Ziemianitch's: it is the news of the peasant's suicide that leads Razumov to confess everything.

To Razumov, Ziemianitch appears the embodiment of the Russian common man. The peasant and Haldin represent two fatal poles of the Russian character, and Razumov, the rational man (as he sees himself) is caught "[b]etween the drunk[en]...peasant incapable of action and the dream-intoxicat[ed]...idealist incapable of perceiving the reason of things, and the true character of men" (31). Like Nostromo, he is suddenly overwhelmed by the sense of his own isolation and loneliness:

> Razumov thought: "I am being crushed—and I can't even run away." Other men had somewhere a corner of the earth—some little house in the provinces where they had a right to take their troubles. A material refuge. He had nothing. He had not even a moral refuge—the refuge of confidence. To whom could he go with his tale—in all this great, great land?
> Razumov stamped his foot—and under the soft carpet of snow felt the hard ground of Russia, inanimate, cold, inert, like a sullen and tragic mother hiding her face under a winding-sheet—his native soil!—his very own—without a fireside, without a heart! (32, 33)

This image of Russia as a dead mother is particularly striking (and poignant) when we remember that Russia is, in fact, Razumov's only mother—his real mother is dead—and when we recall that Conrad's mother died a victim of the cold and heartless Russian winter.

Like Mother Russia herself, Haldin represents death; he is an uninvited evil, a fatality capriciously destructive, like Jones and Ricardo in *Victory*. Any contact with other human beings is potentially dangerous; merely by *knowing* Haldin, Razumov has placed his life in jeopardy. Razumov seems to suffer equally from his sense of isolation and from the sense of danger that human relationships evoke.

Having recognized that Russia is his true mother (even though a spectral and threatening presence), Razumov finds patriotism: "Is not this my country? Have I not got forty million brothers?" (35). From this perception, Razumov moves to a sort of religious conversion:

> The grace entered into Razumov. He believed now in the man who would come at the appointed time.
>
> ...
>
> [A]bsolute power should be preserved—the tool ready for the man—for the great autocrat of the future. (34, 35)

Like Haldin, Razumov believes in Russia's messianic role, but for Razumov the messiah will be "the great autocrat of the future"; Razumov, who until now has considered himself a liberal, discovers his convictions are conservative. He further rationalizes his decision:

> Betray. A great word. What is betrayal? They talk of a man betraying his country, his friends, his sweetheart. There must be a moral bond first. All a man can betray is his conscience. (37)

The decision to betray Haldin, really motivated by Razumov's fear for his own safety, has become "an act of conscience." As the narrator remarks, "Indeed it could hardly be called a decision. He had simply discovered what he had meant to do all along" (38, 39).

But in betraying Haldin, Razumov does not free himself from the threat the police represent; he puts himself into their hands. He is now suspect. Furthermore, he learns that had it not been for him Haldin surely would have escaped: "disappeared like a stone in the water" (47). Worst of all, after going to the police, Razumov is obliged to return to his rooms, and to send Haldin out to meet not a rescuer, but death.

This second interview between Razumov and Haldin is, like the first, replete with ironies, as Haldin misunderstands virtually every word Razumov speaks.[6] When, on Razumov's return, Haldin immediately begins praising the "rough sagacity" of Ziemianitch and the other *misérables* who frequent the inn Razumov has visited, we are struck by the almost comic incongruity between Haldin's perceptions and Razumov's. Razumov is overcome with hatred for Haldin, feeling "an insane temptation to grip [Haldin's] exposed throat and squeeze the breath out of that body," but Haldin misinterprets Razumov's emotion and looks "at Razumov with wistful gratitude for this manifestation of feeling" (57, 58). Razumov is further maddened by Haldin's Christ-like attitude. "They can kill my body but they cannot exile my soul from this world.... As to the destroyers of my mere body, I have forgiven them beforehand," Haldin says (58). Nevertheless, Razumov feels an almost overwhelming temptation to confess everything. He needs to explain himself to Haldin—in words, of course, that Haldin cannot understand.[7] Razumov points out to Haldin the differences in their situations:

> "You are a son, a brother, a nephew, a cousin—I don't know what—to no end of people. I am just a man.... Did it ever occur to you how a man who had never heard a word of warm affection or praise in his life would think on matters on which you would think first with or against your class, your domestic tradition—your fireside prejudices?... I have no domestic tradition. I have nothing to think against. My tradition is historical. What have I to look back to but that national past from which you gentlemen want to wrench away your future? (61)

Haldin has a history, a name, a family; Razumov has only Mother Russia: "You come from your province, but all this land is mine—or I have nothing," he tells Haldin.[8] Haldin has explained to Razumov that his lack of family was one reason he was chosen for this "confidence," and Razumov thinks bitterly: "Because I haven't that, must everything else be taken away from me?" But Haldin does not realize that Razumov resents him; indeed, he completely misinterprets Razumov's words. When, after Razumov's impassioned speech, Haldin asserts "with awe-struck dismay" that he now understands everything, Razumov thinks that Haldin now knows Razumov has betrayed him. Haldin, however has put a different construction on Razumov's words: "I see now how it is, Razumov—brother. You are a magnanimous soul, but my action is abhorrent to you—alas..." (62). Haldin departs to meet his fate, misunderstanding Razumov to the last.

Henceforth, Razumov will be misunderstood by virtually everyone he meets. His fellow students, as well as the police, now believe Razumov was implicated in the assassination. As earlier Razumov felt crushed between the peasant ("incapable of action") and the idealist ("incapable of perceiving the reason of things"), now he is threatened both "by the lawlessness of autocracy—for autocracy knows no law—and the lawlessness of revolution" (77).

Summoned by the police to an interview with the formidable Councillor Mikulin, Razumov suffers another nightmare vision:

> Razumov beheld his own brain suffering on the rack—a long, pale figure drawn asunder horizontally with terrific force in the darkness of a vault, whose face he failed to see. It was as though he had dreamed for an infinistesimal fraction of time of some dark print of the Inquisition. (88)

Razumov feels "anguish at the circumstance that there was no one whatever near the pale and extended figure. The solitude of the racked victim was particularly horrible to behold." It is a waking nightmare of the tortures of isolation. Although Razumov believed that in betraying Haldin to the police he was asserting his membership in the mystical body of Mother Russia, he was in reality cutting himself off from all mankind. In this vision we can also see Razumov beginning to identify with Haldin. By the end of the novel, he has psychically appropriated much of Haldin's experience, which he uses, only partly consciously, to deceive the revolutionaries. Haldin, of course, has been "racked"—tortured by the police before being condemned to death.

Ironically enough, Razumov is finally driven to embrace the isolation he finds so terrifying here, as the consequences of his act of betrayal make any human contact seem "racking." His only possible escape is withdrawal into a world of silence. At this point, however, Razumov still longs for human understanding—he the perpetually misunderstood. Having been led to denounce Haldin partly because of sentiment for his father, who symbolizes the social order Haldin menaces, Razumov has convinced himself that Prince K. truly understands him. He is bitterly disappointed to learn that not only has the Prince agreed to Razumov's being named to Haldin as his betrayer, but also that the Prince knows he has been called in by the police. Diabolically, Mikulin plays on Razumov's longing for understanding and for his father's love, using Prince K. to help induce Razumov to become a spy:

> Prince K– was persuaded to intervene personally, and on a certain occasion gave way to a manly emotion which, all unexpected as it was, quite upset Mr. Razumov. The sudden embrace of that man, agitated by his loyalty to a throne and by suppressed paternal affection, was a revelation to Mr. Razumov of something within his own breast. (307, 308)

So Razumov, the betrayer of a comrade, is betrayed by his own father, who has already betrayed him by his refusal to acknowledge paternity.

Razumov has chosen Prince K. and the autocratic order he represents over Haldin and possible chaos. But Razumov has come within a hair of going the other way. In his quest for understanding—"understanding" is, for Razumov, the single word that defines the solution to his dilemma—Razumov is first tempted to confess all of his confusions to Haldin: a confession "that would end in embraces and tears; in an incredible fellowship of souls"...(40). However, this vision is immediately dispelled by another: "The glimpse of a passing grey whisker, caught and lost in the same instant, had evoked the complete image of Prince K–, the man who once had pressed his hand as no other man had pressed it—a faint but lingering pressure like a secret sign, like a half-willing caress" (40). Razumov's need for fatherly understanding leads him to betrayal, and finally leads him to give over his soul to Mikulin (also a father figure) by becoming a police spy—the most odious of all possible occupations for Razumov, who detests secrecy and lies.

Nevertheless, we are not told specifically that Razumov has become a spy until late in the novel.[9] Part One ends in ambiguity, as Razumov, confused by his first interview with Mikulin, announces his intention "to retire—simply to retire," and the enigmatic Mikulin counters with the question: "Where to?" (99). In contrast to Part One, the rest of the novel presents Razumov as a man of mystery—perceived, or most often misperceived, by others. We are much more conscious, in the Geneva section, of the interventions and interpretations of the first person narrator—who often virtually disappears in Part One, to be replaced by an omniscient consciousness. In the latter part of the novel, the narrator tends to get in the way of the action and to obscure our view of the characters' true motives and emotions. In fact, his presence seems, somehow, to prevent the novel from becoming the love story Conrad originally planned. The direction of the intended plot is reversed. Razumov, who originally was to marry Natalia Haldin in retaliation for her brother's "crime," remains the novel's quintessential victim, instead of becoming a victimizer.

The originally intended victim, Natalia, is surprisingly strong and self-sufficient, in contrast to Razumov, who is often on the verge of hysteria. The narrator, whose emotional involvement with Natalia remains mysterious, describes her in peculiarly bisexual terms. Her voice is "deep, almost harsh, and yet caressing in its harshness." Her glance is "intrepid," and "as direct and trustful as that of a young man..." (102). Elsewhere, her voice is again described as "slightly harsh, but fascinating with its masculine and bird-like quality" (141). The narrator responds to her handshake with: "The grip of her strong, shapely hand had a seductive frankness, a sort of exquisite virility" (118).[10]

The narrator emphasizes the fact that, although he has great admiration and esteem for Natalia, he finds her political beliefs mystifying and disquieting. (Like her brother, Natalia believes in Russia's messianic mission to find a "better way" than the institutions of Western political liberalism to abolish partisan discord.) When Natalia asserts that "occidentals" are unable to understand the Russian political situation, the narrator agrees, but goes on to make a surprisingly strong denunciation of the Russian character:

> I suppose one must be a Russian to understand Russian simplicity, a terrible corroding simplicity in which mystic phrases clothe a naive and hopeless cynicism. I think sometimes that the psychological secret of the profound difference of the people consists in this, that they detest life, the irremediable life of the earth as it is, whereas we westerners cherish it with perhaps an equal exaggeration of its sentimental value. (104)

Earlier, the narrator, searching for the *logos* to define the Russian spirit ("some key-word...a word that could stand at the back of all the words covering the pages...") has discovered it to be "cynicism":

For that it is the mark of Russian autocracy and of Russian revolt. In its pride of numbers, in its strange pretensions of sanctity, and in the secret readiness to abase itself in suffering, the spirit of Russia is the spirit of cynicism. (67)

Razumov himself shares this perception, as he later tells Peter Ivanovitch: "We are Russians, that is—children; that is—sincere; that is—cynical, if you like" (207). The associations Razumov makes seems very strange, but he is speaking out of his experience with the child-like Ziemianitch and with the sincere Haldin, as well as with the cynical Mikulin. For the narrator, however, the meaning of the words Russians use remains impenetrable: "The most precise of [Natalia's] sayings seemed always to me to have enigmatical prolongations vanishing somewhere beyond my reach" (118).

But if speech is incomprehensible, or deliberately obfuscating, Russian silence has its own menace. When Mrs. Haldin is told of her son's arrest, it is her silence that alarms the narrator and Natalia:

> It was the stillness of a great tension. What if it should suddenly snap? Even the door of Mrs. Haldin's room, with the old mother alone in there, had a rather awful aspect. (112)

The threat of silence, the sense of something terrible hidden behind closed doors, looks forward to Miss Haldin's experience on her first visit to Château Borel, the principal meeting place for the Russian emigrés. Here Natalia is also confronted with closed doors and, at first, silence; then she hears a disembodied voice, speaking an incomprehensible language. The scene is dream-like:

> The front door stood wide open. There was no one about. She found herself in a wide, lofty, and absolutely empty hall, with a good many doors. These doors were all shut. A broad, bare stone staircase faced her, and the effect of the whole was of an untenanted house. She stood still, disconcerted by the solitude, but after a while she became aware of a voice speaking continuously somewhere....
> She could not make out the language—Russian, French, or German. No one seemed to answer it. It was as though the voice had been left behind by the departed inhabitants to talk to the bare walls.... An invincible repugnance prevented her from opening one of the doors in the hall. It was so hopeless. No one would come, the voice would never stop. (144)

Natalia's frightening sense of isolation recalls Razumov's earlier vision of the lonely racked victim, and also reflects her real situation in Geneva—cut off as she is from her homeland, from the "Western" natives, and from the other Russian emigrés. Indeed, Natalia's and Razumov's situations are quite similar: both are solitary and vulnerable "orphans" (since Mrs. Haldin, after the shock of her son's death, is unable to provide any motherly support to Natalia).[11]

The numerous closed doors Natalia cannot bring herself to open suggest the story of Bluebeard—with whom the revolutionary writer and "feminist"

Peter Ivanovitch is associated.[12] Peter Ivanovitch has been trying to lure Natalia into his orbit. He is the narrator's *bête noire*.[13] The narrator resents and fears Peter Ivanovitch's influence on Natalia; he hates especially Peter Ivanovitch's speechifying, and he fancies Miss Haldin is "drowning" in the Russian's rhetoric, as the sound of his voice seems to issue grotesquely from somewhere other than his mouth: "The deep sound seemed to rise from under the floor, and one felt steeped in it to the lips" (12). In contrast, the narrator takes pride in his "silent friendship" with Natalia, although he fears his silence can offer her no protection, that he is only a "dumb helpless ghost" (126). Natalia does not appear to need protection, however. She is never in any danger of falling under Peter Ivanovitch's sway. It is the narrator who is obsessed with the "heroic fugitive."

Peter Ivanovitch's characterization has certain resemblances to that of Michaelis in *The Secret Agent:* both have been prisoners and have been profoundly altered by that experience, both have lost their fiancees, and both have been taken up by high-born patronesses.[14] But whereas Michaelis seems eunuch-like and gives an impression of childish innocence, Peter Ivanovitch is most often seen as strongly sexual—although there are, as we shall see, ambiguities in the narrator's view of him, as in the characterization of Natalia. Peter Ivanovitch's sexual relationship with his "great lady," Madame de S., inspires both the narrator and Razumov with intense disgust. Although originally intended to be youthful, Madame de S. becomes, in the final version of the novel, "an ancient, painted mummy."[15] The narrator notes that Peter Ivanovitch "preached generally the cult of the woman. For his own part he practised it under the rites of special devotion to the transcendental merits of a certain Madame de S—... (125)." This implies that the narrator feels strongly that it is not Peter Ivanovitch's "feminism" that constitutes a threat to the innocent Natalia, but his sexuality. The narrator describes the carriage rides the couple takes through Geneva as a "public manifestation," that is "hardly decent."

Razumov's reaction is like the narrator's. On meeting Madame de S., Razumov is struck by "the death-like immobility of an obviously painted face," by her "black, fathomless stare," and by her "smile which made him think of a grinning skull." Peter Ivanovitch's relationship with her seems necrophilic, and Razumov finds it physically sickening.

Peter Ivanovitch wears dark glasses and a high silk hat. The glasses give him a gaze of "glossy steadfastness" that suggests the inhuman. Razumov feels he is being watched from behind those spectacles and, just as the narrator had the illusion that Peter Ivanovitch's voice issued from the floor, Razumov feels the voice "proceed[s] from under the steady spectacles of Peter Ivanovitch, rather than from his lips" (216). The hat, an anomalous garment for a revolutionary, is a reminder that Peter Ivanovitch is an aristocrat, a member of the class he conspires to overthrow. The hat also seems to be something of a sexual symbol. When the narrator encounters the "great feminist" at the Haldins' he notes that the hat rests "on the floor by the side of his chair" (119), and when a few minutes later Peter Ivanovitch picks it up the narrator hopes it is a sign that he is about to depart, "but [he] only... deposit[s] it on his knees" (127). As Peter Ivanovitch exhorts Natalia to join the struggle, the narrator's view of the revolutionary as alternately threateningly sexual and hopelessly impotent is indicated by his mention of the hat: "He raised for a moment one thick arm; the other remained hanging down against his thigh, with the fragile silk hat at the end" (129). The narrator sees Peter Ivanovitch as at once savage and effete:

> He towered before [Natalia], enormous, deferential, cropped as close as a convict; and this big pinkish poll evoked for me the vision of a wild head with matted locks peering through parted bushes, glimpses of naked, tawny limbs slinking behind the masses of sodden foliage under a cloud of flies and mosquitoes. It was an involuntary tribute to the vigour of his writing. Nobody could doubt that he had wandered in Siberian forests, naked and girt with a chain. The black broadcloth coat invested his person with a character of austere decency—something recalling a missionary. (128, 129)

Peter Ivanovitch is both a "pinkish poll" and a beast in the jungle, a missionary and a convict.

The narrator's vision of the "feminist" as bestial fugitive, "naked and girt with a chain"—of the reality (perhaps) behind the broadcloth coat—is described as "an involuntary tribute to the vigour of his writing." The word has power to unleash the beast, as Decoud also discovered in his career as journalist, and as Ossipon knew when he composed his "improper" pamphlets. Peter Ivanovitch is one of a long line of writers Conrad condemns as humbugs or worse.

The narrator vacillates between viewing Peter Ivanovitch as ridiculous and seeing him as menacing, but to Razumov the revolutionary always presents a threat: Peter Ivanovitch may "see through" Razumov at any moment. Razumov, on the occasion of his visit to Madame de S., is also struck by Peter Ivanovitch's hat—or rather by its absence, indicating as it does the sexual license Peter Ivanovitch enjoys.

> The ceremonious black frock-coat and the bared head of Europe's greatest feminist accentuated the dubiousness of his status in the house rented by Madame de S—, his Egeria. His aspect combined the formality of the caller with the freedom of the proprietor. (205)

Again, ambiguously, the hat suggests both Peter Ivanovitch's sexual assertion and his toadying, dependent relationship with Madame de S. A little later, Razumov, maddened by Peter Ivanovitch's claim of psychic kinship with him, and by the need constantly to dissemble, contemplates murder.

> Peter Ivanovitch, meditating behind his dark glasses, became to him suddenly so odious that if he had had a knife he fancied he could have stabbed him not only without compunction, but with a horrible triumphant satsifaction. His imagination dwelt on that atrocity in spite of himself.... "I could get away by breaking the fastening on the little gate in the back wall.... Nobody in the house seems to know he is here with me. Oh yes. The hat! These women would discover presently the hat he has left on the landing. They would come upon him, lying dead in this damp gloomy shade—." (209)

Razumov is bested by Peter Ivanovitch's hat! This hat is the first object Razumov notices on reentering the chateau: "On the balustrade of the first-floor landing a shiny tall hat reposed, rim upwards." (This recalls the similar detail in *The Secret Agent*, where Verloc's hat lies beside his dead body "as if prepared to receive the contributions of pence." Peter Ivanovitch, however, has been murdered only mentally.) As elsewhere, the symbol seems to suggest both masculinity and its opposite—Peter Ivanovitch has been unmanned by Madame de S. When Madame de S. calls for cakes, Peter Ivanovitch produces them from the hat, like a magician.

The narrative ambiguity attached to Peter Ivanovitch is perhaps most evident in the account of his adventures as a fugitive, a "stealthy, primeval savage, pitilessly cunning in the preservation of his freedom from day to day, like a tracked wild beast" (122). He is encumbered with a heavy chain, "wound about his waist"; another sexual symbol carrying somewhat contradictory implications:

> These links, [Peter Ivanovitch] fancied, made him odious to the rest of mankind. It was a repugnant and suggestive load. Nobody could feel any pity at the disgusting sight of a man escaping with a broken chain. (123)

The great rhetorician has even lost the power of speech, having completely reverted to a prehuman condition. Finally, however, the "bestial creature" encounters a woman and, as in the fairy tale, is miraculously restored to humanity:

> He had become a dumb and despairing brute, till the woman's sudden, unexpected cry of profound pity, the insight of her feminine compassion discovering the complex misery of the man under the terrifying aspect of the monster, restored him to the ranks of humanity. This point of view is presented in his book, with a very effective eloquence. She ended, he says, by shedding tears over him, sacred, redeeming tears, while he also wept with joy in the manner of a converted sinner. (124)[16]

The "wild beast" is easily tamed. We are reminded, also, that it is Peter Ivanovitch himself who has created this mythic scene; as a writer, he has transformed his experience into a moral fable—a fable that the narrator finds both menacing and ridiculous.

Although the narrator repeatedly states he fears Natalia will fall under Peter Ivanovitch's influence, there is no indication that she is tempted in the slightest to do so. She only agrees to visit Château Borel because she hopes to meet Razumov, of whom her brother has written glowingly. Peter Ivanovitch tells Natalia that Razumov is "already under the charm" of Madame de S.—a fact Conrad evidently forgot, since later we see Peter Ivanovitch presenting Razumov to the old lady and we are told, "Razumov had never seen Madame de S— but in the carriage" (211).[17]

Peter Ivanovitch describes Razumov as "silent, like a man who has been shown the way of peace," an ironic misinterpretation. However, Razumov's silence contrasts sharply with Peter Ivanovitch's volubility. Natalia hopes Razumov "will have something to give me, if nothing more than a few poor words" (137), but although she expects the gift of words from Razumov it is in his silence that his power resides. His taciturnity inspires confidence. It is not only in his silence that Razumov's character is opposed to Peter Ivanovitch's; whereas the "feminist" is perceived as sexually threatening, Razumov is curiously asexual.

Originally, Conrad conceived the love story as central to the novel, but the final form of the plot is quite different. Not only do Razumov and Natalia not marry, they have virtually no contact with one another; their relationship hardly exists. Most of the meetings between them occur off stage and are recounted at second or third remove.[18] In the earlier plot outline, Natalia was to be Razumov's victim, but in the novel's final version it is Razumov who is the principal victim. It is politics that leads to destruction; the sexual theme is subordinate. In fact, as George Goodin has pointed out, in the first American edition of the novel it is made clear that Razumov has *no* romantic interest in Natalia.[19] Goodin quotes a passage, deleted from later editions, occurring just before Razumov goes to confess to Natalia and her mother.

> The fact that these were women he was going to meet did not trouble him especially. As a matter of fact, he did not recognize women as women. There had been literally no feminine influence in his life. Women were human beings for him and nothing more, somewhat in the background, not to be thought of in any special way. He simply knew nothing of them in any relation; no woman had ever influenced a dream of his, taken up a moment of his time, or awakened any of his dormant feelings; no thought of woman had enriched his life by a touch of amenity, of color, of revery. It may be said that, in a manner, he had never seen a woman, for even Sophia Antonovna was a conspirator, a revolutionist, a dangerous person with whom he must be on his guard more than with anybody else—nothing more.[20]

Goodin also notes that, along with deleting this passage, Conrad *added* these sentences to Razumov's diary: "I felt that I must tell you that I had ended by loving you. And to tell you that I must first confess." Goodin remarks, "This passage is the only one in the novel which authorizes us to say definitely that

Razumov loved Natalia."[21] Conrad may have tried to restore the missing "love interest" at the end of the novel to supply a stronger motivation for Razumov's confession. In any case, in the novel as it stands, the relationship between Razumov and Natalia is quite tenuous.

As we have noted, Razumov and Natalia are similarly situated: exiled, isolated, and effectively orphaned, since each is deprived of parental support. Tekla, who serves as Peter Ivanovitch's amanuensis and as maid-of-all-work at Château Borel, shares these characteristics. Like Razumov and Natalia, furthermore, Tekla has become politically involved because of family influence. But whereas Razumov's political commitment arose out of his frustrated love for his father, and Natalia's out of a family tradition of liberalism, Tekla's devotion to revolution is a form of rebellion against the family she hates. Tekla has devoted herself to the care of a young man who has been crippled by a police beating. (This revolutionary's fate foretells Razumov's: he has betrayed his comrades—but, like Monygham, only under torture—and suffers unbearable mental anguish and terrible physical retribution.) When the young man dies, Tekla drifts into revolutionary activity as a courier, ending up in Geneva. She, too, is given rather contradictory characteristics—a scared slavey, skuttling about, wincing under the careless cruelty of Peter Ivanovitch, on the periphery of revolutionary activity (her main task is tending the cat), she is also strong-willed, determined, selfless, and deeply commited to revolution, in contrast to Peter Ivanovitch and Madame de S., whose "revolution" is mere rhetoric. "The greatest joy of my life has been to hear what your brother had done," Tekla tells Natalia.

Natalia's meeting with Tekla occurs immediately before her first meeting with Razumov, and Tekla's account of her sufferings at the hands of "the great feminist"—as well as Natalia's witnessing Peter Ivanovitch's humiliating rebukes to Tekla—ends the possibility that Natalia might be drawn into Peter Ivanovitch's orbit. So at the moment she first meets Razumov she has already become free of the "threat" Peter Ivanovitch represents, defusing the dramatic tension of the situation (Natalia, in effect, caught between the two men, each of whom wants to "steal her soul") that Conrad seems to have been at pains to establish. (The narrator's concern about Peter Ivanovitch's influence on Natalia always seems exaggerated; she is too strong-minded and independent for us to believe she could be taken in.) In fact, the meeting between Razumov and Natalia is presented in such an incredibly convoluted way it seems hardly dramatized at all. One expects an important confrontation, but Conrad backs away from the scene.

After Natalia catches sight of Razumov approaching Château Borel in the company of Peter Ivanovitch the actual meeting is postponed for a number of pages, first by the narrator's rambling digression on how he has come to know so much about Mme. de S., and then by Natalia's account of Peter Ivanovitch's insults to Tekla. The scene between Natalia and Razumov is recounted at two removes: the narrator has his information from Natalia and from Razumov's journal. There is little direct dialogue reported—in keeping with Conrad's general reluctance to show Razumov and Natalia conversing. Natalia tells the narrator of her own emotional reactions, and describes Razumov sketchily, noting only that he seemed quite moved at meeting her. Of course, she completely misinterprets the reason for Razumov's agitation:

> He was quite overcome. I have told you my opinion that he is a man of deep feeling—it is impossible to doubt it. You should have seen his face. He positively reeled. He leaned against the wall of the terrace. Their friendship must have been the very brotherhood of souls! (172)

We have already been told Razumov's *real* emotion when he learns Natalia's identity:

> It stands recorded in the pages of his self-confession, that it nearly suffocated him physically with an emotional reaction of hate and dismay, as though her appearance had been a piece of accomplished treachery. (167)

The relationship between Razumov and Natalia, like that between Decoud and Antonia, between Winnie and Verloc, between Anthony and Flora in *Chance,* and between Heyst and Lena in *Victory,* is founded on misunderstanding.

Natalia hopes Razumov will somehow take her brother's place, will help her "[find] again a little of what I thought was lost to me forever, with the loss of my brother—some of that hope, inspiration, and support which I used to get from my dear dead..." (273). Most importantly, she hopes he can tell her how Victor came to be captured by the police, since her mother has developed the obsessive conviction that Victor had not planned to escape—that his revolutionary act was a form of suicide. At Natalia's behest, the narrator tries to explain the situation to Razumov, who reacts to the narrator's innocent statements with terror.

> "There was something peculiar in the circumstances of [Haldin's] arrest. You no doubt know the whole truth...."
> I felt my arm seized above the elbow, and next instant found myself swung so as to face Mr. Razumov.
> "You spring up from the ground before me with this talk. Who the devil are you? What do you know what is or is not peculiar?" (186)

When he finally understands the narrator's meaning, Razumov's reaction is immediate: "Must I go then and lie to that old woman!" But, on leaving the narrator, Razumov speculates:

> "Won't the truth do! The truth for the crazy old mother of the—"
> The young man shuddered again. Yes. The truth would do! Apparently it would do. Exactly. And receive thanks, he thought, formulating the unspoken words cynically. "Fall on my neck in gratitude, no doubt," he jeered mentally. (199, 200)

As, earlier, Razumov was tempted to confess to Haldin, here, already buckling under the strain of playing a hateful role—and Razumov has only just arrived in Geneva—he considers casting falsehood aside in favor of truth-telling. In fact, for the remainder of the novel, Razumov is continually on the verge of confession. He is clearly unfit for a life of intrigue and espionage, and the reader may wonder why the astute Mikulin did not see this immediately.

After Natalia's meeting with Razumov at Château Borel, the love story is virtually forgotten. In fact, Natalia hardly appears in the novel again, until the climactic confession. We have instead a series of confrontations between Razumov and various other characters, including the narrator; but most of these confrontations take the form of tests, real or imagined, as Razumov tries to gain acceptance among the revolutionaries and tries, rather half-heartedly, to elicit information. (Razumov actually writes only one report to Mikulin, immediately after his meeting with Mme de S.; it is important to Conrad's moral scheme that Razumov does the revolutionaries little damage.) In all these confrontations, Razumov is continually on the verge of giving himself away. He is seized by a spirit of perversity that, coupled with his hatred of lying, causes him to deal dangerously in double-meanings and in irony. Speaking with Peter Ivanovitch, Razumov chafes under the suspicion that he is being watched and judged:

> "Curse him," said Razumov to himself, "he is waiting behind his spectacles for me to give myself away." Then aloud, with a satanic enjoyment of the scorn prompting him to play with the greatness of the great man—
> "Ah, Peter Ivanovitch, if you only knew the force which drew—no, which *drove* me toward you! The irresistible force.
> ...
> I have been impelled, compelled, or rather sent—let us say sent—towards you for a work that no one but myself can do.... It is absurd to me to talk like this, yet some day you will remember these words, I hope. Enough of this. Here I stand before you—confessed!" (228, 229)

Of course, the force that has driven Razumov to Peter Ivanovitch is Councillor Mikulin. This ironic "confession" presages Razumov's later confession.

In his confrontations with the revolutionaries, Razumov is alternately silent and voluble, fearing self-disclosure, but driven unconsciously to pour out everything. He speaks habitually in a tone of nervous irritation, of barely repressed anger, and of heavy irony. Sophia Antonovna, the most admirable of the revolutionaries, excepting Tekla, finally bursts out: "Leave off railing.... Remember, Razumov, that women, children, and revolutionaries hate irony, which is the negation of all saving instincts, of all faith, of all devotion, of all action" (279). Only with Tekla does Razumov take a gentler tone. Like Razumov, Tekla is an outsider in this milieu: Tekla is deemed of no account; Razumov is not what he pretends. Both are nameless. Tekla tells Razumov:

> No one is told my name.... I have no use for a name, and I have almost forgotten it myself. (235)

Razumov, because he is illegitimate, also has no real name, as he points out more than once. Both are prisoners of their situation: Razumov cannot leave Geneva without Mikulin's permission; Tekla cannot leave because, as Razumov reflects, "the mere fact of leaving the great man [Peter Ivanovitch] abruptly would make her a suspect" (236).

Most important, perhaps, Razumov and Tekla share a distrust of words. After listening for years to Peter Ivanovitch, Tekla has come to hate all rhetoric, just as Razumov finds unbearable the Russian habit of speechifying and gossiping. Razumov will find in deafness a release from the oppression of words, while Tekla says she has no need of speech: "Who would ever want to hear what I could say?" (237).

In contrast to Tekla, who offers Razumov unquestioning support and devotion, Sophia Antonovna, the only one of the revolutionaries Razumov respects, represents "a distinct danger in his path" (242). She alone, of all the emigrés, perceives Razumov's real mood: "What's the matter with you is that you don't like us," she says. "I don't think you understand me," replies Razumov, the perpetually misunderstood—although he fears she understands him all too well. For her part, Sophia Antonovna reproaches Razumov for his typically "masculine" faults: faults conventionally attributed to women:

> Ah! Kirylo Sidorovitch, you like other men are fastidious, full of self-love and afraid of trifles. Moreover, you had no training. What you want is to be taken in hand by some woman. (243)

The sexual ambiguities present in the characterizations of Peter Ivanovitch and Natalia are most evident in this confrontation between Razumov and Sophia. Both use the rhetoric of the war between the sexes here, but the usual sexual stereotypes seem to be reversed. So Sophia (who, like Natalia, has a "manly hand-grasp") accuses Razumov of taking everything personally: "You men are so impressionable and self-conscious," she says (240). And when Razumov responds to her assertion of faith in the final triumph of the revolution with: "And is it to Peter Ivanovitch that you owe that faith?" she counters: "That's just like a man.... As if it were possible to tell how a belief comes to one" (245). In effect, she is reproaching him for assuming that one's ideas result only from one's attachment to another person. She also accuses him of being too subjective: "You've got to trample down every particle of your own feelings..." (245), and with believing that good fortune rather than hard work will carry the day.

> You men are all alike. You mistake luck for merit.... You men are ridiculously pitiful in your aptitude to cherish childish illusions down to the very grave. (246)

She further charges Razumov with being sexually over-delicate, telling him that his dislike of Peter Ivanovitch stems from his disapproval of the liaison with Mme de S.: "some of his [i.e., Razumov's] conventional notions are shocked, some of his pretty masculine standards. You might think he was one of those nervous sensitivities that come to a bad end" (248). When Razumov insists that Peter Ivanovitch's courtship of Mme de S. makes him sick, Sophia bursts out: "Oh, you squeamish, masculine creature." She does concede however, that "when you [men] manage to throw off your masculine cowardice and prudishness you are not to be equalled by us. Only, how seldom..." (25). Razumov himself appears to accept this reversal of sexual stereotyping when he tells Sophia he speaks with "masculine frivolity" (251).

Razumov also uses the epithets of the war between the sexes. When Sophia asks what Haldin was like, Razumov, to whom the mention of Haldin always acts as a red flag, answers:

> How like a woman.... What is the good of concerning yourself with his appearance? Whatever it was, he is removed beyond all feminine influence now. (247)

Sophia Antonovna has not inquired about Haldin's appearance, in fact, but about his character, but the question (and the questioner) recall to Razumov his original jealousy of those "feminine influences" in Haldin's life, of Haldin's position as son and brother. It is the continual reminder of this basest part of Razumov's motivation for betrayal that makes the presence of Natalia and Mrs. Haldin in Geneva so painful for Razumov. Sophia, who is an astute psychologist, recognizes the depth of emotion behind Razumov's outburst, although, of course, not its cause. Her response is, "You suffer, Razumov..." (247).

As the novel's most selfless and committed revolutionary, Sophia Antonovna embodies Conrad's belief that women are often more faithful to a cause, less sentimental about human relationships, and more ruthless in achieving their ends than are men. All the novel's women have a strength of character and of purpose the men seem to lack—even Mme de S., who turns out to have been using Peter Ivanovitch, and who outfoxes him by failing to leave him her money.[22] Sophia alludes to Mme de S. specifically when she tells Razumov: "In life, you see, there is not much choice. You have either to rot or to burn. And there is not one of us [women], painted or unpainted, that would not rather burn that rot" (250).

Although Razumov fears Sophia's perspicacity and realizes that she is his most formidable adversary, he again cannot resist the spirit of perversity that seizes him. He speaks with heavy irony, using words that mean one thing to Sophia and quite another to Razumov. So, when Sophia speaks of "that uncompromising sense of necessity and justice which armed your and Haldin's hands to strike down the fanatical brute," Razumov answers: "I can't speak for the dead. As for myself, I can assure you that my conduct was dictated by necessity and by the sense of—well—retributive justice." He reflects:

> Stripped of rhetoric, mysticism, and theories, [Sophia] was the true spirit of destructive revolution. And she was the personal adversary he had to meet. It gave him a feeling of triumphant pleasure to deceive her out of her own mouth. The epigrammatic saying that speech has been given to us for the purpose of concealing our thoughts came into his mind. (261)

As early as his second interview with Haldin, Razumov has been taking up others' words and giving them an ironic twist, deceiving people out of their own mouths. This compulsion arises from his hatred of lying. Although as a spy his whole life is a lie, he tries always to speak from his own psychological truth, even while he knows his words will be misinterpreted. Because he must continually conceal his thoughts, and because he believes he is fated to be forever misunderstood, Razumov comes to the conviction that all speech is a lie.

Councillor Mikulin has instructed Razumov to "see and hear" (311), but Razumov himself is tormented by the idea that he is being watched and that the falsehoods he utters are not believed. Trying to explain to Sophia Antonovna his actions on the day of the assassination, Razumov feels "the steady curiosity of the black eyes fastened on his face as if the woman revolutionist received the sound of his voice into her pupils instead of her ears" (257)—as Peter Ivanovitch's voice seemed to issue from behind his glasses. (The murderous Nikita's voice, however, "seemed to proceed from that thing like a balloon he carried under his overcoat" [266].) Razumov has the impression that these people are grotesques—fearsome mechanical beings that watch and listen and speak words designed to entrap.[23] Razumov longs for silence and invisibility. "The people that are neither seen nor heard are the lucky ones—in Russia" (258), he tells Sophia. Razumov loathes the idea that he is being discussed by others. As he says to Mikulin, Haldin's unforgivable crime is that: "He went about talking of me" (96).[24] "Oh, we are great in talking about each other," Razumov has cried to Peter Ivanovitch. "Gossip, tales, suspicions, and all that sort of thing, we know how to deal in to perfection. Calumny, even" (206). When Razumov learns that Sophia Antonovna has received a letter from Petersburg describing Razumov's activities at the time of the assassination, he is astounded.

> Who could have written about him...?
> He smiled inwardly at the absolute wrong-headedness of the whole thing, the self-deception of a criminal idealist shattering his existence like a thunder-clap out of a clear sky, and re-echoing amongst the wreckage in the false assumptions of those other fools. (258)

The metaphor prefigures the blow, like a thunder-clap, that will burst Razumov's eardrums, leaving him finally in blessed silence.

The letter, however, brings not exposure but exoneration. It contains the story of Ziemianitch's suicide, convincing the revolutionaries that the peasant is the probable betrayer of Haldin. When Razumov understands that he is finally safe, he is at first relieved:

> No more need of lies. I shall have only to listen and to keep my scorn from getting the upper hand of my caution. (284)

But soon Razumov discovers that his very safety condemns him to go on forever playing this hateful role. His precipitous confession follows. Razumov is also surprised to find that he feels pity for Ziemianitch, "a large neutral pity, such as one may feel for an unconscious multitude, a great people seen from above—like a community of crawling ants working out its destiny" (283, 284). For Razumov, Ziemianitch symbolizes all the enslaved common people of Russia.

Earlier in his conversation with Sophia, Razumov has asserted that their common nationality makes them kin: "don't you think, Sophia Antonovna, that you and I come from the same cradle?"—in answer to her charge that Razumov "must have bitten something bitter in [his] cradle" (253). This claim to brotherhood is in sharp contrast to his earlier denial of kinship with Peter Ivanovitch, who has attempted to claim Razumov as "one of *us*" (208) (meaning that Razumov is a member of the upper class, like himself and Mme de S.). Razumov says:

> The very patronymic you are so civil as to use when addressing me I have no legal right to.... I have no father.... [M]y mother's grandfather was a peasant—a serf. See how much I am one of *you*. I don't want anyone to claim me. But Russia *can't* disown me. She cannot!"
> Razumov struck his breast with his fist.
> "I am *it!*" (209)

Russia is Razumov's only parent, and, he asserts, the only parent he wants. Furthermore, Razumov's Russia is the Russia of the suffering peasants—not the Russia of the privileged, like Peter Ivanovitch and Mme de S., and Razumov's own father. Unlike Razumov, Sophia Antonovna has no tender feelings about the cradle of Mother Russia: "One lies there lapped up in evils, watched over by beings that are worse than ogres, ghouls, and vampires. They must be driven away, destroyed utterly" (254).

Leaving Sophia, Razumov has yet another encounter—this time with the journalist Laspara, one more contemptible wordsmith. The title of Laspara's journal, the *Living Word,* parodies the novel's characters' search for the *logos* that will explain things Russian. His request that Razumov write something for the journal enrages Razumov, reminding him of his former ambitions. In a gesture of contempt, Razumov determines that he will write instead his first–and last–report to Mikulin.

In Part Three, and in much of Part Two, the narrator is not in evidence; the point of view is omniscient, and we are presented with Razumov's thoughts and feelings directly. The remainder of the novel, except for an excerpt from Razumov's journal and the scene of Razumov's confession to the revolutionaries, is told from the narrator's point of view—he is relating events he himself has witnessed.[25] After the long, drawn-out, often circuitous conversations that comprise Part Three, the conclusion seems startlingly abrupt.[26] The final section opens with a brief "retrospect," explaining how Mikulin induced Razumov to become a spy, and emphasizing Prince K.'s role in the scheme. Razumov, who has never known affection, is very vulnerable to his father's pretended concern. In a gesture of resentment toward fathers in general, Razumov persuades his friend Kostia to steal money from his indulgent father; Razumov then throws the money away.[27] Razumov is intensely conscious of his own lack of human ties, and intensely envious of those who have family; the perceived contrast between his own situation and Haldin's in this respect was central to his act of betrayal. His unpremeditated confession to Natalia comes about after his painful meeting with Mrs. Haldin, which serves to remind him of his original envy of Haldin. He feels

> the old anger against Haldin reawakened by the contemplation of Haldin's mother. And was it not something like enviousness which gripped his heart, as if of a privilege denied to him alone of all the men that had ever passed through this world? It was the other who had attained to repose and yet continued to exist in the affection of that mourning old woman, in the thoughts of all these people posing for lovers of humanity. (341)

Razumov has gone to the Haldins' house to repeat the story of Ziemianitch's suicide, the story Razumov believes will make him safe and put to rest forever the ghost of Haldin. But Razumov finds he will never be free of Haldin's phantom; Razumov envies Haldin both his death (he has "attained to repose") and his continued existence in the thoughts of those who loved him.

When Natalia tells Razumov that she had hoped he could help console her mother with some news of Victor, Razumov explains that he is inexperienced in the matters of the heart, never having known love.

> In order to speak fittingly to a mother of her lost son one must have had some experience of the filial relation.... Your hopes have to deal with 'a breast unwarmed by any affection,' as the poet says. (344)

Just before he confesses to Natalia that he is the betrayer of her brother, Razumov says:

> "Do you know why I came to you? It is simply because there is no one anywhere in the whole great world I could go to.... Do you conceive the desolation of the thought—no one—to—go—to?" (353, 354)

By confessing, Razumov hopes not only to break out of the prison of living a lie, but also to escape, if only for a moment, his terrible sense of isolation.

Yet both the narrator and Miss Haldin misunderstand Razumov right up to the moment of his self-denunciation. The narrator thinks he is witnessing a love scene: "The period of reserve was over; he was coming forward in his own way. I could not mistake the significance of this late visit..." (347). The narrator has, in fact, completely mistaken the significance of the scene. He is wrong both about Razumov's political convictions and about his feelings for Natalia. Natalia herself has been "utterly misled by her own enthusiastic interpretation of two lines in the letter of a visionary [i.e., Haldin]..." (354), and has no idea that Razumov is indicting himself, even though he has, throughout the conversation, insisted that he is not the man she thinks he is, and that he does not share her opinions.

> "You must expect nothing from me. [Razumov tells her]...you have given yourself up to vain imaginings while I have managed to remain amongst the truth of things and the realities of life—our Russian life—such as they are....
> "One must look beyond the present." Her tone had an ardent conviction.
> "The blind can do that best. I had the misfortune to be born clear-eyed." (344, 345)

Paradoxically, Razumov is too clear-eyed to be a visionary. Natalia reminds him that her brother believed "that men serve always something greater than themselves—the idea" (352). Later Razumov picks up her words in an almost mocking way, as he asserts he knows the real story of Haldin's betrayal:

> "There is a staircase in it, and even phantoms, but that does not matter if a man always serves something greater than himself—the idea. I wonder who is the greatest victim in that tale?" (353)

Haldin is the victim of his own vision, which has "blinded" him to reality. Razumov and even Ziemianitch are victims of Haldin's "idea," as are Natalia and her mother, who have come to believe Haldin's deed "not worth the price"—furthermore, innocent bystanders were victims in the assassination. Nevertheless, Razumov comes to accept that Haldin's idea—revolution—is the way of the future. He writes in his journal, "it is they [the revolutionaries] and not I who have the right on their side!—theirs is the strength of invisible powers" (361). He goes on, however, "Only don't be deceived, Natalia Victorovna, I am not converted. Have I then the soul of a slave? No! I am independent—and therefore perdition is my lot." Razumov feels only contempt for these "idealists," who are "doomed by [their own] folly and... illusion... they being themselves the slaves of lies" (360). The eternal solitary, Razumov cannot blindly adopt a cause or lose himself in a communal effort. Like Decoud and Heyst, he is condemned by his lack of illusions to remain cut off from life. Razumov even comes to embrace this isolation, since to be alone is to be free of others' incessant demands and misinterpretations of one's conduct and, especially of one's words.

Earlier, as Razumov sat writing on the tiny Ile Jean Jacques Rousseau, he realized that only the sounds of nature were bearable to his ears:

> the sound of water, the voice of the wind—completely foreign to human passions. All the other sounds of this earth brought contamination to the solitude of a soul. (291)

In making his confession to the revolutionaries, he hopes to "escape from the prison of lies" (363), but he also seeks annihilation. As he writes in his letter to Natalia, he will "Confess, go out—and perish" (361).[28] To escape from lies, Razumov must escape words. On entering Laspara's house to make his confession, Razumov is assaulted by sound: "Loud talking was going on in all three [rooms]..." (364). After telling his story,

> Razumov expected to be torn to pieces, but [the revolutionists] fell back without touching him, and nothing came of it but noise. It was bewildering. His head ached terribly. (366)

The tumult ends when Razumov is deafened by the sadistic Nikita. "[The blow] seemed to split his head in two, and all at once the men holding him became perfectly silent—soundless as shadows" (369).

Nikita (who, as it turns out, is also a police spy) has conceived a hatred for Razumov even before meeting him. He is jealous of Razumov's instant reputation, "exasperated like a fashionable tenor by the attention attracted to the performance of an obscure amateur" (267). One may innocently inspire malevolent hatred as well as trust, even in a stranger.

This theme takes on major importance in the two novels that follow, in which the heroes are unwitting victims of the hatred and envy of men they barely know: Heyst is victimized by Schomberg in *Victory*, and Captain Anthony by de Barral in *Chance*. Here, as well, we are reminded that there is no evading the threat that any human relationship involves; even though Razumov asserts that his confession has made him "free from falsehood, from remorse—independent of every single human being on this earth," this is not the case. Razumov becomes Tekla's dependent. Only in death can one be "independent of every single human being." Living on, deaf and crippled, Razumov is more dependent than he has ever been. As Bernard Meyer notes, in Tekla Razumov at last finds the mother he has sought.[29]

For Conrad, confession may be ultimately good for the soul, but its immediate consequences are always unpredictable. Nostromo hoped his confession to Mrs. Gould would free him from the curse of the silver, but she refused to learn the secret of the silver's location and thus declined to assume Nostromo's burden, leaving him unshriven. Verloc's confession brings about his murder; Winnie's delivers her into Ossipon's hands. Razumov hopes his confession will bring him independence and peace, the peace of death, instead it brings silence and a comforter, Tekla. At the end of the novel we are told that she, "the good Samaritan," tends "him unweariedly with the pure joy of unselfish devotion" (379). (Samaritanism is viewed a good deal more skeptically in the novels that follow.) The revolutionaries have—unbelievably—forgiven Razumov; he has even become a sort of oracle, as Sophia Antonovna tells the narrator:

> Some of *us* always go to see him when passing through. He is intelligent. He has ideas.... He talks well, too. (379)

One wonders how Razumov likes this role.

Nevertheless, Razumov's confession *has* freed him from the "prison of lies"; he can now presumably speak the truth—whatever truth he has settled on. We remember that Razumov shares the narrator's belief that "words... are the great foes of reality." On the other hand, silence can also be a weapon—as Conrad emphasized in *Nostromo* and in *The Secret Agent*. Razumov's habit of silence was a root cause of the original misunderstanding with Haldin and, much later, Mrs. Haldin's silence during Razumov's interview with her is a precipitating factor in Razumov's confession to Natalia. In fact, Mrs. Haldin's stubborn silence is a torment to Natalia as well. The narrator finds himself "angry with the broken-hearted old woman passing away in the obstinacy of her mute distrust of her daughter (372).[30] Since either speech or silence can lead to destruction there is little to choose.

Analogously, in the political sphere Razumov is unable finally to choose between revolution and the status quo, between action and resignation. After his meeting with Ziemianitch, Razumov felt himself caught between "the drunkenness of the peasant incapable of action and the dream-intoxication of the idealist incapable of perceiving the reason of things, and the true character of men" (31). Later, he asks Mikulin:

> What is a sober man to do, I should like to know? To cut oneself entirely from one's kind is impossible. To live in a desert one must be a saint. But if a druken man runs out of the grog-shop, falls on your neck and kisses you on both cheeks because something about your appearance has taken his fancy, what then—kindly tell me? (96)

The two threats—Ziemianitch and Haldin—have become one in Razumov's image of the drunken man who bestows an unwelcome kiss. Finally, Razumov will conclude that the only escape from the misunderstanding of others is "to live in a desert."

The novel's emphasis on Razumov as victim of fate and on his unremitting suffering makes quite unbelievable the journal entries in the novel's last pages, where Razumov claims demonic possession and speaks of plans to steal Natalia's soul. One speculates that Conrad, in his haste to conclude the novel, returned unconsciously to his original idea for the plot—in which Razumov was to marry Natalia and their son was to be the agent of Razumov's unmasking. But the notion of a Razumov "given up to evil" (359) does not accord with his behavior in the rest of the novel.[31] And although Razumov tells Natalia that she is a "predestined victim," in his journal he asserts that he is, in fact, *her* victim:

> You were appointed to undo the evil by making me betray myself back into truth and peace. You! And you have done it in the same way, too, in which he ruined me: by forcing upon me your confidence. (358)

Razumov sees Natalia as another agent of his destruction. It is evident that the love story the reader is led to expect cannot be forthcoming. Razumov asserts that he has intended to revenge himself on Natalia by stealing Natalia's soul. Presumably he will accomplish this by marrying her.

> Victor Haldin had stolen the truth of my life from me, who had nothing else in the world, and he boasted of living on through you on this earth where I had no place to lay my head. She will marry some day, he had said—and your eyes were trustful. And do you know what I said to myself? I shall steal his sister's soul from her.... If you could have looked then into my heart, you would have cried out aloud with terror and disgust.
> Perhaps no one will believe the baseness of such an intention to be possible. (359)

Razumov believes that to cause Haldin's sister to fall in love with his betrayer would be an enormous crime in itself, but it is hard to imagine what devilish plan Razumov intended to put into effect after the marriage: just what is it that would make Natalia cry out "with terror and disgust?" Although Razumov writes: "I felt that I must tell you that I had ended by loving you" (361), this sentence (as noted earlier) was added to the book after the publication of the first American edition. Furthermore, Razumov has just written, "I was afraid of your mother. I never knew mine. I've never known any kind of love" (360). Razumov's relationship with Natalia, like his relationship with Haldin, is founded on misunderstanding and on misplaced confidence. Meeting Natalia forces Razumov to relive and reenact the most terrible experience of his life. He could hardly be expected to love her.

Razumov's feelings about both Haldin and Natalia are ambiguous, however. Although Razumov feels Haldin has robbed him of his life, he also identifies with him; he sees Haldin's "phantom" everywhere, is haunted by him, and finally is almost possessed by him. Earlier, in describing the events after the assassination to Sophia Antonovna, Razumov has appropriated Haldin's experiences, passing them off as his own. Now Razumov plans to take over Haldin's life, replacing him in the affections of his mother and sister. Razumov unconsciously seems to seek the family he has never had. Were Razumov to succeed in taking Haldin's place, he would be both brother and husband to Natalia. Perhaps it is the fear of "incest" that prompts Razumov's extravagant horror here—"no one will believe the baseness of such an intention to be possible."

It is, we are told, Haldin's mother Razumov fears most. When he goes to her with the false story of Ziemianitch's guilt, Razumov finds her immobility and silence ominous.

> The fifteen minutes with Mrs. Haldin were like the revenge of the unknown: that white face, that weak, distinct voice; that head, at first turned to him eagerly, then, after a while, bowed again and motionless—in the dim, still light of the room in which his words which he tried to subdue resounded so loudly—had troubled him like some strange discovery. And there seemed to be a secret obstinancy in that sorrow, something he could not understand; at any rate, something he had not expected. Was it hostile?... He had said all he had to say to her, and when he had finished she had not uttered a word. She had turned away her head while he was speaking. (340)[32]

Mrs. Haldin's silence constitutes a rejection of Razumov. He suddenly realizes that he will never be free of Haldin because Haldin still "exist[s] in the thoughts of that mourning old woman" (341)—while Mrs. Haldin declines to recognize Razumov's existence. This final rejection makes clear to Razumov that he is doomed to remain an outsider, that his situation is indeed hopeless. "It's myself whom I have given up to destruction," he concludes. Meeting Natalia, he blurts out the confession he has been ever on the verge of making.

Razumov's situation, as a man without human ties, perpetually misunderstood and unequal to the demands others make of him, has poignance; his moral dilemma and its implications are fascinating. Yet, as a character, Razumov is far from engaging and, indeed, less than believable. His characterization obviously owes a great deal to Dostoevsky's Raskolnikov—some of Razumov's speeches teeter on the brink of parody.[33] Razumov seems one-dimensional, and the attempt to suggest a more complex character at the very end of the novel, in Razumov's assertion that he was "given up to evil," is startling but unconvincing.

Like *Nostromo* and *The Secret Agent,* this novel sees politics as the domain of the self-deluded and personal relationships as inherently dangerous and invariably founded on misunderstanding, but *Under Western Eyes* lacks the earlier novels' power to move the reader (except, perhaps, in the opening section). Moreover, the novel's view of human relationships, and especially sexual relationships, is even bleaker than *The Secret Agent*'s. While *Nostromo* sees love as powerless against the human capacity for self-deception and *The Secret Agent* sees love itself as an act of self-deception, *Under Western Eyes* finds love virtually unthinkable. Razumov, who has never experienced affection of any sort, cannot believe in its possibility, and he finds any hint of sexuality profoundly disquieting.[34] The novelist seems to share this malaise with sexuality; we have noted the ambiguities surrounding the characterization of Peter Ivanovitch and the androgynous features attributed to Natalia and Sophia Antonovna. Peter Ivanovitch's affair with Mme de S. inspires intense disgust in the narrator, as well as in Razumov. Even in the case of a very minor character like Julius Laspara, it is sexual license that is condemned: one of Laspara's daughters has had an illegitimate child and, Conrad remarks sardonically, "he had refrained from asking her for details—no, not so much as the name of the father, because maternity should be an anarchist function" (286)—a possible motto for *The Secret Agent.*

Peter Ivanovitch's "feminism" is made to represent everything ridiculous and fuzzy-minded in revolutionary philosophizing, but it also represents the menace of sexuality, both for Razumov and for the narrator.[35] Ziemianitch, "a lifelong lover," is associated in Razumov's mind with Peter Ivanovitch as "a feminist of a different stamp" (283). The two are further associated when, at the very end of the novel, Sophia Antonovna tells the narrator that Mme de S. has died, leaving Peter Ivanovitch nothing, but that he has now "united himself to a peasant girl," a surprise since Peter Ivanovitch prides himself on his aristocratic antecedents. "He just simply adores her," adds Sophia. The narrator makes a peculiar response: "Does he? Well, then, I hope that she won't hesitate to beat him" (382). This comment suggests another sexual role reversal, and also recalls the narrator's tendency to view Peter Ivanovitch as alternately sexually threatening and impotent. It also recalls Ziemianitch's beating by Razumov. That other "feminist," Ziemianitch, has as Razumov knows committed suicide not out of remorse (as the revolutionaries believe) but out of unrequited love. Ziemianitch's story is a "drama of love, not of conscience" (283); Razumov's is the reverse.

5

Chance

> "Transcendental good intentions...cause often more unhappiness than the plots of the most evil tendency."
> —Joseph Conrad, *Chance*

Conrad interrupted the writing of *Chance* to compose *Under Western Eyes*, so it is not surprising that the novels share many of the same preoccupations: with isolation, misunderstanding, and betrayal; with the inevitably baleful effect of parental influence; and with the difficulties inherent in the relationship between the sexes—here, as in the previous novel, embodied in Conrad's condemnation of feminism. Both novels have heroines who at first appear predestined victims but later prove strong; they are the survivors. Both novels have heroes who avoid sexuality, though for different reasons: Razumov out of a feeling of active repugnance, Anthony out of a combination of wounded vanity and high-minded self-sacrifice. Anthony's self denial is central to the misunderstanding on which the plot of *Chance* turns, however. Razumov's inability to love is only one facet of his extreme isolation. Both novels have narrators who claim detachment from the story they tell yet often imply an almost obsessive (and unexplained) personal involvement—although Marlow has considerably less contact with the central characters in *Chance* than does the narrator of *Under Western Eyes* with Razumov and Natalia.

Like *Under Western Eyes*, *Chance* emphasizes the destructive power of words. "We live at the mercy of a malevolent word," says Marlow.[1] Both Flora and Captain Anthony suffer brutal verbal assaults that shatter their lives almost irrevocably. Flora's governess tells the young girl she is unlovable; Anthony's brother-in-law declares that Anthony is caddishly taking advantage of Flora's helplessness and forcing her to prostitute herself in marriage. Both Flora and Anthony allow themselves to be defined by others (as do Razumov and Nostromo) and accept others' false definitions. Analogously, Marlow's role in the novel is to define the characters. As we shall see, his definitions are often contradictory and sometimes clearly false.

In fact, Marlow is a problem. Are we meant to take his pronouncements at face value? To what extent is he Conrad's mouthpiece? To what extent a character in his own right?[2] Numerous readers have found this Marlow quite different from the Marlow of the earlier works. Bernard Meyer notes that while "the early Marlow is a thoughtful, troubled man endowed with a remarkable capacity for sympathy and understanding...[the Marlow of *Chance* is] transformed into a stuffy, cantankerous, and opinionated man, giving to sweeping generalizations and particularly to intemperate misogyny."[3] Thomas Moser observes that Marlow is not directly involved in the story, remarking: "What Marlow's irony shows most conspicuously is his lack of rapport with the story he is hearing and recounting, rather than, as in *Lord Jim,* the conflict of his moral judgment with his inherent sympathy."[4] This Marlow exhibits little sympathy with any of the characters—indeed, he often professes amusement at their suffering. He is cynically ready to believe the worst about anyone, especially about women.

Marlow's frequent denunciations of womankind in general and his, at best, ambiguous attitude toward the ostensible heroine, Flora, have led some critics to argue that the "role of woman" is the real subject of the novel.[5] But Marlow is cynical about men as well—he finds Mr. Fyne just as ridiculous as Mrs. Fyne (although his attitude towards both of them is far from consistent), and he finds something perverse in Anthony's attraction to Flora. At bottom, Marlow distrusts everyone's motives; he particularly distrusts the impulse to samaritanism. Would-be-saviors have, at best, mixed motives, Marlow believes, and furthermore, every action, even the best intended, is bound to have unforeseen consequences. As Conrad says in the Author's Note: "it is only for their intentions that men can be held responsible. The ultimate effects of whatever they do are far beyond their control" (x).

We have noted the skepticism about "doing good" pervades the preceding novels. In *Nostromo,* the title character saves Sulaco, but sacrifices Decoud, as Monygham sacrifices Hirsch to save Mrs. Gould; even Mrs. Gould's benevolence to the poor is qualified, since it only serves to perpetuate their enslavement to the mine. *The Secret Agent* is ironic not only about such "protectors of society" as Verloc, but also about such sanctioned protectors as government officials and the police, and Winnie's altruistic self-sacrifice for Stevie's sake ends in disaster. *Under Western Eyes* takes a dim view of Haldin's noble mission. Although he claims he has acted for Razumov's benefit, he has really brought Razumov's whole life crashing down. In *Chance,* the beneficient acts of almost everyone—the Fynes, Anthony, Flora, Powell, and even Marlow—miscarry, either because the actors do not understand their own motives, or because they misread others'.

Marlow's sardonic skepticism is thus appropriate to the novel's deeply pessimistic view of human nature (in spite of the ostensibly happy ending). The opening chapter offers a striking example of Marlow's cynicism in his response to the sailor Powell's story of how he got his first berth—as mate of Captain Anthony's ship, as it turns out. By a coincidence, the Shipping Master also was named Powell, and had allowed Captain Anthony to assume that the younger Powell, whom he had just met, was a relative, thereby providing an implicit character reference. When young Powell had tried to thank the Shipping Master, the latter had checked him with: "Don't be in a hurry to thank me.... The voyage isn't finished yet" (22). Marlow remarks: "It's certainly unwise to admit any sort of responsibility for our actions, whose consequences we are never able to foresee" (23)—setting forth the pervasive theme. He goes on to reassert the point, telling Powell:

> I wouldn't suggest... that your namesake, Mr. Powell, the Shipping Master, had done you much harm. Such was hardly his intention. And even if it had been he would not have had the power. He was but a man, and the incapacity to achieve anything distinctly good or evil is inherent in our earthly condition. Mediocrity is our mark. And perhaps it's just as well, since, for the most part, we cannot be certain of the effect of our actions. (23)

Although Marlow here declares human beings are powerless to do "anything distinctly good or evil," he later contradicts this dictum—indeed, he is all too ready to assign blame (but rarely praise), in spite of his stated belief that people should not be held responsible for the results of their actions. He continues with a startling interpretation of the Shipping Master's motives. Powell, who is uncomfortable with Marlow's cynicism, insists that the Shipping Master "did something uncommonly kind," but Marlow reiterates:

> I cannot help thinking that there was some malice in the way he seized the opportunity to serve you.... This was an excellent occasion to suppress you altogether. For if you accepted he was relieved of you with every appearance of humanity, and if you made objections (after requesting his assistance, mind you) it was open to him to drop you as a sort of impostor. (23, 24)

The most damaging possible interpretation of the Shipping Master's "uncommonly kind" action![6] A more plausible explanation is that the Shipping Master merely enjoys playing a little joke on Captain Anthony, while at the same time doing young Powell a good turn. Are we meant to accept Marlow's view of the situation, or Powell's? Powell was, after all, the person directly involved. Yet Marlow has also been acquainted with the Shipping Master, whom he describes as "not exactly remarkable... In a general way it's very difficult for one to become remarkable [he continues]. People won't take sufficient notice of one, don't you know" (7, 8). This is an extremely peculiar statement for Marlow to make, since the entire action of the novel has Marlow himself taking inordinate notice of the affairs of people whose lives touch him only tangentially. Later Marlow several times bemoans the fact that we may, all unwittingly, become objects of interest to others, even to strangers.[7]

In any case, the opening chapter proves to have limited relevance to the rest of the novel, as Conrad himself recognized.[8] Powell's history is of little consequence. (As in *Nostromo,* many pages elapse before we are allowed to discover the center of interest.) But Powell's anecdote does exemplify one of the novel's central insights: that one's fate, for better or worse, is often shaped by another's perverse impulse. Furthermore, Marlow's cynical interpretation of the anecdote may serve to alert us to his propensity to believe the worst of everyone, and may even cause us to question some of his subsequent judgments—which are not notable for their consistency. Nevertheless, it is not clear that Marlow is *meant* to be an unreliable narrator; he seems to have insisted on becoming one in spite of Conrad. At the end of this chapter, the primary narrator (unnamed) appears eager to establish Marlow's authority. Sailors are particularly clear-sighted, the narrator claims:

> A turn of mind composed of innocence and skepticism is common to them all, with the addition of an unexpected insight into motives, as of disinterested lookers-on at a game. (33)

But if Marlow's mind is a blend of "innocence and skepticism," it is the skeptical side that predominates as he pieces together the story of Captain Anthony and Flora de Barral. His stance is that of a "disinterested looker-on at a game," and he even finds the lovers' difficulties a source of amusement—in spite of the fact that he makes clear Flora and Anthony suffer almost completely at the hands of others, beginning as so often in Conrad, with their mistreatment by their fathers. Flora's father, who claims to be a financier but is really a confidence man, has neglected her as a child but fastens on her parasitically after his release from prison, tormenting her with his jealousy of Anthony. The father of Roderick Anthony and his sister, Mrs. Fyne, is a famous poet, who has been sadistically cruel to his two wives (both dead) and children. Like Peter Ivanovitch, he combines a threatening and overbearing manner with a suggestion of the effete:[9]

> His poems read like sentimental novels told in verse of a really superior quality. You felt as if you were being taken out for a delightful country drive by a charming lady in a pony carriage. But in his domestic life that same Carleon Anthony showed traces of the primitive cave-dweller's temperament. He was a massive, implacable man with a handsome face, arbitrary and exacting with his dependants, but marvelously suave in his manner to admiring strangers. (38)

The elder Anthony's over-bearing manner may be the root cause of Captain Anthony's excessive deference with Flora, since both Anthony and his sister have shaped their personalities in reaction to their father. Both children finally escaped the "savage sentimentalist" by running away: Anthony, Marlow notes, "as if disgusted with the amenities of civilization, threw himself, figuratively speaking, into the sea" (39), while his sister "remained in bondage to the poet for several years, till she too seized a chance of escape by throwing herself into the arms, the muscular arms, of the pedestrian Fyne" (39), a man as unlike her father as possible.

It is through his acquaintance with the Fynes that Marlow comes to know Flora de Barral—he never meets Anthony. Marlow speaks of them with extreme condescension; he finds them ridiculous. He is particularly incensed by Mrs. Fyne's feminism, and he seems suspicious about her relations with the "girl-friends" who come to hear her preach the doctrine, and who take but "scanty notice" of Mr. Fyne and ignore Marlow altogether, much to his annoyance. Marlow also notes that Mrs. Fyne "always walked off directly after tea with her arm around the girl-friend's waist." These hints, together with the fact that Mrs. Fyne's dress is mannish (she wears "blouses with a starched front like a man's shirt, a stand-up collar and a long necktie") have led many critics to assume Conrad intended to portray her as a lesbian.[10] It seems more likely, however, that Marlow means to poke fun at Mrs. Fyne's assumption of the "masculine" role of ideologue and political activist—although, as Moser points out, her feminism "seems to have no specific program."[11] Moreover, we are told that the Fyne marriage is "perfectly successful and even happy, in an earnest, unplayful fashion" (39). The girl-friends most probably satisfy only Mrs. Fyne's need for disciples.[12]

Although Marlow, on first meeting Flora at the Fynes', takes her for a "girl-friend," this is not strictly the case. Flora is not a disciple—indeed this is a contributing factor to Mrs. Fyne's anger at Flora and Anthony's elopement, for Flora's explanatory note parrots Mrs. Fyne's feminism, a doctrine to which Mrs. Fyne knows Flora does not subscribe. Flora views Mrs. Fyne instead as a surrogate mother; the Fynes have rescued Flora after the brutal attack by her governess, and have remained concerned with her welfare. In spite of the fact that Marlow's attitude toward the Fynes verges on contempt, in reality they have behaved rather admirably. They respond quite unselfishly to Flora's plight: they shelter her after her governess has abandoned her; they suffer the humiliation of dealing with Flora's suspicious "mercantile" relatives; they go to considerable trouble to find her respectable positions of employment after her relatives cast her out. Furthermore, they do all this out of completely disinterested benevolence—Mrs. Fyne, at least, does not find Flora particularly likeable.

It is this lack of genuine feeling for Flora that Marlow seems to find culpable in Mrs. Fyne (although Marlow's own reactions to Flora are quite ambivalent), for Flora already suffers from the conviction she is unlovable. But the contradictions inherent in Marlow's attitude toward Mrs. Fyne are apparent in the following passage:

> Mrs. Fyne...told me that the children had never liked Flora very much.... Mrs. Fyne assured me that she often found it very difficult to have her in the house.
> 'But what else could we do?' she exclaimed.
> That little cry of distress, quite genuine in its inexpressiveness, altered my feeling towards Mrs. Fyne. It would have been so easy to have done nothing and to have thought no more about it. My liking for her began while she was trying to tell me of the night she spent by the girl's bedside, the night before her departure with her unprepossessing relative. That Mrs. Fyne found means to comfort the child I doubt very much. (138)

On the one hand, Marlow admits that the Fynes have put themselves to considerable trouble for Flora out of pure, disinterested kindness ("It would have been so easy to have done nothing and to have thought no more about it"), but he also seems to condemn Mrs. Fyne for her lack of feeling. It is hard to believe Marlow feels the liking for Mrs. Fyne he professes here. Marlow finds her something of a Job's comforter. When Flora begs her to agree the governess must have been insane, Mrs. Fyne cannot bring herself to lie. Marlow says: "Mrs. Fyne was unflinching in her idea that as much truth as could be told was due in the way of kindness to the girl, whose fate she feared would be to live exposed to the hardest realities of unprivileged existences" (139). Marlow is surely being ironic, pointing out that Mrs. Fyne hurts Flora in the name of "kindness," but Mrs. Fyne's foresight is correct; nevertheless, she misjudges Flora's ability to bear up to the truth.

Marlow's tone, especially when dealing with the Fynes, is such a mixture of irony, condescension, sentimentality, and self-conscious intellectualizing that it is difficult to know what his true feelings are. Consider the following:

> [Mrs. Fynes's] patient immobility by the bedside of that brutally murdered childhood did infinite honour to her humanity. That vigil must have been the more trying because I could see very well that at no time did she think the victim particularly charming or sympathetic. It was a manifestation of pure compassion.... (139, 140)

Surely the phrases Marlow applies to Mrs. Fyne here ("infinite honor to her humanity," "a manifestation of pure compassion") are spoken sardonically, while Marlow himself is prepared to sentimentalize Flora's situation ("brutally murdered childhood"). Yet, again, Mrs. Fyne is really being kind, and the words she actually says to Flora are not lacking in understanding or sympathy.

> It is your former governess who is horrid and odious. She is a vile woman. I cannot tell you that she was mad, but I think she must have been beside herself with rage and full of evil thoughts. You must try not to think of these abominations, my dear child. (140)

Further, Marlow himself does not find Flora "particularly charming or sympathetic," and indeed speculates that she somehow invites victimization. But Marlow persists in his implicit condemnation of Mrs. Fyne. Flora has asked Mrs. Fyne for reassurance that her father is not a swindler, as the governess has claimed. Mrs. Fyne explains her response:

> Silence would have been unfair. I don't think it would have been kind either. I told her that she must be prepared for the world passing a very severe judgment on her father....

Surely this is only sensible—Flora is, after all, not a small child, but sixteen years old. Marlow, however, responds with a burst of sarcasm:

> As they say of an artist's work: this was a perfect Fyne. Compassion–judiciousness–something correctly measured. None of your dishevelled sentiment. (141)

Marlow here seems to be condemning Mrs. Fyne for her lack of "sentiment"—elsewhere found a vice, as in the "savage sentimentalist," Carleon Anthony. He finds Mrs. Fyne's strong principles inhumane; later he faults her for spending her time writing instead of entertaining her brother:

> It was indeed a very off-hand way of treating a brother come to stay for the first time in fifteen years. I suppose she discovered very soon that she had nothing in common with that sailor, that stranger, fashioned and marked by the sea of long voyages. In her strong-minded way she had scorned pretenses, had gone to her writing which interested her immensely. A very praiseworthy thing your sincere conduct,—if it didn't at time resemble brutality so much. (158)

There is even a hint that Marlow associates Mrs. Fyne with the evil governess who "brutally murdered" Flora's childhood.

> A something which was not coldness, nor yet indifference, but a sort of peculiar self-possession gave her the appearance of a very trustworthy, very capable and excellent governess; as if Fyne were a widower and the children not her own. (41, 42)

Of course, as a feminist, Mrs. Fyne is bound to be something less than a "real woman," Marlow believes. But elsewhere, Marlow makes it clear her attitude of detachment has been taken on in self-defense:

> Having seen two successive wives of the delicate poet [i.e., her father] chivied and worried into their graves, she had adopted that cool, detached manner to meet her gifted father's outbreaks of selfish temper. It had now become second nature. (51)

For Marlow, Mrs. Fyne's sincerity, her devotion to total honesty, her compulsion to speak the truth whatever the circumstances, is selfish, and "resemble[s] brutality." "Real women," Marlow asserts, know that men cannot stand the truth.

> The women's rougher, simpler, more upright, judgment embraces the whole truth, which their tact, their mistrust of masculine idealism, ever prevents them from speaking in its entirety. And their tact is unerring. We could not stand women speaking the truth. (144)

Thus Marlow categorizes women as a sex as liars, while condemning Mrs. Fyne for telling the truth. Marlow's misogyny is never far below the surface of the narrative. While there was a good deal of rhetorical sexual warfare in the second half of *Under Western Eyes,* here virtually the whole story is couched in these terms. Marlow's attacks on women are so intemperate—and embody such errant nonsense—that they make us question his reliability about other matters.[13]

Late in the novel, Marlow offers what is seemingly a summary judgment on the Fynes' samaritanism: "There is a kind way of assisting our fellow-creatures which is enough to break their hearts while it saves their outer envelope" (353). As we noted, Marlow condemns the Fynes for being unable to undo the governess's evil. Because Mrs. Fyne was unable to like Flora, she was unable to restore the girl's self-esteem. But there is another side to the equation—Flora herself. Marlow speculates: "Perhaps she had not the power of evoking sympathy, that personal gift of direct appeal to the feelings" (142). In fact, only Captain Anthony and Powell find Flora appealing; she elicits the hostility of the ship's crew, and even her father appears to dislike her. Conrad hints at this ambivalence toward Flora in the Author's Note, in which he attributes to Flora his initial inspiration for the novel and remarks that chance often manifests itself in "the charm, *true or illusory,* of a human being." (Author's emphasis.) If Anthony is only under the illusion that Flora is appealing, he is, in effect, self-intoxicated. He has worked up a passion for his own romantic idea, and his suffering is, therefore, of his own making.

Marlow's own initial impression of Flora is unfavorable. Surprising her on the edge of a precipice (where she has gone intending to commit suicide), Marlow, ignorant of her intention, feels her behavior exemplifies "the foolhardiness of the average girl" (43). When she replies to his expression of concern with: "I don't see why I shouldn't be as reckless as I please," Marlow is "nettled by her brusque manner of asserting her folly." He adds:

> I don't like rude girls. I had been introduced to her only the day before—at the round tea-table—and she had barely acknowledged the introduction. (45)

But noticing that Flora is weeping, Marlow reappraises her—rather callously:

> She looked unhappy. And—I don't know how to say it—well—it suited her. The clouded brow, the pained mouth, the vague fixed glace! A victim. And this characteristic aspect made her attractive; an individual touch—you know. (45, 46)

It is as a victim that Flora exerts her attraction—for Anthony as well as for Marlow. Reconstructing the scene of Anthony's declaration of love to Flora, Marlow speculates:

> It was obvious the world had been using her ill. And even as he spoke with indignation the very marks and stamp of this illusage of which he was so certain seemed to add to the inexplicable attraction he felt for her person. It was not pity alone, I take it. It was something more spontaneous, perverse and exciting. It gave him the feeling that if only he could get hold of her, no woman would belong to him so completely as this woman. (224)

That there is an element of the perverse in Anthony's love is implied several times. It is because Flora seems utterly helpless and alone that Anthony finds the courage to declare his love, for like Flora he believes himself unlovable.

> You told me you had no friends. Neither have I. Nobody ever cared for me as far as I can remember. Perhaps you could. (224)

Among the people who have neglected to care for Anthony is his sister, one assumes. Yet their relationship is puzzling. Mrs. Fyne asserts that, as children, they were close friends.

> We were very fond of each other.... It is no use concealing from you that neither of us was happy at home.... Well, I was made still more unhappy and hurt—I don't mind telling you that. He made his way to some distant relations of our mother's....(184)

Mrs. Fyne seems to believe that her brother deserted her; "I felt myself very much abandoned," she tells Marlow. And, since their lives have taken such divergent paths, Mrs. Fyne and Anthony find themselves virtual strangers. Mrs. Fyne is made uncomfortable by her brother, with whom she can find nothing to talk about, while Anthony, in turn, is hurt by her neglect. He tells Flora:

> Look at my sister. She isn't a bad woman by any means. She asks me here because it's right and proper, I suppose, but she has no use for me. There you have your shore people. I quite understand anybody crying. I would have been gone already, only, truth to say, I haven't any friends to go to. (221)

Anthony assumes Mrs. Fyne is somehow responsible for Flora's tears, which is not the case. Flora answers Anthony by saying:

> "Mrs. Fyne is my best friend."
> "So she is mine,' [Anthony] said without the slightest irony or bitterness, but added with conviction: 'That shows you what life ashore is. Much better be out of it." (221)

One is struck by Anthony's seeming depression here and elsewhere; he seems almost as suicidal as Flora. The words "much better be out of it" have an ominous ring. There is a hint that, for Anthony, life at sea is a sort of death—certainly it is a withdrawal from the complexities of life on shore, with its confusing human relationships. He tells Flora there is "no rest and peace and security but on the sea," and we are told that Flora "thought suddenly that there was peace and rest in the grave too" (221).

Although Anthony suffers pain from his sister's perceived neglect—his discovery of his own intense loneliness precipitates his attachment to Flora—Mrs. Fyne does not realize he is hurt. She is insensitive, not malicious. There is no evidence that she "does not love her brother," as Moser asserts.[14] Moser argues that it is implausible that Mrs. Fyne should oppose the match between Anthony and Flora, but there are many reasons for her to do so. First, as Moser points out, Mrs. Fyne does not like Flora (nor is her reaction an isolated phenomenon; Flora inspires almost universal rejection). Furthermore, Flora, as the daughter of a notorious convict, is hardly a socially desirable sister-in-law. Mrs. Fyne is also angered by Flora's letter, stating that she is marrying Anthony not out of love, but out of necessity—to provide for herself and her father. Mrs. Fyne's preachings have thus come home to roost in a very unpleasant way. Still, she assures Marlow that her "feelings are mostly concerned with [her] brother" (184), and there is no reason to doubt her—especially as she goes on to tell Marlow of her childhood love for Anthony. Yet Marlow comes up with another interpretation of Mrs. Fyne's motives for opposing the match:

> It might have been unconscious on Mrs. Fyne's part, but her leading idea appeared to me to be not to keep, not to preserve her brother, but to get rid of him definitely. She did not hope to stop anything.... She wanted the protest to be made, emphatically, with Fyne's fullest concurrence in order to make all intercourse for the future impossible. Such an action would estrange the pair forever from the Fynes....
>
> Yes. That must have been her motive. The inspiration of a possibly unconscious Machiavellism! (194)

Marlow's judgment recalls his earlier appraisal of the Shipping Master—who, Marlow judged, really wanted to be rid of Powell. It is difficult to believe that Mrs. Fyne, even unconsciously, chooses to estrange her brother forever. Marlow's view of human nature is relentlessly cynical.

Our view of Marlow's reliability may be further qualified by the fact that when he participates in events his actions have untoward results. It is he who persuades Fyne to bow to his wife's wishes and go to see Anthony because Marlow believes it "cannot do any harm to anybody whatever" (191). But the visit precipitates the nearly fatal misunderstanding between Anthony and Flora, since Fyne convinces Anthony not only that Flora does not care for him in the least, but also that he (Anthony) is taking advantage of Flora's dependency to satisfy his carnal desires.[15] Marlow, who views Fyne as insignificant, cannot foresee that the little man could have such a telling effect; nor could Marlow foresee Anthony's reaction, since he has never met Anthony. Marlow himself realizes that he has too few facts about Anthony to know his real character.

> [I]nsired by secret antagonism to the Fynes, I said to myself that Captain Anthony must be a fine fellow. Yet on the facts as I knew them he might have been a dangerous trifler or a downright scoundrel. (193)

Marlow *decides* to see Anthony in a certain light.

> I imagined to myself Captain Anthony as simple and romantic. It was much more pleasant. Genius is not hereditary but temperament may be. And he was the son of a poet with an admirable gift of individualizing, or etherealizing the common-place; of making touching, delicate, fascinating the most hopeless conventions of the so-called, refined existence. (193)

Conrad usually judges people who want to "etherealiz[e] the commonplace" quite harshly; it is odd that Marlow seems to endorse this tendency in Anthony.

Perhaps Marlow's most disconcerting trait, however, is his habit of giving way to laughter at unseemly moments.[16] Marlow first becomes embroiled in the search for Flora out of "the unworthy hope of being amused by the misfortunes of a fellow-creature" (49). When Marlow and Fyne go to the quarry, where Marlow really expects to find Flora's dead body, Marlow is repeatedly amused by Fyne's concern, and when Fyne falls into a hole Marlow bursts into laughter, finding it "the comic relief of an absurdly dramatic situation" (53, 54). Later, when Flora tells him how she was saved from suicide by the appearance of Anthony, Marlow "cough[s] down the beginning of a most improper fit of laughter" (315). To the narrator's chiding comment that Marlow seems to find Flora's plight comic, Marlow responds:

> Oh, I laughed—did I? But don't you know that people laugh at absurdities that are very far from being comic?... we laugh from a sense of superiority. Therefore, observe, simplicity, honesty, warmth of feeling, delicacy of heart and of conduct, self-confidence, magnanimity are laughed at, because the presence of these traits in a man's character often puts him into difficult, cruel or absurd situations, and makes us, the majority who are fairly free as a rule from these peculiarities, feel pleasantly superior. (283, 284)

And Marlow does feel superior—not only to the Fyne, but to Flora and Anthony and Powell as well. What one expects to be the central figures are reduced to marionettes, whose drama is played out on the stage of Marlow's mind, and Marlow can change the thoughts and motives he attributes to these figures seemingly at will. Marlow never really decides if the story is "a farce or... a tragedy" (55), but he chooses most often to emphasize the farcical.

This tendency is perhaps nowhere more evident than in Marlow's account of de Barral's rise and fall. Like many other Conrad characters, de Barral has made a career out of the seductive power of words—although he is neither a writer nor an orator. Marlow explains:

> The fellow had a pretty fancy in names: the 'Orb' Deposit Bank, the 'Sceptre' Mutual Aid Society, the 'Thrift and Independence' Association. Yes, a very pretty taste in names; and nothing else besides—absolutely nothing—no other merit. (69)

But de Barral not only trades in meaningless labels; he is himself insubstantial, an empty husk, "a mere sign, a portent." And although the collapse of de Barral's financial empire has tragic consequences—for the financier himself, for his daughter Flora, and for those who invested money with him—it is the absurdity of the situation Marlow chooses to emphasize:

> As the grotesque details of these incredible transactions came out, one by one, ripples of laughter ran over the closely packed court—each one a little louder than the other. The audience ended by fairly roaring under the cumulative effect of absurdity. (81, 82)

The confidence man de Barral's parody version of capitalism is one of Marlow's social targets; the other, of course, is feminism, as expounded by Mrs. Fyne. Marlow believes that she, like de Barral, uses words without regard for their meaning: "She had got hold of words as a child might get hold of some poisonous pills and play with them for 'dear, tiny little marbles'" (61), Marlow asserts, and he doubts "whether she really understood herself the theory she had propounded to me" (61). Again, Marlow does not know if he should be horror-struck by her philosophy or merely amused. He characterizes her thoughts as "lurid, violent, crude reveries," and notes "There were no limits to her revolt" (62), but on balance he decides mirth is the proper response to her revolutionary doctrine. Her book, "a sort of handbook for women with grievances... made you laugh at its transparent simplicity" (65, 66).

Marlow's reaction to Flora is similarly ambiguous. On the one hand, Flora seems a pitiful victim, utterly alone and, except for the Fynes, friendless. Everyone with whom she comes in contact does her an injury: her father, the governess and her "nephew," the vulgar relatives who take her in for a time, the elderly lady to whom she is companion, the German family who employ her as governess, the Fynes (although they do harm unintentionally), and even Captain Anthony, whose chivalric renunciation Flora finds the ultimate humiliation. On the other hand, Marlow implies that Flora invites victimization. He himself finds her annoying, at least on first acquaintance, and is put off by her "brusque manner." As noted, Mrs. Fyne finds Flora personally unsympathetic; the "mercantile" relatives believe Flora considers herself their better; the old lady is made uncomfortable by Flora's lugubrious manner—she feels Flora does not have an affectionate nature. This is most certainly true; Flora has, in fact, a tremendous store of resentment and hostility. When Marlow surprises her on the precipice, he chides her with the fact that, had she fallen, the local populace would have suspected suicide. Flora replies, "with infinite contempt," that "once one [is] dead, what horrid people thought of one d[oes] not matter"(45). Later, speaking of her relatives, she asserts: "I could not stand being liked by any of these people. If I thought [my uncle] liked me I would drown myself rather than go back with him"(166). Flora's anger and her streak of stubborn independence make her something other than a passive victim.[17]

Indeed, in many ways Flora seems incredibly strong. She opposes the formidable Mrs. Fyne, who has been her mentor and faithful friend, when she elopes with Anthony. (Marlow describes her as "a fugitive carrying off spoils"; her disappearance is the "flight of a raider—or a traitor" [148].) Although the crew of the Ferndale resents her presence and her destructive effect on Captain Anthony, it is Flora who saves the ship from a potentially disastrous collision (its cargo is dynamite) when she lights a warning flare after Powell is unable to do so. Finally, it is she who takes the sexual initiative with Anthony, thereby ending the rather ridiculous mutual misunderstanding on which the plot hinges. But it is perhaps in her dealings with her father that we see Flora at her most determined. In another reversal of the traditional roles of parent and child, Flora makes herself responsible for de Barral's welfare and protection after his release from prison; she also must steel herself to withstand his relentless bullying, for de Barral, like Carleon Anthony, is ruthlessly egotistical.

Flora marries Anthony to provide her father a place of refuge. During de Barral's years of imprisonment, Flora has consoled herself with the belief that he is a victim of gross injustice; her concern for him has become obsessive. Unloved by anyone around her, Flora is convinced that her father loves her unreservedly, but once father and daughter are reunited de Barral proves incapable of love or understanding. He is outraged that Flora, whom he considers his property, has married.

> "Here I am, overthrown, broken by envy, malice and all uncharitableness. I come out—and what do I find? I find that my girl Flora has gone and married some man or other, perhaps a fool, and how do I know.... [A] very suspicious thing it is too, on the part of a loving daughter.'...
> She gazed into his faded blue eyes as if yearning to be understood, to be given encouragement, peace—a word of sympathy. He declared without animation:
> "I would like to break his neck." (362, 363)

Like Charles Gould, Flora has shaped her life in response to a father's misfortune. Like Razumov, she longs for a father's understanding.[18]

This longing is doomed to frustration, and the rescue Flora has planned is repudiated. De Barral persists in regarding the marriage as an act of prostitution on Flora's part—he is, of course, unaware of Anthony's renunciation. On first boarding the Ferndale, de Barral "follow[s] his daughter into [the] ship's cabin... as if into a house of disgrace" (371); he tells Flora: "you've sold yourself; you know you have" (379). And later:

> You can't care for [Anthony]. Don't tell me. I understand your motive. And I have called you an unfortunate girl. You are that as much as if you had gone on the streets. (384)

This view of marriage as a transaction, a rather disreputable affair of buying and selling, pervades the novels from *The Secret Agent* to *Victory*.[19] The Goulds' marriage is the last we see entered into idealistically.

Flora endures her father's cruel taunts because she believes he loves her—and she is convinced that no one else in the world *can* love her: "she did not want to quarrel with her father, the only human being that really cared for her, absolutely, evidently, completely—to the end" (380). But de Barral's love is far from absolute; it is thoroughly egocentric.

> [O]nce, out of patience, she said quite sharply "Leave off. It hurts me. One would think you hate me."
> "It isn't you I hate... But if I saw that you loved that man I think I could hate you too."
> That word struck straight at her heart. "You wouldn't be the first then," she muttered bitterly. (381)

Marlow notes that de Barral "in the seclusion of his prison had thought himself into such a sense of ownership of that single human being he had to think about, as may well be inconceivable to us who have not had to serve a long... sentence of penal servitude" (371). We remember that de Barral also "thought himself into... a sense of ownership" of others' money. The financier seems the very emblem of paternalistic capitalism.

Caught between the conflicting claims of father and husband, fated to be forever the outsider, viewed with suspicion and even hostility, Flora, for Marlow, epitomizes the plight of the "woman for whom there is no clear place in the world" (281).

> And this is the pathos of being a woman. A man can struggle to get a place for himself or perish. But a woman's part is passive, say what you like, and shuffle the facts of the world as you may, hinting at lack of energy, of wisdom, of courage. As a matter of fact, almost all women have all that—of their own kind. But they are not made for attack. Wait they must. I am speaking here of women who are really women. And it's no use talking of opportunities, either. I know that some of them do talk of it. But not the genuine women. Those know better. Nothing can beat a true woman for a clear vision of reality; I would say a cynical vision if I were not afraid of wounding your chivalrous feelings—for which, by the by, women are not so grateful as you may think, to fellows of your kind.... (281)

As is usual in Marlow's expatiations on women, ambiguities are rife. It is pathetic that women are powerless. But "true women" know better than to strive for power—presumably because they know it is hopeless. Yet that "clear vision of reality" is also "cynical." Do women lack energy, wisdom, and courage? Well, no. They have those qualities, but "of their own kind." And although Marlow is making an implicit contrast here between women like Mrs. Fyne, who seek "opportunities," and women like Flora, who are meant to wait passively for rescue, it is clear that Flora is far from passive. She is a good deal more active than Anthony, or Powell, or de Barral.

While Marlow recommends passivity here, later he states that women's seeming passivity is only a mask, and that masculine distrust of the emotions that passivity cloaks is a root cause of misogyny.

> In this world as at present organized women are the suspected half of the population.... the part falling to women's share being all "influence" has an air of occult and mysterious action, something not altogether trustworthy, like all natural forces....
> If women were not a force of nature, blind in its strength and capricious in its power, they would not be mistrusted. As it is one can't help it. (327)

On the one hand, women have only "influence"; on the other hand, they are a "force of nature, blind in its strength and capricious in its power." Although Marlow seems eager to assure us—and himself—that women are powerless, rather ridiculous creatures, he really finds them terrifying. He compares a man's capture of a woman to the "capture" of electricity:

> It lights him on his way, it warms his home, it will even cook his dinner for him—very much like a woman. But what sort of conquest would you call it? He knows nothing of it. He has got to be mighty careful what he is about with his captive. And the greater the demand he makes on it in the exultation of his pride the more likely it is to turn on him and burn him to a cinder.... (327)

Not only do women possess an annihilating, "occult" power, they have no ethical restraints.

> As to honour–you know–it's a very fine mediaeval inheritance which women never got hold of.... In addition they are devoid of decency. I mean masculine decency. Cautiousness too is foreign to them—the heavy reasonable cautiousness which is our glory. (63)

"Perhaps you didn't know that my character is upon the whole rather vindictive," Marlow remarks at one point. He goes on:

> For myself it's towards women that I feel vindictive mostly.... Mainly I resent that pretence of winding us round their dear little fingers, as of right. Not that the result ever amounts to much generally.... It is the assumption that each of us is a combination of a kid and an imbecile which I find provoking.... (150)

Again, Marlow's attitude is curious. He dislikes women's manipulative tendencies, but finds them only a "pretence"—the result never "amounts to much generally." Similarly, the denunciation of women as unprincipled is followed by another self-reassurance:

> [W]hat prevents women... from "coming on deck and playing hell with the ship" generally, is that something in them precise and mysterious, acting both as restraint and as inspiration; their femininity, in short, which they think they can get rid of by trying hard, but can't, and never will. Therefore we may conclude that, for all their enterprises, the world is and remains safe enough. (63)

But Marlow does not really seem to find a world that includes women "safe enough." He is horrified at Mrs. Fyne's feminist doctrine. When Marlow remarks that Flora is a "most wrongheaded, inconsiderate girl," Mrs. Fyne says: "Why should a girl be more considerate than any one else? More than any man, for instance?" Marlow is shocked:

> I asked Mrs. Fyne if she did not think it was a sort of duty to show elementary consideration, not only for the natural feelings, but even for the prejudices of one's fellow-creatures.
> Her answer knocked me over.
> "Not for a woman."
> Just like that. I confess that I went down flat. And while in that collapsed state I learned the true nature of Mrs. Fyne's feminist doctrine. It was not political, it was not social. It was a knock-me-down doctrine—a practical individualistic doctrine.... it was something like this: that no consideration, no delicacy, no tenderness, no scruples should stand in the way of a woman (who by the mere fact of her sex was the predestined victim of conditions created by man's selfish passions, their vices and their abominable tyranny) from taking the shortest cut towards securing for herself the easiest possible existence. She had even the right to go out of existence without considering anyone's feelings or convenience, since some women's existences were made impossible by the short-sighted baseness of men. (59)

While Marlow professes himself horror-struck by Mrs. Fyne's "practical individualistic doctrine," her feminism seems, to the modern reader, to proceed from simple egalitarianism: "Why should a girl be more considerate than any one else? More than any man, for instance?" And although Marlow is ridiculing Mrs. Fyne's doctrine here, elsewhere he too sees women as predestined victims "by the mere fact of [their] sex."

Marlow also seems to agree with Mrs. Fyne that women have "even the right to go out of existence," to commit suicide, "without considering anyone's feelings." Flora's suicide attempt is central to the novel's action. It brings her to Marlow's attention initially, and causes him to become enmeshed with the Fynes and their affairs, and it is because she is on the verge of suicide that Flora accepts Anthony, an alternative she chooses as a fate *not* worse than death. Marlow spends a great deal of time speculating about Flora's urge to self-destruction, and although, in the passage quoted above, Marlow seems to condemn (female) suicide as a potential consequence of feminism, he later concludes differently. When Flora tells him she is deeply ashamed at having considered suicide, Marlow observes, rather callously: "why she, that girl who existed on sufferance, so to speak—why she should writhe inwardly with remorse because she had once thought of getting rid of a life which was nothing in every respect but a curse—*that* I could not understand." Marlow attributes this remorse to "some obscure influence of common forms of speech, some traditional or inherited feeling—a vague notion that suicide is a legal crime; words of old moralists and preachers which remain in the air and help to form all the authorized moral conventions" (214). But in fact Flora is totally unconcerned with "the authorized moral conventions"; she is remorseful because she has temporarily forgotten her father's need of her. "I was so miserable that I could think only of myself. This was mean. It was cruel too," she tells Marlow (213). Marlow's elaborate interpretation of Flora's motivation is false, and may lead to a further erosion of our trust in his reliability.

Our view of Marlow is further qualified by his rather comic insistence that he has been responsible for saving Flora from suicide—a belief in which he persists despite Flora's repeated denials. Marlow explains to Flora that the Fynes thought she might have killed herself because he had told them of encountering Flora on the cliff.

> "I told them that you were making up your mind and I came along just then. I told them that you were saved by me. My shout checked you...." She moved her head gently from right to left in negation.... "No? Well, have it your own way."
> I thought to myself: She has found another issue. She wants to forget now. (201)

Flora tries again to enlighten Marlow:

> "No, it wasn't your shout. I had been there some time before you saw me. And I was not there to tempt Providence, as you call it. I went up there for—for what you thought I was going to do."
> What had kept her back all that time [says Marlow], till I appeared on the scene below, she went on, was neither fear nor any other kind of hesitation.... But something did keep her back. I should have never guessed what it was. She herself confessed that it seemed absurd to say. It was the Fyne dog. (202)

The dog had followed Flora to the edge of the precipice and Flora imagines it will either jump after her or be overcome with grief at her disappearance. She envisions "the creature sitting on the brink, its head thrown up to the sky and howling for hours" (203). But when Marlow appears, the dog immediately deserts her, to Flora's extreme vexation and humiliation. "Not even that animal cared for her—in the end" (203). The unhappy Flora has spared her life for the sake of a dog—who then spurns her. This happenstance effectively desentimentalizes the entire incident, and makes both Marlow and Flora appear ridiculous.

Marlow continues to insist that he is responsible for saving Flora's life. It is the source of his feeling of involvement with her, as he tells the narrator: "the fact of having shouted her away from the edge of a precipice seemed somehow to have engaged my responsibility as to this other leap [i.e., the elopement]" (209). Finally Flora bursts out, with some asperity:

> I see you will have it that you saved my life. Nothing of the kind. I was concerned for that vile little beast of a dog. (213)

The Fynes' perfidious dog points up the absurdity of the situation: Flora, the perpetual victim, is finally betrayed even by man's best friend. And Marlow is absurd in his continuing insistence that he, and not the dog, is Flora's savior.

Earlier, when the Fynes and Marlow are discussing Flora's disappearance, Marlow feels that he and the Fynes resemble

> three trained dogs dancing on their hind legs. I don't know why. Perhaps because of the pervading solemnity. There's nothing more solemn on earth than a dance of trained dogs. (57, 58)

Struck by this insight, Marlow, steadfastly refusing to take the situation seriously, declares himself "out of the dance and down on all-fours so to speak, with liberty to bark and bite" (58). If human beings are no better than dogs, acting out of blind instinct or fawning on others out of self-interest, Marlow chooses to be a "natural" dog rather than a trained one. (Conversely, dogs are no better than people: fickle, unpredictable, and prone to having fun at others' expense.)

Although Marlow, having given himself "liberty to bark and bite," insists that Flora's suicide, had it in fact occurred, would have been no tragedy, but merely the logical end to her cursed existence, and although he repeatedly reminds us that he, like almost everyone else, finds Flora less than totally sympathetic ("dead or alive, I thought of her as minx," he remarks as he recalls searching for her body in the quarry), nevertheless her attempted suicide is his almost obsessive concern. Marlow's narrative continually circles back to the vision of Flora as potential suicide, as though it is this, and only this, he finds interesting about her. As noted earlier, her suicidal bent is the mainspring of the plot. Her engagement to Anthony results from a misunderstanding that occurs when Anthony, encountering her in the garden late in the evening, assumes she has come to meet him, when in fact she has gone out intending to make another attempt at suicide. This initial misunderstanding between Anthony and Flora prefigures the later mutual misunderstanding in which Flora interprets Anthony's sexual renunciation as rejection. It is notable too that misunderstanding also comes into play when this dilemma is resolved, since Flora does not realize that Anthony's decision to "let her off" arises from his shock at de Barral's murder attempt (of which she never learns).

The meaning and consequences of suicide are as central here as in *Nostromo*.[20] And there is in *Chance,* as in *Nostromo,* a sense of fatality, in which catastrophes, narrowly averted, tend finally to occur. Flora does not commit suicide, but her father, for whose sake she decides to live, does take his own life; the threatened ships' collision is avoided by Flora's quick action, but later the *Ferndale* is rammed by another ship and sinks, taking Anthony down with her; Powell's first experience of being mistaken for someone else has happy consequences—he gets his berth as mate—but the second, when after the fatal collision he is taken for the Captain, leads to Anthony's death. This sense that though we may avoid one potential tragedy another always waits around the corner makes the ostensibly happy ending ring rather hollow.

The tone of hearty jocularity Marlow assumes in the concluding pages further contributes to their hollow reverberation. At the end, Marlow has become a do-gooder himself, bringing Powell and Flora together for a promised marriage presumably intended to set the seal of normality on this strange tale. But it is hard to have much faith in this happy outcome when we recall the consequences attempted benevolence has had throughout the novel. The Fynes have suffered the unhappy results of their own samaritanism as Flora, the object of their kindness, repays them by "purloining" Anthony. Flora has suffered from Anthony's misguided chivalry, as well as from the Fynes' attempts to find her a place in the world—always with uncongenial patrons. De Barral has suffered from his daughter's self-sacrifice; as it turns out, her marriage is the one thing in the world he can not bear to experience. And Captain Anthony has suffered, perhaps most deeply, from his brother-in-law's well-meaning attempt to save him from making a fool of himself by marrying a girl the Fynes believe is a ruthless adventuress.

In this last incident, the pervasive theme of misunderstanding is given an added twist. Fyne is stung to denounce Flora and to question Anthony's motives by Anthony's own brusque manner and lack of tact. Angered by Anthony, Fyne is driven to utter the cruel words that plant the sword of self-doubt in Anthony's heart—that self-doubt that will serve to confirm Flora in her own sense of unworthiness. Because he misinterprets Anthony's manner, the normally kind and considerate Fyne unconsciously reenacts the earlier scene between the governess and Flora. A verbal attack once again results in the victim's altered perception of his own character and place in the world.

"His manner was offensive, derisive, from the first. [Fyne tells Marlow.] . . . [H]e was exulting at having got hold of a miserable girl."

> "I told the fellow very plainly that he was abominably selfish in this...."
>
> "You did! Selfish!" I said, rather taken aback, "but what if the girl thought that, on the contrary, he was most generous?"
>
> "Generosity! I am disposed to give it another name. No Not folly," he shot out at me as though I had meant to interrupt him. "Still another. Something worse. I need not tell you what it is," he added with grim meaning.
>
> "I told him it was a shame,' said Fyne.... Yes! A shame to take advantage of a girl's distress—a girl that does not love him in the least."
>
> "I had sufficient authority to tell my brother-in-law that if he thought he was going to do something chivalrous and fine he was mistaken. I can see very well that he will do everything she asks him to do—but, all the same, it is rather a pitiless transaction."
>
> For a moment I felt it might be so. (250, 251, 252)

Even Marlow, who is determined to view Anthony in the best light, is momentarily persuaded that there is something sordid in this "transaction." Marriage is again seen as a disreputable bargain, but whereas in *The Secret Agent*, for instance, Winnie ends the contract by murder when she fears Verloc will "want to keep her for nothing," here Flora is moved to take the opposite tack: she assures Anthony she does not want to be "let off" her compact.

But up until that moment of resolution, Anthony has accepted Fyne's appraisal of his motives. Words, both written and spoken, have immense destructive power. Although, in *Chance*, it is most often the spoken word—the careless observation or the deliberately planted barb—that festers into a psychic wound, the written word can also be pernicious. Mrs. Fyne's writings are misinterpreted by Flora, and Flora's letter, composed under the influence of those writings, is misinterpreted by Mrs. Fyne. Marlow, who does not know the actual contents of the letter, believes it must have been "an unreserved confession," and this supposition occasions another curious rhetorical outburst.

> [T]here's nothing like a confession to make one look mad; and ... of all confessions a written one is the most detrimental all round. Never confess! Never, never! An untimely joke is a source of bitter regret always. Sometimes it may ruin a man; not because it is a joke, but because it is untimely. And a confession of whatever sort is always untimely.... You seek sympathy, and all you get is the most evanescent sense of relief—if you get that much. For a confession, whatever it may be, stirs the secret depths of the hearer's character. Often depths that he himself is but dimly aware of. And so the righteous triumph secretly, the lucky are amused, the strong are disgusted, the weak either upset or irritated with you according to the measure of their sincerity with themselves. And all of them in their hearts brand you for either mad or impudent.... (212)

The narrator remarks that he "had seldom seen Marlow so vehement, so pessimistic, so earnestly cynical before," and indeed Marlow's speech is a startling indictment of human nature. A confession is an absurdity, an "untimely joke," because those to whom it is made will always have a venal response, of one sort or another. Human beings are not to be trusted—not even with a confidence, and certainly not with a confession. As we noted in considering the previous novels, confessions never bring the anticipated response, nor does confession bring redemption.

Marlow's vehemence here seems unrelated to Flora's situation; she has not told him that she in fact made a confession; Marlow is merely speculating, and the narrator implies that Marlow's denunciation is excessive. Marlow appears to project his own experiences, as well as his own interpretations, onto the story of Flora and Anthony. This is clearest, perhaps, when Marlow admits that he, like Flora and Anthony, has suffered from an undeserved and unexpected calumnious attack. Marlow is speaking of the effect of Fyne's accusation on Anthony:

> [N]o man comes out of such a 'wrangle'... without showing some traces of it.... For my own part I'll tell you that once, many years ago now, it came to my knowledge that a fellow I had been mixed up with in a certain transaction—a clever fellow whom I really despised—was going around telling people that I was a consummate hypocrite. He could know nothing of it. It suited his humour to say so. I had given him no ground for that particular calumny. Yet to this day there are moments when it comes into my mind, and involuntarily I ask myself, 'What if it were true?'... See the might of suggestion? We live at the mercy of a malevolent word. A sound, a mere disturbance of the air, sinks into our very soul sometimes. (263, 264)

Anthony and Flora accept others' negative assessments of their characters because their traumatic childhoods have left them with a very precarious sense of identity, but here we see that even Marlow is vulnerable to self-doubt. He too has a somewhat shaky sense of self: "involuntarily I ask myself, 'What if it were true?'" Marlow's sensitivity to the power of the "malevolent word" often seems to border on the paranoid. He notes: "There are on earth no actors too humble and obscure not to have a gallery, that gallery which envenoms the play by stealthy jeers, counsels of anger, amused comments or words of perfidious compassion" (278).[21] In fact, this constitutes a perfect description of Marlow's role as storyteller in *Chance*. The very form of the novel—Marlow and the narrator's speculations on the meaning of Flora and Anthony's story—is a form of the activity Marlow condemns: gossip. The narrator makes this clear when, earlier in the novel, he responds to Marlow's assertion that "people...are for the most part quite incapable of understanding what is happening to them," with:

> But we, my dear Marlow have the inestimable advantage of understanding what is happening to others.... Is that too a provision of nature? And what is it for? Is it that we may amuse ourselves gossiping about each other's affairs? (117)

By taking Flora to sea, Captain Anthony has sought to escape the interference of others, but although Marlow asserts that "at sea...there is no gallery," this does not prove true. Anthony's affairs do not escape notice, even "in an isolation so complete that if it had not been for the jealous devotion of the sentimental Franklin stimulating the attention of Powell, there would have been no record, no evidence of [the trouble between the newlyweds] at all" (326). Flora and Anthony's "gallery" consists not only of Franklin (the first mate), Powell, and the other members of the *Ferndale*'s crew, but also of Marlow, the narrator, and the reader. Marlow, however, is the primary interpreter of events; the other members of the audience confine themselves most often to reporting.

If Marlow's perceptions of the Fynes and of Flora seem at times contradictory, unconvincing, or even willfully perverse, his conclusions about Anthony's motives, although less ambiguous than his judgments of other characters' motives, may yet be more questionable, since Anthony, as we have him, is virtually a creation of Marlow's imagination. As noted, Marlow never meets Anthony; what Marlow knows about him comes from relatively brief conversations with the Fynes, Flora and Powell (who knows nothing of Anthony's history or inner life), and from these hints Marlow creates a personality—based largely on what Marlow feels must have been Anthony's reaction to being "the son of the poet":

> He certainly resembled his father, who, by the way, wore out two women without any satisfaction to himself, because they did not come up to his supra-refined standard of the delicacy which is so perceptible in his verses. That's your poet. He demands too much from others. The inarticulate son had set up a standard for himself with that need for embodying in his conduct the dreams, the passion, the impulses the poet puts into arrangements of verses, which are dearer to him than his own self—and may make his own self appear sublime in the eyes of other people, and even in his own eyes. (328)

Like his father, Captain Anthony confounds life with art, and this romantic and idealistic self-conception, really a form of overweening vanity, leads him to his "chivalric" renunciation. Anthony is also like his father, Marlow implies, in that his capacity to love another, sexually, is inferior to his capacity for self-love:

> If Anthony's love had been as egoistic as love generally is, it would have been greater than the egoism of his vanity—or of his generosity, if you like—and all this could not have happened. He would not have hit upon that renunciation at which one does not know whether to grin or shudder. (331)

But Anthony is at once impotent (over-sentimental, "womanish") and sexually threatening, as was Peter Ivanovitch for the narrator of *Under Western Eyes*. Flora, at least, is often frightened of him (although she also finds his violence perversely attractive).

> What seemed most awful to her was the elated light in his eyes, the rapacious smile that would come and go on his lips as if he were gloating over her misery. But her misery was his opportunity and he rejoiced while the tenderest pity seemed to flood his whole being. (223, 224)

When Anthony attempts to declare his love, Flora interprets it as an attack:

> He growled at her in a savage passion. She felt certain that he was threatening her and calling her names. She was no stranger to abuse, as we know, but there seemed to be a particular kind of ferocity in this which was new to her. She began to tremble. (226)

In fact, Anthony's words are not exactly the usual endearments: "you white-faced wisp, you wreath of mist, you little ghost of all the sorrow in the world." He goes on: "'What makes your cheeks always so white as if you had seen something.... Don't speak. I love it....'" (226, 227) Shades of Krafft-Ebing! Flora even thinks Anthony is capable of murdering her. When she steals out of the Fyne house to attempt yet again to commit suicide and encounters Anthony, we are told:

> She did not understand the mood of that man clearly. He was violent.... [T]he thought came into her mind that should he get into ungovernable fury from disappointment, and perchance strangle her, it would be as good a way to be done with it as any. (229)

Marlow observes:

> This makes one shudder at the mysterious ways girls acquire knowledge. For this was a thought, wild enough, I admit, but which could only have come from the depths of that sort of experience which she had not had, and went far beyond a young girl's possible conception of the strongest and most veiled of human emotions. (230)

Marlow accepts the association of sexuality with murder—an association Anthony also makes.

> Possessed by most men's touching illusion as to the frailness of women and their spiritual fragility, it seemed to Anthony that he would be destroying, breaking something very precious inside that being. In fact nothing less than partly murdering her. (332, 333).

Having sexual relations with Flora would be tantamount to murder, Anthony believes, and in fact it seems to prove so, as their sexual union is finally brought about by de Barral's intended murder of Anthony. Furthermore, de Barral commits suicide while Flora and Anthony consummate the marriage. After the marriage, the life of husband, wife, and father-in-law on board ship is repeatedly described as deathly. Flora looks in a mirror and "her own face looked far off like the livid face of a drowned corpse at the bottom of a pool"

(384). She tells Anthony, who has asked if she objects to going on a long voyage:

> I assure you I haven't the slightest wish to evade my obligations.... Even if I could. Even if I dared, even if I had to die for it! (388)

Her statement, of course, has a deeper meaning—which Anthony chooses to ignore. He responds: "Oh, no. You won't die. You don't mean it. You have taken kindly to the sea." (389) Flora goes on to tell him she is crushed by his magnanimity, but still Anthony does not grasp her meaning.

For his part, de Barral finds life at sea "just sitting down to look at the death that's coming, coming." And he tells Flora, "Some day you will jump overboard" (394). Anthony himself feels that "death was not an unfriendly visitor after all" (397). When he discovers that de Barral has tried to murder him, he reacts as though he had, in fact, received a deadly blow. Instead of becoming energized by anger, he indulges in a veritable orgy of renunciation:

> I can't fight any longer for what I haven't got.... I give up.... I must learn to live without you.... I have done fighting, or waiting, or hoping. Yes. You shall go.... Your father has found an argument which makes me pause.... He shall have his way with you—and with me.... I renounce not only my chance but my life.... I shall let you go. (428, 429)

Only when Flora throws herself into his arms, declaring that she does not want to be let off, does Anthony come back to life, giving Powell "a glance of unwonted fire," and speaking in a "ringing" voice. Although Marlow asserts that Anthony, when he first proposes to Flora, is in the grip of a passion that drives him "into all sorts of adventures, to the brink of unfathomable dangers, to the limits of folly, and madness, and death" (329), Anthony does not fight for Flora. Indeed, he seems to welcome the opportunity to renounce her sexually—even before the marriage, Anthony feels his love is "lifted up into a higher and serene region by its purpose of renunciation" (334). Marlow views this renunciation sometimes as noble and at other times as reprehensible.

> [W]ho could have suspected Anthony of being a heroic creature. There are several kinds of heroism and one of them at least is idiotic. It is the one which wears the aspect of sublime delicacy. It is apparently the one of which the son of the delicate poet was capable. (328)

Anthony may have a rough, "vehement," exterior, but his soul is fatally soft. Marlow alludes to Anthony's "violent conquest" of Flora, and Flora finds him a "whirlwind," but when checked by a word from his dense brother-in-law, Anthony's passion cools—or moves into a "higher and serene region." Marlow also asserts, elsewhere, that it is Flora who has captured Anthony and carried him off "like a buccaneer." Anthony is, in turn, admirable and idiotic, a simple sailor and a perverse sensualist, a sexual threat (even unto murder) and impotent—just as Marlow finds Flora at one point appealing, at another charmless, a victim and an adventuress, an innocent child and a prostitute, helpless and preternaturally powerful.

The form of the novel, in which Marlow and the narrator are engaged in the "old-maiden-lady-like occupation of putting two and two together" (326), emphasizes the watery nature of identity. Marlow's multifarious and often contradictory interpretations of characters and motives serve finally to suggest that human beings may exist *only* as they are perceived by others. People have no "real" identity; they may seem to be anyone. This is the point of Powell's otherwise irrelevant anecdote in the opening chapter—and Flora herself goes under an assumed name. This concern with identity is central to the earlier novels as well. We recall Decoud's loss of identity when he is forced to confront himself in solitude; Nostromo's change of name and occupation and self-image in response to what he believes to be his public's changed perception of him (as a failure, who has "lost a lighter"); Verloc's multiple identities; and Razumov's change of identity—from student to spy—while playing the false role of revolutionary.

But whereas Razumov fought against others' false assessments of his character, Flora and Anthony passively accept the judgment that they are unworthy. There is an indication that Flora, having been pronounced unlovable, does indeed become so, and Anthony, on being told he is about to do Flora a grave injury, hits upon a scheme that serves to confirm Flora's self-hatred. The characters in *Chance* seem to dwell in a severely determined universe. Constrained by their pasts, they are all too eager to take on the roles in which others have cast them; they appear condemned to play out a scenario they had no hand in writing. Moreover, if this is meant to be a drama of love triumphant, Marlow's acerbic comments from the gallery serve continuously, as we noted, to "envenom the play." It is Marlow's corrosive skepticism, his intensely cynical view of human nature that we take away from *Chance*. For Marlow, to put oneself into another's hands is insane: even (or especially) in the name of love. As Marlow watches Flora walk toward Anthony's hotel to enter into her bargain, he sees her as walking toward "the edge of a ninety-foot sheer drop" (249). Marriage is but another form of suicide, and acts of "transcendental good intention," of purest self-sacrifice, lead invariably to misery.

6

Victory

"I only know that he who forms a tie is lost. The germ of corruption has entered into his soul."
—Joseph Conrad, *Victory*

As in *Chance,* the plot of *Victory* hinges on an elopement that is, in fact, a rescue, and the heroes and heroines of the two novels exhibit some striking similarities. Lena, like Flora, is motherless and, effectively, fatherless: Flora's father is in prison; Lena's is in a home for "incurables." Both are described as waif-like, friendless, and predestined victims of others' casual cruelties. Both women are rescued just when they are at the point of giving up their very lives, yet both finally prove stronger than their rescuers. Neither is presented as a stock romantic heroine; Conrad emphasizes the fact that not everyone finds Flora and Lena attractive, and in each case it is the heroine's misery, rather than any more positive characteristic, that enchants the hero. Anthony and Heyst also have similar histories. Both have withdrawn from the world; both are orphans who have been psychically deformed in youth by their powerful fathers; both claim to have no experience of love; and both wish to deny the sexual component in their impulse to "rescue." All four central characters are victims of the "malevolent word," but whereas Flora and Anthony passively accept others' misreading of their characters and motives, Heyst is tortured by the sense of injustice—Schomberg's lie is so outrageous that the fact that people have put credence in it shakes Heyst's faith in the reality of existence itself. (He has difficuty believing in the villains' existence even when they are on his doorstep.) In any case, the result is the same as with Anthony: immobility and self-doubt. In contrast, Lena, whose character has also been grossly misread by Ricardo, is able to use that misinterpretation as a weapon because she cares for no one's opinion but Heyst's.

But it is not only the concern with false reputation that *Victory* shares with *Chance* and with the other novels we have considered. *Victory* also looks at the various forms betrayal can take, at the dangers inherent in action and in any form of human commitment, and particularly at what Douglas Park has termed "the gulf between those who are fully conscious and those whose simplicity or imagination allows them to function in a world of illusions."[1] the novel further continues the progressive narrowing of social focus in these novels, as we have moved from the chaotic political conflicts of the immensely populated *Nostromo* to a world of two who have tried to cut themselves off from all the complexities of the wider world. As Donald Dike has noted, the novel's "landscape is nearly barren of the immediate forms of social life: of manners, for example, the intimate form of social motives, and of politics, their public form.... the scene of action in *Victory* is significant in the measure of its abstraction from history."[2]

When the book begins, Heyst has already withdrawn from the social sphere—after the failure of his brief career as capitalist (manager of the Tropical Belt Coal Company). After the collapse of this enterprise, Heyst remains alone at the abandoned mine (except for a providentially provided Chinese cook), withdrawn from the world, secure in the belief that "an inert body can do no harm to any one, provokes no hostility, is scarcely worth derision."[3] This does not prove true. Although Heyst fancies himself virtually invisible, in reality he is an object of great interest; his withdrawal is so extreme it makes him a public figure.

> He was out of everybody's way, as if he were perched on the highest peak of the Himalayas, and in a sense as conspicuous. Every one in that part of the world knew him, dwelling on his little island. An island is but the top of a mountain. (3,4)

We see Heyst initially through the eyes of the gallery—a crowd of expatriate drifters who occupy their idle moments with gossip. The narrator is one of this group; he has no other identity and no name. (The first person narrator is soon abandoned, however, and the point of view becomes omniscient.)[4] The opinions of these gossips are volatile; at one moment Heyst is dubbed "Enchanted," at another, "Hard Facts." Their general view of Heyst as an eccentric, but harmless, moony romantic changes abruptly when he becomes involved with the coal scheme: he becomes positively satanic, "the Enemy." But, the narrator makes clear, it is not just Heyst who is the object of uninformed speculation. Anyone may occasion gossip; even the pious Morrison is suspected of having a wife in each of the native villages he visits.

The narrator addresses the reader conversationally. He offers the snippets of information he has gathered about Heyst in a playful, almost mocking tone, asserting again and again that Heyst is a "queer chap," a fellow whose antics most often occasion amusement. The events of Heyst's life, as the narrator knows them, are presented in a jumble: Heyst as loafer, aimless wanderer, eccentric (who voyages into the wilds of New Guinea to make sketches), entrepreneur, apostle of progress, and hermit. The effect is to make Heyst seem important, mysterious, and interesting, but at the same time a bit ridiculous. The narrator, as the voice of the collective expatriate colony, has an impulse to demean the object of interest, a tendency also very evident in the Marlow of *Chance*. This view of Heyst, pervasive in Part One, serves to qualify our perception of him later in the novel when the point of view becomes predominately omniscient, even as Heyst's consciousness becomes our primary point of reference. Furthermore, the emphasis in the opening chapters on gossip as a way of life and as a way of apprehending reality in this society prepares us for the climactic moment when Heyst, learning of Schomberg's calumny, is psychically destroyed. Another narrative device that prevents our over-identification with Heyst—and with Lena—is a symbolic doubling; Heyst and Lena share unexpected traits with the "bad" characters.[5] Lena and Ricardo are associated, and Heyst shares certain characteristics with Schomberg, Ricardo, and Jones.

The narrator's account of Heyst's rescue of Morrison, although emphasizing Heyst's unpremeditated kindness and generosity, yet hints at certain deficiencies in Heyst's character. Heyst's habitual courtly politeness acts, it is implied, as a barrier to real fellowship. When Morrison is overcome with despair at the knowledge he can never repay Heyst's loan, Heyst is unable to find the words to reassure him. "Consummate politeness is not the right tonic for an emotional collapse," the narrator remarks (18). Indeed, Heyst's elaborately polite tone leads Morrison to believe, at first, that Heyst's offer of money is a joke—as Lena believes Heyst is making fun of her when he tries to express indignation at her ill-treatment. As a further illustration of the ambiguous responses one may expect to a samaritan impulse, Morrison can't decide if Heyst is an emissary of God or the Devil. Heyst assures him: "I have no connection with the supernatural...Nobody has sent me. I just happened along" (17).

The narrator appears to believe firmly that people act only out of self-interest, not out of altruism and, as was the case with Marlow's cynical appraisals in *Chance,* it is hard to decide if we are to take this skepticism at face value. For instance, the narrator makes clear that the rumour that Heyst has fastened parasitically on Morrison arose because the two men decided to keep the facts of Heyst's act of rescue a secret, since Morrison is ashamed at having got into financial difficulties and Heyst is embarrassed by Morrison's excessive gratitude. Yet the narrator hints at another, less worthy, motive for secrecy on Heyst's part: "And perhaps he did not care that it should be known that he had some means, whatever they might have been—sufficient, at any rate, to enable him to lend money to people" (19). There is however, no evidence that Heyst values money to the extent of fearing robbery—or perhaps of being touched for a loan by others. But the narrator's interpretation of Mrs. Schomberg's motive for aiding Lena and Heyst ("she must have had some interest of her own to serve. She was too lifeless to be suspected of impulsive compassion") proves right on the mark. She wants to get Lena away from the infatuated Schomberg.

In any case, whatever Heyst's motive for keeping secret the reality of his relationship with Morrison, the result is that Heyst becomes first the object of gossip then the object of a murderous plot. The gallery's propensity to believe the worst can lead to tragedy. Nevertheless it is clear that however well-intentioned Heyst's charity, his relationship with Morrison is founded on a misunderstanding for which Heyst must bear some degree of blame. Morrison sincerely believes that he is doing Heyst a favor by making him a partner in the coal scheme, yet Heyst knows from the beginning the enterprise has little chance of success. Heyst's "delicacy" prevents his being honest with Morrison. Heyst drifts along with Morrison out of inertia and, perhaps most worthy of blame, he allows Morrison to assume a degree of friendship Heyst does not really feel—he later tells Lena worst thing about living with Morrison was that he was so boring; Morrison's simple-minded faith contrasts strongly with Heyst's inbred skepticism.

Heyst's relationship with Lena is similarly founded on misunderstanding. Startled to witness the wife of Zangiacomo (in whose orchestra Lena is incarcerated) pinch the girl, Heyst approaches her to express his concern, and Lena responds by asking: "What are you going to do about it?" Heyst, taken aback, responds: "I am grieved to say that I don't know. But can I do anything? What would you wish me to do? Pray command me." (73) Lena takes these polite phrases literally and does command: "*You* do something! You are a gentleman." Heyst is once again committed to an unforeseen action. Heyst is touched by "something indefinably audacious and infinitely miserable" (74) in Lena's expression. Lena's audacity, like Flora's, arises out of desperation; both women throw in their lot with men they scarcely know as a way out of an intolerable situation. Heyst's response, like Anthony's, is a tenderness that arises partly from pity and partly from sexual desire. Heyst feels that his involvement with Lena is a great danger, greater even than his adventure with "the New Guenea cannibals... the most exciting of his *earlier futile adventures*" ... (82). [My italics; the implication is that this adventure will also prove futile.] (Ironically, the narrator, on hearing of Heyst's elopement with Lena, predicts: "he may end yet by eating her" [45].) Nevertheless, Heyst is able to argue himself into a decision to "steal" Lena, "accustoming his mind to the contemplation of his purpose, in order that by being faced steadily it should appear praiseworthy and wise. For the use of reason is to justify the obscure desires that move our conduct, impulses, passion, prejudices and follies, and also our fears" (83).

Lena, of course, is unaware of Heyst's doubts, nor does she realize the extent to which he mistrusts her. Only at the end of the novel, as she prepares for her encounter with Ricardo, does Lena know that she has "been for [Heyst] only a violent and sincere choice of curiosity and pity—a thing that passes" (394). But from the first Heyst fears there is something deceitful about Lena (and Lena does later prove adept at deceit). As they converse in Schomberg's music hall, Heyst asks Lena to smile so that onlookers will not perceive the seriousness of their talk:

> [T]he effect of the mechanical, ordered smile was joyous, radiant. It astonished Heyst. No wonder, it flashed through his mind, women can deceive men so completely. The faculty was inherent in them; they seemed to be created with a special aptitude. (81)

The cynical misogny of this reflection associates Heyst symbolically with Jones. The cynicism seems unwarranteed, however. Lena has a simpler explanation. Later, when Heyst has explained why he asked her to smile, she says:

> Oh, I was ready enough to smile then. That's the truth. It was the first time for years I may say that I felt disposed to smile. I've not had many chances to smile in my life, I can tell you; especially of late. (89)

Lena's simplicity, candor, and direct expression of feeling is contrasted with Heyst's coldness, caution, and propensity to generalize in the oft-quoted passage where Lena asks him to give her a new name:

> Think of one you would like the sound of—something quite new. How I should like to forget everything that has gone before, as one forgets a dream that's done with, fright and all! I would try. (88)

Heyst's response seems rather callous. "I understand that women easily forget whatever in their past diminishes them in their eyes." This suggests that Heyst assumes Lena wants to forget a shady past.[6] Lena emphatically corrects Heyst's interpretation of her words:

> It's your eyes that I was thinking of, for I'm sure I've never wished to forget anything till you came up to me that night and looked me through and through. (88)

Lena wants Heyst to re-create her. She would like to exist only in the form he would find most pleasing. Later she tells him, "if you were to stop thinking of me I shouldn't be in the world at all" (187).

But the island retreat is not really "in the world" to begin with; it is an attempted escape from the world, a separate universe, as the sea was for Anthony in *Chance*. And as in *Chance* the sea was associated not only with freedom and with escape from the hypocrisies of the social world but also with depression, withdrawal, and death, Heyst's island refuge has similar ambiguous associations. The first indication that Heyst has determined to assume responsibility for Lena occurs when she says she has "no one to care if I make a hole in the water the next chance I get or not," and Heyst tells her "that he thought she could do a little better than that, if it was only a question of getting out of the world" (78). As an escape from the world, Samburan is an alternative to suicide. It is clear that Heyst sees Samburan as "out of the world." He tells Davidson: "The world is a bad dog. It will bite you if you give it a chance; but I think that here we can safely defy the fates." (57) Although Heyst believes he and Lena have left behind the impulses to destruction and aggression the world represents, this is not so. The world still has power to bite; an unexpected word can set it to gnawing one's very vitals, as Heyst discovers when Lena tells him of Schomberg's lie, and somehow, given that initial bite, the lovers are doomed to become a veritable cannibal feast for the world's bad dogs, as the symbolic evils of Jones, Ricardo, and Pedro are called up, seemingly out of a moment of misunderstanding between Lena and Heyst.

While the plot of *Chance* also turned on misunderstanding between lovers, there, once Flora was startled into revealing her true feelings, into speaking honestly and from the heart, all could be well. In *Victory,* Lena and Heyst misunderstand each other to the end: Lena dies in the mistaken belief she has won Heyst's love, and it is by no means clear that Heyst ever realizes what Lena has been up to with Ricardo. That the gulf between them is too great ever to be bridged is indicated repeatedly. Heyst is a Swedish baron, an intellectual with an inherited income; Lena is totally uneducated, "almost a girl of the streets," raised in grinding poverty. Of their first meeting the narrator remarks: "as to the conversation, it had been perfectly insignificant, because naturally they had nothing to say to each other" (74). They are alike only in that each is a solitary, cut off from the company in which they find themselves.

> [Lena] perceived how different [Heyst] was from the other men in the room. He was as different from them as she was different from the other members of the ladies' orchestra. (73)

Lena knows, as Heyst does not, how difficult it will be for them to understand, or even to communicate, with one another. "What could I ever talk to you about?" she asks. Heyst answers in his drawing-room manner: "Don't let it trouble you.... Your voice is enough. I am in love with it, whatever it says" (88). In fact, he wishes later she could speak to him in some unknown language, so that he could be seduced by the beauty of sound without having to attend to the sense of her words. In the face of Lena's heartfelt expressions of emotion, Heyst inevitably retreats into the posture of mockingly playful politeness, often with the intention of putting Lena in the wrong by making her honesty and directness seem somehow in bad taste. When Lena says:

You should try to love me!...[S]ometimes it seems to me that you can never love me for myself, only for myself, as people do love each other when it is to be forever....Do try!

Heyst, though touched, turns away from the meaning of her words:

> These last words went straight to his heart—the sound of them more than the sense. He did not know what to say.... But he managed a smile...the well-known Heyst smile of playful courtesy, so familiar to all sorts and conditions of men in the island.
> "My dear Lena," he said, "it looks as if you were trying to pick a very unnecessary quarrel with me—of all people!" (221)

There is a similar rather querulous exchange a bit earlier, after Lena has made the statement that if Heyst were to stop thinking of her she would cease to exist. He asks: "What is it?... Is it a reproach?"

> "A reproach! Why, how could it be?" she defended herself.
> "Well, what did it mean?" he insisted.
> "What I said—just what I said. Why aren't you fair?"
> "Ah, this at least is a reproach!" (187)

Heyst and Lena are always asking each other, "What do you mean?"

From the beginning, Heyst is aware that he has not been completely candid with Lena; he has allowed her to assume that he has been overwhelmed by her physical charms, when if fact his "rescue" is more complexly motivated. As with Morrison, Heyst's impulsive expression of concern has arisen from pity, and although there is a strong component of sexual desire in Heyst's attraction to Lena, he shrinks from that recognition. He physically recoils from Lena when she seems to associate his interest in her with Schomberg's. Lena says:

> ...I will tell you straight that I have been worried and pestered by fellows like this before. I don't know what comes to them...Is it my fault? I didn't even look at them, I tell you straight. Never! Have I looked at you? Tell me. It was you that began it. (84, 85)

Heyst is immediately "ashamed of his fastidiousness," and tells Lena a "compassionate lie"—that he thinks they are being observed—to explain his recoil. Although Heyst wants to deny any symbolic association with Schomberg, there are resemblances between the two men: both are attracted to Lena because she seems helpless, and both feel Lena has made it impossible to withstand Jones and his disciples—Schomberg because he doesn't have her; Heyst because he does![7] After he and Lena have escaped to Samburan, Heyst is able to admit to himself that his response to Lena was sensual as well as altruistic. "There must be a lot of the original Adam in me, after all," he reflects (173).

Yet his original commitment to Lena grew out of a misunderstanding—her taking literally his words, "Pray command me"—and the lovers are fated to continue in misunderstanding. After living with Lena for some weeks, Heyst is still conscious of "the sensation of something inexplicable reposing within her; stupidity or inspiration, weakness or force—or simply an abysmal emptiness, reserving itself even in the moments of complete surrender" (192). To Heyst, Lena seems deeply mysterious. While she continues to insist that she is his creation, existing only as he defines her, Heyst sees her as a creature almost of another species; he cannot tell if she is stupid or inspired, weak or strong; he even fears she may be "hollow at the core." Understandably enough, Lena feels that Heyst keeps her psychically off balance: "her tone betrayed always a shade of anxiety, as though she were never certain how a conversation with him would end" (186).

We have noted that Heyst often twists Lena's words to deflect the conversation from serious matters, since he is uncomfortable with the direct expression of emotion, being congenitally unable to respond in kind. He can also, however, exhibit an almost brutal insensitivity, as in the pivotal conversation in which Heyst tells Lena the history of his relationship with Morrison, eliciting in turn the unwelcome news of Schomberg's interpretation of that relationship. Throughout the conversation, Heyst remains unaware that Lena associates her own situation with Morrison's. When Heyst describes Morrison as "cornered," Lena (who has been cornered by Schomberg) assumes Morrison has also been the victim of sexual importunities.

> "What do you say?" she whispered, astounded. "A man!"
> Heyst laughed at her wondering eyes.
> "No! No! I mean in his own way."
> "I knew very well it couldn't be anything like that," she observed under her breath. (197)

Heyst himself compares Lena's situation to Morrison's, still without understanding how painful Lena must find his words.

> "[Morrison] was really a decent fellow, he was quite unfitted for the world, he was a failure, a good man cornered—a sight for the gods; for no decent mortal cares to look at that sort." A thought seemed to occur to him. He turned his face to the girl. "And you, who have been cornered too—did you think of offering a prayer?"
> Neither her eyes nor a single one of her features moved the least bit. She only let fall the words:
> "I am not what they call a good girl." (198)

But Heyst, oblivious to Lena's pain, goes on to emphasize "the comicality of the situation," in which he inadvertently found himself saddled with Morrison's company. Lena bursts out:

"You saved a man for fun—is that what you mean? Just for fun."
"Why this tone of suspicion?" remonstrated Heyst. (199)

But as Heyst tells her of his reaction to life with Morrison, Lena must fear for her own future:

[H]is gratitude was simply frightful. Funny position, wasn't it? The boredom came later, when we lived together on board his ship. I had, in a moment of inadvertence, created for myself a tie. How to define it precisely I don't know. One gets attached in a way to people one has done something for. But is that friendship? I am not sure what it was. I only know that he who forms a tie is lost. The germ of corruption has entered into his soul. (199, 200)

Lena, in turn, unintentionally wounds Heyst's feelings when she is startled into revealing Schomberg's lie. At first, Heyst is simply stunned: "as much surprised as if he had believed himself to be a mere gliding shadow among men" (206). Heyst has really hoped to be a "gliding shadow among men"; he has believed his ethic of detachment would provide "the means of passing through life without suffering and almost without a single care in the world—invulnerable because elusive" (90). But his attempt to exist apart from others has, ironically, made him the object of intense interest. And Heyst is surprised to find himself smarting at the calumny: "Strange that it should hurt me [he thinks]... yet it does" (208). Heyst feels the slander is a violation of his innermost being, since his whole life has been an attempt to create an existence that would be proof against such casual blows, but he also reacts with immoderate anger because of his own repressed feelings of guilt—he does feel remorse about Morrison's fate. He is also angry with Lena because he suspects she has put some credence in the tale. Heyst is forced to the realization that he does care about others' opinions—particularly Lena's. "[H]e who forms a tie is lost," Heyst has said, and his association with Lena has opened a pandora's box of painful emotions. "[W]hen one's heart has been broken into in the way you have broken into mine, all sorts of weaknesses are free to enter—shame, anger, stupid indignations, stupid fears—stupid laughter, too" (210), Heyst remarks after Lena expresses surprise at hearing him laugh—for the first time, as she says.[8] Heyst's laugh, like Marlow's, expresses irritation rather than mirth. Lena responds by asking, "But why are you angry with me?"

Throughout the scene the gulf of misunderstanding between the lovers deepens. Heyst suspects Lena has really believed him capable of murder:

"[W]hen you understood that it was of me that these things had been said, you showed a strange emotion. I could see it."
"I was a bit startled," she said.
"At the baseness of my conduct?" he asked.
"I wouldn't judge you; not for anything."

"Really?"

"It would be as if I dared to judge everything that there is." With her other hand she made a gesture that seemed to embrace in one movement the earth and the heaven. "I wouldn't do such a thing." (213)

Because Lena has given over her life to Heyst, she needs to believe that he is a being of a different order. It would be a sacrilege to judge him; it would be like judging God. She has given Heyst mental authority to do whatever he likes. If he in fact has cast off Morrison, as Schomberg charged, then he must have done so for a good reason—but because Lena identifies with Morrison, she fears the same fate may befall her:

> [W]hy shouldn't you get tired of that or any other—company? You aren't like any one else and—and the thought of it made me unhappy suddenly; but indeed, I did not believe anything bad of you. (214)

This is Lena's explanation for her "strange emotion," but Heyst is too indignant to understand.

> "No, this earth must be the appointed hatching planet of calumny enough to furnish the whole universe! I feel a disgust at my own person, as if I had tumbled into some filthy hole. Pah! And you—all you can say is that you won't judge me that you—"
> . . .
> "I don't believe anything bad of you," she repeated. I couldn't."
> All at once, without a transition, he detested her. (215)

Heyst wants Lena to declare unequivocally her belief that he is incapable of the evil with which Schomberg has charged him.

Heyst's momentary feeling of hatred for Lena is followed immediately by love-making, as if to underscore the connection between aggression and sexuality that is implicit throughout this scene. Donald Dike, finding in Lena a symbolic Eve, who "introduces evil to the island" when she repeats Schomberg's gossip, asserts that Heyst's angry moment of hatred "frees their relation for sexuality"—something of an overstatement, since this is certainly not the lovers' first sexual encounter.[9] Yet it is clear that Lena's revelation is, for Heyst, a loss of innocence. His inexperience has made him unfit "for the encounters of a world in which love itself rests as much on antagonism as on attraction" (222). Heyst explains to Lena that he is equally inexperienced in love and in death-dealing:

> I've never killed a man or loved a woman—not even in my thoughts, not even in my dreams.... To slay, to love—the greatest enterprises of life upon a man! And I have no experience of either. (212)

Dike points out that this statement associates Heyst with Ricardo, who makes "an ambivalent physical attack" on Lena ("ravish or kill—it was all one to him").[10] But while Ricardo claims the capacity for passion and for murder that Heyst disclaims, he too is easily disarmed; the raging tiger becomes a house cat.

Ricardo's pose of detachment also associates him with Heyst, ironically enough. Terrorizing Schomberg, Ricardo states:

> ...I am not friendly to you. I just don't care. Some men do say that; but I really don't. You are no more to me one way or another than that fly there. (129)

Heyst asserts that he is indifferent to life itself: "And I may say truly, too, that I never did care, I won't say for life—I had scorned what people call by that name from the first—but for being alive" (212). Clearly Heyst is, at least unconsciously, much in love with easeful death; his father has, after all, taught him that life is meaningless. Heyst communes with his father through the latter's voluminous writings. After making love to Lena, Heyst returns with her to the house, and sending Lena to rest, Heyst turns immediately to one of his father's books for a restorative draught of nihilism:

> He turned the pages of the little volume... It seemed to him that he was hearing his father's voice... a ghostly voice, audible to the ear of his own flesh and blood. With what strange serenity, mingled with terrors, had that man considered the universal nothingness! He had plunged into it headlong, perhaps to render death, the answer that faced one at every inquiry, more supportable. (219)

This ironic summing up of Heyst's father's philosophy—a pessimism about life so deep as to make death itself seem an ameliorative state—reminds us again of the source of Heyst's own death-in-life (for that is what his attempt to pass through life without suffering and without cares amounts to, in the end). Heyst's father is perhaps the most reprehensible of all the reprehensible philosopher-writers in Conrad, just as he seems the most destructive of all the gallery of Conrad's destructive fathers; certainly the fact that it is fatherly influence that has maimed Heyst is underscored most clearly here.

Like the Professor in *The Secret Agent,* Heyst's father has become a nihilist as an angry response to others' failure to recognize his genius; he is "dissatisfied with his country and angry with all the world, which had instinctively rejected his wisdom" (91).[11] Heyst Sr. is described as a "destroyer of systems, or hopes, or beliefs" (175), a force of pure destruction, like Jones and his minions. There is an implication that by taking up his father's book, by listening to his father's ghostly voice, Heyst has somehow invoked these evil spirits. His father has written:

> Clairvoyance or no clairvoyance, men love their captivity. To the unknown force of negation they prefer the miserably tumbled bed of their servitude. (220)

This is also Ricardo's opinion, as he tells Schomberg. Ricardo thinks himself a hero because he has chosen negation, in the person of Jones, instead of servitude. Jones is the very personification of death, called up perhaps as retribution for Heyst's apostasy from his father's doctrine, or perhaps the emanation of Heyst's own devout desire to escape life.

This disgust with life is at its most intese in the moment just before Wang announces the arrival of the villains. Remembering Schomberg's calumny, Heyst feels physically poisoned, and he has come to believe his tender feelings for Lena constitute a danger—he reads in his father's book: "Of the strategems of life the most cruel is the consolation of love—the most subtle, too; for the desire is the bed of dreams" (219). (The wording recalls the elder Heyst's reference to "the miserably tumbled bed of ... servitude" and seem to associate the ties of love with loss of freedom, as well as with destructive illusion.) Turning from the book to Lena, Heyst looks on her as "on a piece of writing which he is unable to decipher, but which may be big with some revelation" (222), and is "struck afresh by the physical and moral sense of the imperfections of their relations." Heyst is trying to avoid the implications of Lena's plea— "You should try to love me!"—and feigns misunderstanding:

> "I don't see clearly what you mean. Is your mind turned toward the future?
> ...
> "Because if it is so there is nothing easier than to dismiss it. In our future, as in what people call the other life, there is nothing to be frightened of." (222)

Having gone out of the world, Heyst and Lena are as though dead, and the dead need have no worry about the future. Heyst again insists that they are cut off from humanity as he tenders an indirect reproach: "Surely you don't suspect after what I have heard from you, that I am anxious to return to mankind." (223)

Lena, whose "victory," is the ostensible moral of the tale, is meant to provide a counter-weight to Heyst's ethic of withdrawal and disengagement—to represent a life force that can overcome her lover's unconscious death wish. While initially presented as a child-like waif, physically insignificant, indeed almost a spectre in her white dress, Lena seems to become larger as the narrative progresses, until at the end she is seen as a sort of enormous idol, sitting on Heyst's veranda, with the worshipping Ricardo recumbent at her feet. She possesses supernatural physical strength as well; she easily subdues the savage Ricardo, who is capable of breaking the head of Pedro (who, in turn, we are told, is stronger than any mere human being). She symbolically unmans Ricardo when she gains possession of his knife, as she unmans Heyst when she repeats Schomberg's gossip. And, it is implied, Lena bears ultimate responsibility for the visitation of evil, in the persons of Jones et al., to the island, since Schomberg has sent them in retaliation for Heyst's theft of Lena. (Lena assumes this guilt: "Woman is the tempter," she tells Heyst.)

But it is not just Lena's repetition of Schomberg's lie that troubles Heyst; it is her inability to state that she has never, for a minute, believed it. The situation is reminiscent of the Lear-Cordelia impasse, as the need for self-justification runs up against the impulse for scrupulous honesty. Heyst sees the lie and the arrival of the villains as equally unprovoked, and unthinkable, assaults, but the fact that he thinks Lena "only half disbelieves" Schomberg's story constitutes a "moral stab in the back" that "seemed to have taken some of his strength from him, as a physical wound would have done. He had no desire to do anything..."(259). Heyst is unable even to summon the moral indignation necessary to combat the villains:

> They ought to have aroused my fury. But I have refined everything away by this time—anger, indignation, scorn itself. Nothing's left but disgust. Since you have told me of that abominable calumny, it has become immense—it extends even to myself." [Heyst tells Lena.] (330)

The repeated references Heyst makes to his continual suffering because of Lena's unwise words certainly constitute an implicit reproach and confirm Lena's sense of guilt. Heyst even offers Schomberg's calumny as a further reason to avoid killing the menacing trio. Even though he has told Lena a number of times that he is physically incapable of murder, he says:

> [Murder] may be—my duty to you, to myself.... Do you know what the world would say?... It would say, Lena, that I—that Swede—after luring my friend and partner to his death from mere greed of money, have murdered these unoffending shipwrecked strangers from sheer funk. That would be the story whispered—perhaps shouted—certainly spread out, and believed—and *believed,* my dear Lena!... [T]he power of calumny grows with time. It's insidious and penetrating. It can even destroy one's faith in oneself—dry-rot the soul. (361, 362)

When Lena has first told Heyst of Schomberg's story, he has exclaimed: "What power there must be in words.... What were they?... If you were to try to remember, they would perhaps convince me, too" (214). Like Marlow, in *Chance,* Heyst is forced to ask himself if there might be a grain of truth in this cruel assessment of his character. But, in a sense, by asserting that it is the calumny that has destroyed his faith in himself and made him unable to take action, Heyst is placing the responsibility for their plight on Lena. Heyst's words seem almost a rationalization, since he has never been capable of physical violence. It is also difficult to accept that, in this extremity, as he and

Lena are threatened with death, he would most dread being the subject of further gossip.

Heyst, as the object of gossip, is associated symbolically with both Schomberg and Jones. The calumniating Schomberg has been himself the object of gossip (which is seen as self-perpetuating) and that gossip has brought Jones, Ricardo, and Pedro to his door. Jones tells Schomberg he learned of the hotel-keeper from a man who

> was anything but a friend of yours. He called you all the names he could think of. He said you set a lot of scandal going about him once, somewhere.... (96)

And Jones, whose homosexuality is strongly implied, has also been the butt of gossip. Ricardo says to Schomberg:

> The girls... would ask me if the English *caballero* in the *posada* was a monk in disguise, or if he had taken a vow to the *sanctissima madre* not to speak to a woman or whether—You can imagine what fairly free-spoken girls will ask when they come to the point of not caring what they say; and it used to vex me. (160)

During his final interview with Heyst, Jones repeatedly associates himself with his intended victim, even hinting that he suspects Heyst shares his sexual bent. (This is before Jones learns of Lena's existence.) Jones says:

> It's obvious that we belong to the same—social sphere.... Someting has driven you out—the originality of your ideas, perhaps. Or your tastes. (378)

Jones goes on to point out other similarities. Not only are both "gentlemen," both are outcasts from society as well, and both are attended by "faithful retainers"—Jones brags of Ricardo's superiority to Wang in this respect. Jones also is as loathe to take physical action as Heyst has been. Heyst taunts him:

> "He who deliberates is lost.... You don't seem to have quite enough pluck for your business. Why don't you do it at once?"
>
> "Strange as it may seem to you, it is because of my origin, my breeding, my traditions, my early associations, and such-like trifles." [Jones answers.] (383)

These are just the sort of reasons Heyst has offered Lena for his failure to act.

Heyst is still unable to take action, even though Jones, deranged at the news there is a woman in the case, has become so distracted as to be easily overpowered, as Heyst recognizes. But Heyst, having gone to see Jones with the intention of somehow ending the standoff, is immobilized when Jones reveals that Schomberg was responsible for their arrival; Heyst is struck afresh by the power of words: "This diabolical calumny will end in actually and literally taking my life from me," he thinks (381). As Heyst explains to Jones that Schomberg has sent them on a fool's errand in retaliation for the loss of Lena, he seems to place responsibility for the unwelcome visit on Lena as well: "If it had not been for that girl whom he persecuted with his insane and odious passion, and who threw herself on my protection, he would never have—" (386). Jones later makes the same point when he refers to Lena as "that fascinating creature to whom you owe whatever pleasure you can find in our visit" (391). After Lena is mentioned Heyst seems to lose all capacity for action. He tells Jones, as he earlier told Lena, that he has no love of life: "from which I have divorced myself long ago—" (388). Heyst has lost the sense of reality. "It seemed to him that all this was an elaborate other-world joke, contrived by that spectre in a gorgeous dressing-gown.... His feelings had become so blunted that he did not care how soon he was shot in the back" (389, 390). Heyst is suddenly under Jones's psychic influence:

> His very will seemed dead of weariness. He moved automatically, his head low, like a prisoner captured by the evil power of a masquerading skeleton out of a grave. Mr. Jones took charge of the direction. (390, 391)

Jones has become the symbolic embodiment of Heyst's father—as "a masquerading skeleton out of a grave," "a spectre in a gorgeous dressing gown." Jones forces Heyst to a revelation. "If I have to shoot you in the end, then perhaps you will die cured," he says (391). And Heyst unquestioningly accepts Jone's interpretation of the scene:

> Doubt entered into him—a doubt of a new kind, formless, hideous. It seemed to spread itself all over him, enter his limbs, and lodge in his entrails. He stopped suddenly, with a thought that he who experienced such a feeling had no business to live—or perhaps was no longer living.
> ...
> A great shame descended upon Heyst—the shame of guilt, absurd and maddening. (391, 392)

Clearly it is shame at his apostasy from his father's doctrine that Heyst feels, and the whole voyeuristic scene, as Heyst and Jones watch Lena and Ricardo, suggest a parody of Heyst Sr.'s famous dictum: "Look on—make no sound." The incipient impulses to love and trust that Lena has awakened in Heyst are extinguished, as his father's power reasserts itself.

But Lena is an ambiguous symbol of the life force. She inspires mistrust not only in Heyst but also in Mrs. Schomberg, who thinks Lena will steal her husband; in Wang, whose misinterpretation of the scene he overhears between Lena and Ricardo prefigures Heyst's misinterpretation of the scene between those two at the end of the novel; in Jones, of course; and even in the benign Davidson, who although he has never seen Lena, assumes she will bring Heyst trouble. Even Ricardo believes Lena is eager to betray Heyst. There is also a strong implication that Lena's sexual attraction is a danger. We have noted earlier that Heyst associates love and death ("To slay, to love..."), but in Ricardo the tendency to oscillate between tender protestations of love and murderous impulses is most pronounced. Early in the novel Ricardo tells Schomberg that he enjoys the idea that he is capable of killing as well as loving; he exults in his own barely repressed ferocity:

> Once I was courting a girl. I used to kiss her behind the ear and say to myself: "If you only knew who's kissing you, my dear, you would scream and bolt!" Ha! Ha! Not that I wanted to do them any harm; but I felt the power in myself. (129)

After falling under Lena's spell, Ricardo becomes more and more eager to "rip up" Heyst: "His passions being thoroughly aroused, a thirst for blood was allied in him with a thirst for tenderness—yes, tenderness" (336). But Ricardo also has a strong masochistic streak. Lena wins his heart by strangling him. Although he has attacked her, with a "feral spring," intending to "ravish or kill," when she physically overpowers *him*, he reacts rather strangely.

> Ricardo, feeling his throat with tender care, breathed out admiringly:
> "You have fingers like steel. Jimminy! You have muscles like a giant!" (291)

He declares that he and Lena are soul-mates:

> You and I are made to understand each other. Born alike, bred alike, I guess. You are not tame. Same here! You have been chucked out into this rotten world of 'yporcrits. Same here! (297)

When Lena helps him escape through the window of her room and then throws after him the shoe he has lost in their scuffle, Ricardo asserts that she has saved him. Their sexual roles have become reversed, and what began as a murderous attack ends as a rescue. ("You forgave me. You saved me. You got the better of me, too," says Ricardo [399,400].)

The symbolic connection between sexuality and death is made most explicit, of course, in the scene where Lena gains possession of Ricardo's knife.[12] Lena is convinced that if she can only obtain the knife Heyst will be saved. Ricardo's surrender of his knife is described as a sexual encounter.

> "When we are going about the world together, you shall always call me husband. Do you hear?"
> "Yes," she said, bracing herself for the contest, in whatever shape it was coming.
> The knife was lying in her lap. She let it slip into the fold of her dress, and laid her forearms with clasped fingers over her knees, which she pressed desperately together. The dreaded thing was out of sight at last. She felt a dampness break out all over her. (400)

Ricardo himself recognizes that Lena has obtained his manhood:

> She had his knife. It was she now who was deadly, while he was disarmed, no good for the moment. (402)[13]

Although we are repeatedly reminded of Ricardo's ferocity, these references to his aggressive power invariably contain an ambiguity. When Lena forbids his approach, he stops "with a smile of imbecile worship on his lips, and with the delighted obedience of a man who could at any moment seize her in his hands and dash her to the ground" (395). We remember that Ricardo associates sexuality with the consciousness of power to do physical harm—but we also remember that it was Lena who overpowered him in their earlier encounter, and that he discovered his love for her as she was strangling him. This same confusion is evident in Ricardo's: "What you want is a man, a master that will let you put the heel of your shoe on his neck...." (397). As the image suggests, Ricardo is a foot fetishist.[14]

> "I am dog-tired.... I went tired this morning, since I came in here and started talking to you—as tired as if I had been pouring my life-blood here on these planks for you to dabble your white feet in." (396)
>
> ...
>
> "Give your foot," he begged in a timid murmur, and in the full consciousness of his power."
>
> ...
>
> Ricardo, clasping her ankle, pressed his lips time after time to the instep, muttering gasping words that were like sobs, making little noises that resembled the sounds of grief and distress. (400, 401)

Ricardo's attitude of subjection, the sounds he makes that suggest physical suffering, and especially the image of "pouring [his] life-blood here on these planks for you..." indicate that Ricardo, pierced by Cupid's arrow, has been metaphorically stabbed to death. Possessed of a knife (like Winnie Verloc) Lena represents destruction.

Our view of Lena as heroine, savior of Heyst, and life-force is thus qualified in several ways. As Heyst is associated in certain ways with Schomberg and Jones and Ricardo, so Lena is associated with Ricardo in their common origin in the lower depths, in their devotion to a gentleman, and in their capacity for deception.[15] Moreover, Lena like Ricardo seems pathologically eager for self-immolation. We have noted that Heyst often expresses his disdain for life, but Lena too seems to have a death wish. The island itself represents a retreat from life, but Lena further seeks out darkness and shade, avoiding the sun and exhibiting a dread of open spaces; she is also frightened at viewing the open sea: "all that water and all that light—" (191).

> The flaming abyss of emptiness, the liquid, undulating glare, the tragic brutality of the light, made her long for the friendly night.... (216)

In an image that prefigures the holocaust that ends the novel, Lena feels the sun is "all aquiver with the effort to set the earth on fire, to burn it to ashes" (305). This last observation is made immediately after Ricardo's attempted sexual assault, which finally awakens Lena to the danger the strangers represent.

Until she is attacked, Lena has shown a strange lack of interest in the visitors, preoccupied as she is with her discovery of the immensity of the misunderstanding between herself and Heyst. Now, seeing that Heyst is helpless, without a weapon, and more importantly, temperamentally unfit for action, Lena determines to save him from death. As in the preceding novels, Conrad asserts that it is women who are capable of dealing with unpleasant reality, which men's finer sensibilities prefer to ignore:

> [W]ith the consciousness of her love for this man, of that something rapturous and profound going beyond the mere embrace, there was born in her a woman's innate mistrust of masculinity, of that seductive strength allied to an absurd, delicate shrinking from the recognition of the naked necessity of facts, which never yet frightened a woman worthy of the name. (308)

The vagueness of the writing here and elsewhere in the passages describing Lena's reaction to Heyst, makes it difficult to know what Lena's real motives and feelings are meant to be. In any case, Lena's reaction to the villains' threat seems peculiar:

> Out of the appeased enchantment of the senses she had found with him, like a sort of bewitched state, his danger brought a sensation of warmth to her breast. She felt something stir in there, something profound, like a new sort of life. (303)

Paradoxically, the intruders, emissaries of death, also bring a sense of life, upsetting the stasis of Heyst and Lena's relationship. Indeed, the image suggests a pregnancy—but it is Heyst whom Lena wants to mother. She determines to reverse their previous roles: she will be the rescuer this time.

> [A] thrill went through her at the sudden thought that it was she who would have to protect him, to be the defender of a man who was strong enough to lift her bodily, as he was doing even then in his two arms. (309)

Earlier, when Heyst had become angry with Lena, she realized for the first time how completely dependent she was on him: suspended "between the abysses of earth and heaven in the hollow of his arm" (209). If he were to grow "weary of the burden," she would be plunged into the void. Lena hopes to alleviate her anxiety by taking on Heyst's role, but she is also intoxicated with the idea of self-sacrifice:

> ...all her energy was concentrated on the struggle that she wanted to take upon herself, in a great exaltation of love and self-sacrifice, which is woman's sublime faculty; altogether on herself, every bit of it, leaving him nothing, not even the knowlege of what she did, if that were possible. (317)

The idea of self-sacrifice as "woman's sublime faculty" would have been pooh-poohed by Mrs. Fyne (and by Marlow): here it is gospel.

But while Lena is exulting in her plan to sacrifice her life for Heyst, he is bemoaning the fact he cannot just surrender to death, as he would like to do, because he has Lena to worry about:

> He considered himself a dead man already, yet forced to pretend that he was alive for her sake, for her defence. He regretted that he had no Heaven to which he could recommend this fair, palpitating handful of ashes and dust—warm, living, sentient, his own—and exposed helplessly to insult, outrage, degradation, and infinite misery of the body. (354, 355)

This is another reminder that Heyst is one of the living dead, yet the passage also implies that Heyst wishes Lena were dead; the language suggests a funeral service (although Heyst immediately reminds himself that she is "warm, living, sentient..."). The description of Lena as "ashes and dust" is, in fact, not very different from Jones's angry denunciation of Lena and Ricardo as "Mud souls, obscene and cunning! Mud bodies, too—the mud of the gutter" (392).

Lena also seems to anticipate death—but she looks forward to it with a certain sensual pleasure. As she waits for Ricardo, "the man of violence and death," she feels "the anguish of her disobedience to her lover, which [is] soothed by a feeling she had known before—a gentle flood of penetrating sweetness" (394). At the same time she has come to realize that she has "been for [Heyst] only a violent and sincere choice of curiosity and pity—a thing that passes. She did not know him" (394). "Violent and sincere" seem peculiar adjectives here until we recall that violence "means" sensuality in the novel, and that sincerity indicates that Heyst has truly been emotionally touched by Lena's plight. But the fact that pity was one of Heyst's motives makes the rescue a form of degradation. (Heyst's father has advised him to "cultivate that form of contempt which is called pity" [174].) There is even an implication that Heyst himself finds the feelings of pity Lena awakens unpleasant. We are told that "always when looking into her unconscious eyes, he tasted something like the dregs of tender pity" (366). And at the moment when Heyst bursts in on Lena and Ricardo, believing himself betrayed by Lena: "He would have pitied her, if the triumphant expression of her face had not given him a shock which destroyed the balance of his feelings" (403).

This final encounter between the lovers is compounded with multiple misunderstandings; Lena and Heyst remain incomprehensible to one another to the end. Heyst mininterprets Lena's "triumphant expression." He speaks with bitter misogyny:

> No doubt you acted from instinct. Women have been provided with their own weapon. I was a disarmed man, I have been a disarmed man all my life as I see it now. You may glory in your resourcefulness and your profound knowledge of yourself; but I may say that the other attitude, suggestive of shame, had its charm. (404)

Lena has no idea what Heyst means by these words; she is too exultant at her victory to realize how the scene must have appeared to him. She is convinced she has captured Heyst's heart at last. She is deceived in this, as she is deceived in her belief she has saved Heyst's life—her self-immolation merely frees him for death (the death which he seems to have been seeking all along). Death is seen here as the result of a symbolically sexual encounter, as Davidson, who arrives on the scene unexpectedly, picks up the phallic knife and asks, "Has she been stabbed with this thing?" Lena immediately demands the knife as her prize, ordering Heyst: "Kill nobody" (405). And Lena dies in a "flush of rapture flooding her whole being," while "seeking for [Heyst's] glance in the shades of death" (407). But the lovers have been dwelling in the shades of death all along, as Lena finally seems to realize, crying out to Heyst, "I've saved you! Why don't you take me into your arms and carry me out of this lonely place?" Ironically, only at the moment of death does Lena choose life.

Lena claims credit as Heyst's rescuer here, but the saving gesture can lead only to death. In fact, the novel is an even more radical condemnation of samaritanism than is *Chance*. Not only Heyst, but all those who are rescued meet death: Lena, Morrison, Jones, Ricardo, and Pedro. Furthermore, the very intentions of the rescuer are called in question. Sharon Kaehele and Howard German have pointed out that the novel's "four rescue scenes...[are] presented with the same patterns of detail."[16] These four scenes are Heyst's rescues of Morrison, Lena, and the villains (whose lives he saves when they arrive nearly dead from lack of water), and Jones and Ricardo's rescue of Pedro. (I would argue that Lena's saving Ricardo from being detected by Heyst constitutes yet another rescue.) In each case, the person about to be saved thinks at first he or she is the intended victim of the rescuer: both Lena and Morrison initially assumed Heyst was making sport of them, and Ricardo, hearing Heyst send Wang to fetch a crowbar, is terrified, assuming Heyst means to use it to kill them, just as Pedro had assumed Ricardo's approach with a knife meant death, though Ricardo was only intending to cut his bonds. Indeed, Ricardo as savior serves to parody Heyst. While Heyst has found Morrison's gratitude unbearable, Ricardo tells Pedro, whose head he has just broken open, "You ought to kiss my hands!... Yes! You ought to burn a candle before me as they do before the saints in your country. No saint has ever done so much for you as I have, you ungrateful vagabond" (240).

The comic irony here is intentional, as it is in Ricardo's description of a gentleman as "sometimes that familiar you might think he would eat out of your hand, and at others [apt to] snub you sharper than a devil—but always quiet" (139), and his corollary assertion: "I know a gentleman at sight. I should know one drunk, in the gutter, in jail, under the gallows" (125). But it is not clear exactly how seriously we are meant to take the villains, on balance. Most of Ricardo's speeches are mirth-provoking, as are Jones's grandiloquent claims to be a force of cosmic evil, especially coupled with his physical weakness and tendency to lose all emotional control. Also Conrad's rather over-explicit emphasis on the villains' allegorical significance ("Here they are before you— evil intelligence, instinctive savagery, arm in arm. The brute force is at the back" [329]) prevents our accepting them as real, menacing figures. Furthermore, as we noted, the resemblances many critics have found between aspects of the villains' characters and tendencies in Heyst's and Lena's personalities tend to qualify our view of the lovers and to make it difficult to accept either Lena's proclaimed victory or Heyst's *cri de coeur* (the much-quoted moral of the story): "Ah, Davidson, woe to the man whose heart has not leaned while young to hope, to love—and to put its trust in life" (410)! But instead of commending trust in life, the novel's bleak conclusion seems to indicate that to trust in life is to invite betrayal. It is the spirit of Heyst's father's nihilism that prevails. (Indeed, the old man seems symbolically to be given the last word, since the novel's final word, spoken by Davidson, is "Nothing!")

Douglas Park has remarked that the novel's abrupt conclusion "seems designed to prevent resolution, to freeze the extremes of despair and delusion" Heyst and Lena represent.[17] He also notes that Davidson has a deflationary effect: "That the man who trusts most solidly in life bemusedly reports Heyst's yearning for trust as the utterance of a 'queer chap' (410) provides *Victory*'s final irony."[18] At the end of the novel, as at the beginning, we see Heyst from a critical distance. We are not permitted to identify with his suffering and, in fact, he remains almost as much a mystery to the reader as he is to Davidson. We are left with a wasteland vision, among the ashes of the lovers' demi-Eden: even in a community of two—two people with the most benign intentions toward one another—mutual destruction is inevitable.

Notes

Chapter 1

1. Frederick R. Karl, *Joseph Conrad: The Three Lives* (New York: Farrar, Straus and Giroux, 1979), p. 626.
2. See Bernard C. Meyer, *Joseph Conrad: A Psychoanalytic Biography* (Princeton: Princeton Univ. Press, 1967), pp. 213-19, 338.
3. Meyer, pp. 216-217.
4. See Karl, p. 683.
5. Decoud and Heyst have a number of similarities: both are detached and skeptical observers of others, loathe to take action; both are moved to uncharacteristic behavior by a woman's influence; both are extremely conscious of family heritage; both are suicides.

Chapter 2

1. *Conrad the Novelist* (Cambridge, Mass.: Harvard Univ. Press, 1958), p. 175.
2. In G. Jean-Aubry, *Joseph Conrad: Life and Letters* (New York: Doubleday, Page, 1927), II, 296.
3. *Joseph Conrad: A Critical Biography* (London: Weidenfeld and Nicolson, 1960), p. 301.
4. See F. R. Leavis, *The Great Tradition* (New York: G. W. Stewart, 1948), p. 240.
5. Joseph Conrad, *Nostromo* (New York: Modern Library, 1951), p. 582. Following Eloise Hay, *The Political Novels of Joseph Conrad* (Chicago: Univ. of Chicago Press, 1963) and Claire Rosenfield, *Paradise of Snakes* (Chicago: Univ. of Chicago Press, 1967), among others, I use the Modern Library edition in preference to the Dent edition because it contains some passages, particularly dealing with Nostromo, which are illuminating, although Conrad cut them from the later edition. In the revised edition Conrad generally aimed at making Nostromo more heroic, excising a number of references to his lack of intelligence, and de-emphasizing his vanity somewhat. Page references to the novel follow quotations.
6. Viola's characterization has occasioned critical debate. For instance, Michael Wilding, "The Politics of Nostromo," *Essays in Criticism*, 16 (1966), 441, says Viola is meant to "illustrate the inadequacy of nineteenth-century liberal nationalism in the 'modern world.'" Avrom Fleishman, *Conrad's Politics* (Baltimore: Johns Hopkins Press, 1967) offers two rather contradictory assessments of Viola. He says Viola "represents the real proletariat of the port

and the mine," p. 169n, but later states: "The idealist Viola fails to recognize Nostromo because of both literal and symbolic poor vision. The faded radical is out of touch with the new proletariat and is himself ridden by class prejudices..." p. 175.

7. The shift of focus to the Goulds is inaugurated when, at the end of chapter 5, Sir John asks the engineer what sort of a person Charles Gould is. The engineer remarks that Gould "must be immensely wealthy" (46). This phrase is picked up again on page 102, after another long parenthesis detailing the history of the mine, when the omniscient narrator remarks that the Goulds were "by no means so wealthy as the engineer-in-chief of the new railway could legitimately suppose."

8. Both Guerard and Lewis make this point. Guerard, p. 199, argues persuasively that "Conrad may be condemning Decoud for a withdrawal and skepticism more radical than Decoud ever shows; which are, in fact, Conrad's own."

9. Owen Knowles, "Commentary as Rhetoric: An Aspect of Conrad's Technique," *Conradiana*, 5 (1973), 5-27, notes that Avellanos is first seen as "an object of gossip and criticism by others," not entirely to be taken seriously, until we learn of his ordeal under Bento. Knowles remarks that the "omniscient revaluation does not wholly reverse our view of Don Jose—there are still hints of irony in Conrad's analysis of him—but it does alert us to fresh possibilities, complicating our interest in the emerging man," p. 10. Dr. Monygham's presentation is very similar, of course.

10. *Joseph Conrad: A Psychoanalytic Biography* (Princeton: Princeton Univ. Press, 1967), p. 605.

11. The conversation between Monygham and Nostromo in the Custom House is marked by a series of misunderstandings between the two men, who have a "temperamental enmity." Monygham continually says precisely the wrong thing, first telling Nostromo the silver was of no importance, then refusing to hear the details of the adventure, then revealing his complicity in Hirsch's death, and finally asserting that Decoud has hoodwinked Nostromo: "[Y]ou allowed Decoud to lead you into all this.... Did you imagine Decoud cared very much for what would happen to you?" (511). All these tactless statements lead to Nostromo's sacrifice of Decoud. The scene may be compared to the climactic confrontation between Winnie and Verloc in *The Secret Agent*, where Verloc effectively precipitates his own murder.

12. I think Fleishman, p. 175, is mistaken when he states that Nostromo's ride to Cayta represents a break "with his role of upper-class factotum." Fleishman goes on to say: "It is at this point that Nostromo identifies himself with the community most fully and most altruistically—at precisely the time of his greatest egoism, when he is already absorbed in his own plans to become rich." But Nostromo has *not* yet determined to become rich. He has only just left Decoud and the silver. It is on his return from Cayta that he discovers Decoud's disappearance, and the fact that four silver ingots are missing. I do not, in any case, think there is much evidence that Nostromo ever "identifies himself with the community"; his tragedy is his invincible isolation.

13. Few critics have recognized that Nostromo feels he has no other choice than to keep the silver—even though the novel says this explicitly. For example, John A. Palmer, *Joseph Conrad's Fiction* (Ithaca: Cornell Univ. Press, 1968), pp. 152-53, gives "three distinct motives...for his stealing the silver," but does not mention the four missing ingots.

14. Fleishman, p. 174.

15. Nostromo is also revolutionary "in another manner" in that the politics of the secret societies are not Giorgio's politics. Giorgio, we are told, "would have understood nothing" of the "hater of capitalists'" speech.

16. Quoted by Frederick R. Karl in *Joseph Conrad: The Three Lives* (New York: Farrar, Strauss and Giroux, 1979), p. 811. The letter was written in 1918.

17. Thomas Moser, *Joseph Conrad: Achievement and Decline* (Cambridge, Mass.: Harvard Univ. Press, 1957), p. 87, notes that this is a typical Conradian situation, "with the older relative trying, in this case successfully, to prevent consummation of the love. The once henpecked, now senile, Viola with the inevitable weapon, 'his old gun,' destroys Nostromo, the stalwart lover."

Chapter 3

1. *Joseph Conrad: The Three Lives* (New York: Farrar, Straus and Giroux, 1979), p. 592. Karl also notes that in all the novels from *The Secret Agent* through *Victory* "the family is in an antagonistic relationship, leading to destructive consequences, and children are themselves 'unrelated' to the people who have borne them...." Karl does not, however, expand on the point.

2. *Joseph Conrad: A Psychoanalytic Biography* (Princeton: Princeton Univ. Press, 1967), p. 128n.

3. Joseph Conrad, *The Secret Agent* (London: J. M. Dent, 1923), p. 3. Subsequent page references follow quotations.

4. Conrad uses "amateur" in the sense of "devotee" here and elsewhere in the novel.

5. Norman Sherry, *Conrad's Western World* (Cambridge: The Univ. Press, 1971), p. 367, argues persuasively that Conrad's principal source for Winnie was his wife Jessie, who was famous for "holding her tongue."

6. Meyer, p. 195, notes that in his stage directions for the dramatization of *The Secret Agent*, Conrad emphasized the "similarit[ies] in their personal appearance—both big men, clothes same sort of cut, dark blue overcoats and round hats on."

7. Irving Howe, *Politics and the Novel* (New York: Horizon Press, 1957), p. 96, argues that there is no "moral positive" in the novel, and finds this a grave flaw. Eloise Hay, *The Political Novels of Joseph Conrad* (Chicago: Univ. of Chicago Press, 1963), p. 255, on the other hand, believes English society itself functions as a moral positive, asserting: "This is Conrad's only novel in which England comes off as what the deceased Poland had tacitly been to him before—the highest example of political rectitude." Hay reads the passage quoted (dealing with the proper functions of the police) differently than I. She feels that Winnie's answer to Stevie's question indicates that "rock-bottom social justice is really the standard on which the melodrama rests and turns." I fail to see how one can call letting the hungry remain unfed in the name of law and order "social justice." Surely Conrad is satirizing this concept of social justice.

    Taking the opposite tack, Elliott B. Gose, Jr., "'Cruel Devourer of the World's light': *The Secret Agent*," *Nineteenth-Century Fiction*, 16 (1960), p. 40, says the novel shows "the failure of a whole society disintegrating into a state of unconscious anarchy."

8. Madness is epidemic in *The Secret Agent*; most of the major characters are described as mad, at one time or another: Winnie, Stevie, the Professor, Ossipon, Michaelis, Yundt and his wife—even the Great Lady. For a perceptive study of madness as a theme in the novel, see Michael Haltresht, "The Dread of Space in Conrad's *The Secret Agent*," *Literature and Psychology*, 22 (1972), 89-97.

9. Joseph I. Fradin, "Anarchist, Detective and Saint: The Possibilities of Action in *The Secret Agent,*" *PMLA,* 83 (1968), 1414-22, argues against viewing the Assistant Commissioner as a standard in the novel, since he sees the Assistant Commissioner as morally compromised by his marriage. This is a particularly important and fascinating article, but Fradin bases some of his analysis of the Assistant Commissioner's character on a misreading of a passage in the novel where the Assistant Commissioner is thinking about his wife and her relationship with the Great Lady. The "improper thought" that occurs to him does not have to do with his wife's sexual preferences, as Fradin assumes, but is merely the reflection: "If the fellow [Michaelis] is laid hold of again... she [the Great Lady] will never forgive me" (113).
10. Stallman, p. 240.
11. *Joseph Conrad: Achievement and Decline* (Cambridge, Mass.: Harvard Univ. Press, 1957), p. 92.
12. Stallman, pp. 242, 243.
13. See Leo Gurko, *Joseph Conrad: Giant in Exile* (New York: Macmillan, 1962), p. 176.
14. The theme of the aborted confidence that would have prevented catastrophe, a staple of melodrama, also appears in *Nostromo,* when Nostromo's failure to confide to Monygham that Decoud is alive leads to Decoud's suicide.
15. Robert G. Jacobs, "Comrade Ossipon's Favorite Saint: Lombroso and Conrad," *Nineteenth-Century Fiction,* 23 (1968), 74-83, notes that Conrad himself uses Lombroso's system of classification in many of his works.
16. Stevie shares certain physical characteristics with the Professor—both are very small in stature and thin; both have large "transparent" ears—while Stevie resembles Michaelis in that both are ingenuous and child-like. (Michaelis is "mild-voiced and quiet, with no more self-consciousness than a very small child, and with something of a child's charm—the appealing charm of trustfulness" [107].)
17. Albert Guerard, *Conrad the Novelist* (Cambridge, Mass.: Harvard Univ. Press, 1958), p. 230, has perhaps been the first to make this point. He says, "Verloc rather than his wife takes the initiative in each important step toward his murder."
18. In an essay extremely unsympathetic to Winnie, Arnold E. Davidson, "The Open Ending of *The Secret Agent,*" *Ariel,* 7 (1976), 84-100, asserts that her belief she would have been happy with her butcher boy is an illusion. There seems to me no textual evidence for this.
19. Conrad uses a veil as a symbol in a very similar way in the climactic confession scene in *Under Western Eyes.*
20. As Fradin, p. 1421, remarks, in *The Secret Agent* "Conrad allows us to take no more comfort in compassion as a motive for action than other more obvious manifestations of the human ego."
21. John Hagan, Jr., "The Design of Conrad's *The Secret Agent,*" *English Literary History,* 22 (1955), p. 156, also compares these passages—not, however, to associate Winnie with the Professor, but to underscore "the theme of the hidden or buried life flowing beneath the conventional amenities, reticences, and superficial accords of daily affairs."

Chapter 4

1. Joseph Conrad, *Under Western Eyes* (London: J.M. Dent, 1923), p. 10. Subsequent page references follow quotations.

2. The narrator's limitations as observer and recorder are evident from the start. In the opening pages he remarks of Razumov: "In discussion he was easily swayed by argument and authority." The narrator has no way of knowing this; his source is Razumov's journal, and Razumov would hardly have had this insight about himself. (Furthermore, this statement does not accord with the Razumov we see in the rest of the novel.) Similarly, the narrator tells us how Razumov was perceived by his fellow students, which again he would have had no way of knowing.

3. Ironically enough, Razumov also adopts Russian messianism as a rationale for his decision to inform on Haldin. For an excellent discussion of Conrad's use of the Russian messianic myth, see Eloise Hay, *The Political Novels of Joseph Conrad* (Chicago: Univ. of Chicago Press, 1963).

4. In a letter to Galsworthy, in G. Jean-Aubry, *Joseph Conrad: Life and Letters* (New York: Doubleday, Page, 1927), 64, 65, Conrad sketched the projected plot:

> The Student Razumov (a natural son of a Prince K.) gives up secretly to the police his fellow student, Haldin, who seeks refuge in his rooms after committing a political crime (supposed to be the murder of de Plehve). First movement in St. Petersburg. (Haldin is hanged of course.)
>
> 2d in Genève. The student Razumov meeting abroad the mother and sister of Haldin falls in love with that last, marries her and, after a time, confesses to her the part he played in the arrest of her brother.
>
> The psychological developments leading to Razumov's betrayal of Haldin, to his confession of the fact to his wife and to the death of these people (brought about mainly by the resemblance of their child to the late Haldin), form the real subject of the story.

The novel's final form is quite different, of course. Razumov and Natalia never marry; indeed, we hardly see them together. The only emotional confrontation between them Conrad dramatizes is the confession scene. Furthermore, the novel focuses on the *immediate* consequences of the betrayal, rather than on its later implications. Razumov's career as a spy is very short—only a matter of a month or two, at most—and the novel emphasizes Razumov's unceasing suffering.

5. Morton Zabel, Introd. *Under Western Eyes,* by Joseph Conrad (New York: New Directions, 1951), argues that the revolutionaries act as reflectors of Razumov's complexities, as the subsidiary characters reflect Jim's, but I do not find this persuasive. (Zabel's introduction was very influential in bringing about a resurgence of interest in the novel. It is significant that *Under Western Eyes* was promoted to major status in the Conrad canon during the Cold War.) Many critics have noted the similarities in situation and structure between this novel and *Lord Jim*.

6. Although Hay, p. 270, finds that "Haldin's whole conduct during his two interviews with Razumov, especially in the second... must convince the reader of his acute human sensitivity," I think she overlooks the tremendous amount of irony directed at Haldin, who almost perversely misinterprets Razumov's words.

7. The scene is rendered very much in the manner of Dostoevsky; Razumov here strongly resembles the Dostoevskian hero, particularly Raskolnikov. For more of Conrad's debt to

Dostoevsky, see Hay, Jocelyn Baines, *Joseph Conrad: A Critical Biography* (London, Weidenfeld and Nicolson, 1960), and Frederick R. Karl, *Joseph Conrad: The Three Lives* (New York: Farrar. Straus and Giroux, 1979), especialy pp. 678-80.

8. The opposition here of the isolated orphan and the pampered only son recalls that between Nostromo and Decoud.

9. Albert Guerard, *Conrad the Novelist* (Cambridge, Mass.: Harvard Univ. Press, 1958), p. 236, notes: "By delaying as long as he does the formal revelation that Razumov is Mikulin's agent, Conrad preserves a sympathy that would (with a more abrupt procedure) have been lost."

10. For a fuller discussion of bisexuality in the novel, see Bernard C. Meyer, *Joseph Conrad: A Psychoanalytic Biography* (Princeton: Princeton Univ. Press, 1967), p. 217.

11. See Meyer, p. 267n.

12. Jessie Conrad's memoir, *Joseph Conrad As I Knew Him* (Freeport, N.Y.: Books for Libraries Press, 1925), has as epigraph a quotation from "Bluebeard"—unexplained and, as far as I can ascertain, critically unremarked.

13. The narrator's antipathy towards Peter Ivanovitch seems unmotivated, largely because Conrad cut out passages that detailed confrontations between the two men. According to Davis, Conrad's revisions in the Geneva section of the novel tended to soften the portraits of the revolutionaries, especially of Peter Ivanovitch, and to make Razumov more sympathetic. Davis also notes that Conrad excised passages that made overt his own identification with Razumov.

14. There has been considerable speculation about the sources for Peter Ivanovich's characterization. Baines thinks he is modeled primarily on Tolstoy; Hay, on Tolstoy, Bakunin, and Kropotkin. Jeffrey Berman and Donna VanWagenen, *"Under Western Eyes: Conrad's Diary of a Writer?" Conradiana*, 9 (1977), 269-74, argue that he most resembles Dostoevsky, particularly in his "feminism," while Thomas C. Moser, "Ford Madox Hueffer and *Under Western Eyes*," *Conradiana*, 15 (1983), 163-80, finds a resemblance to Conrad's friend and collaborator Ford.

15. Roderick Davis, "*Under Western Eyes:* 'The Most Deeply Meditated Novel,'" *Conradiana*, 9 (1977), p. 64, notes that Conrad deleted a passage that described Mme de S. as a "rigid and youthful figure ... a fashionably elegant Sybil," having evidently decided to make her a more grotesque figure. Conrad, however, neglected to change the reference to her youthful figure on page 125.

16. Thomas C. Moser, *Joseph Conrad: Achievement and Decline* (Cambridge, Mass.: Harvard Univ. Press, 1957), p. 96, remarks of this passage: "Never did Conrad more effectively satirize his own tendency to sentimentalize women."

17. There is another seeming lapse of memory when we are told Razumov has never been sick in his life (289), then given an account of the illness he suffered after betraying Haldin (298).

18. Conrad probably avoided presenting the meetings of Razumov and Natalia to retain the reader's sympathy for Razumov. Razumov's conversations with Natalia would have had to be a tissue of lies, and Conrad tries to avoid showing Razumov actively engaged in deception. As it is, as Moser, p. 94, points out, "... Razumov and Natalia appear in only three scenes together, of seven, four, and nineteen pages respectively...."

19. "The Personal and the Political in *Under Western Eyes*," *Nineteenth-Century Fiction*, 25 (1970), 327-42.

20. Goodin, p. 337.
21. Ibid.
22. In the novels under consideration, strong women include Mrs. Gould, Teresa Viola and her daughter Linda, Antonia Avellanos, Winnie Verloc, Mrs. Fyne and Flora in *Chance*, and, in *Victory*, Lena and even, perhaps, Mrs. Schomberg. The capacity for single-minded devotion Conrad attributes to women has as its corollary the tendency to set aside certain masculine values, such as honor and fair play; this misogynistic view is particularly evident in *Chance*. For more on Conrad's views on women, see Meyer.
23. For a fuller discussion see Elsa Nettels, "The Grotesque in Conrad's Fiction," *Nineteenth-Century Fiction*, 19 (1974), 144-63.
24. This obsession with the opinion of others, the fear that an unknown, malevolent gossip may wreck one's life, becomes a central concern in *Chance* and *Victory*.
25. The narrator's presence at some of these scenes is quite incredible. Razumov would hardly have confessed to Natalia with the narrator present, and it is equally unlikely that the revolutionaries would have admitted the narrator to their conclave planning the "Balkan operation."
26. Frederick Karl, p. 677, believes Conrad concluded the novel so abruptly because his publisher would not advance any more money.
27. Later, in his journal, Razumov explains this act as the result of demonic possession:

> I was given up to evil. I exulted in having induced that silly innocent fool to steal his father's money. He was a fool, but not a thief. I made him one. It was necessary. I had to confirm myself in my contempt and hate for what I betrayed. (359)

Razumov's character is introduced only in these few pages at the end of the novel, and seems to contradict what we have been told about him previously.

28. Razumov's confession does not seem to me to be motivated by a desire for understanding from, or community with, the revolutionaries, as Avrom Fleishman, *Conrad's Politics* (Baltimore: Johns Hopkins Press, 1967), p. 237, has suggested.
29. Meyer, p. 205.
30. Earlier, the narrator has said of Mrs. Haldin:

> I confess she frightened me a little. She was one of those natures, rare enough, luckily, in which one cannot help being interested, because they provoke both terror and pity. One dreads their contact for oneself, and still more for those one cares for, so clear it is that they are born to suffer and to make others suffer, too. (318)

While Mrs. Haldin initially seems a kindly, wise, and nurturing mother, by the end of the novel she is a virtual Medusa, whose very glance can strike terror. She is a good example of the tendency for Conrad's parental figures to become threatening and destructive, even when they seem originally to have been intended as benign and positive forces.

31. For further discussion, see Guerard, pp. 241, 242. for a contrary view, see Harriet Gilliam, "The Daemonic in Conrad's *Under Western Eyes*," *Conradiana*, 9 (1977), 219-36.
32. Meyer, p. 267, remarks that although Mrs. Haldin is one of the few living mothers portrayed in Conrad's fiction, "aside from her depiction as a grief-stricken woman...she has no convincing identity." Meyer also notes the strongly autobiographical character of the novel:

"Perhaps of all of Conrad's writings *Under Western Eyes* conveys most poignantly his own sense of isolation, his intense longing for human warmth and that unappeasable hunger for physical contact which confers such profound and unspoken significance upon the memory of a hand pressed by a father's hand and of a head cradled within the soft embrace of a mother's arms," p. 218.

33. For a contrary view see Hay (among others), p. 309n, who finds an "enormous difference between Dostoevsky's and Conrad's characterization," and Fleishman.

34. This theme of sexual disgust is further explored in *Chance* and *Victory*, whose immature heroes—perpetually their fathers' sons—are hopelessly ambivalent about sexuality.

35. For a discussion of feminism in the novel, see Maureen Fries, "Feminism-Antifeminism in *Under Western Eyes*," *Conradiana*, 5 (1973), 56-65. She argues that Peter Ivanovitch is really an antifeminist, who wants to make use of women for his own ends, and that it is Conrad who is the real feminist here, having created women who are the "industrial, mental, political, social and sexual equals of men.... in fact, largely superior in industry, mind, political commitment, and social responsibility to any man in the novel," p. 63. She feels that "in *Under Western Eyes*, androgyny seems to pose no threat either to Conrad or to his sympathetic male characters," p. 64.

Chapter 5

1. Joseph Conrad, *Chance* (London: J.M. Dent, 1923), p. 264. Subsequent page references follow quotations.

2. W.Y. Tindall, "Apology for Marlow," in *From Jane Austen to Joseph Conrad*, ed. R.C. Rathburn and Martin Steinmann, Jr. (Minneapolis: Univ. of Minnesota Press, 1959), pp. 274-85, cautions against confusing Marlow with Conrad.

3. *Joseph Conrad: A Psychoanalytic Biography* (Princeton: Princeton Univ. Press, 1967), p. 235.

4. *Joseph Conrad: Achievement and Decline* (Cambridge, Mass.: Harvard Univ. Press, 1957), p. 165.

5. See, for example, Paul Kirschner, *Conrad: The Psychologist as Artist* (Edinburgh: Oliver and Boyd, 1968).

6. Royal Roussel, *The Metaphysics of Darkness* (Baltimore: Johns Hopkins Press, 1971), p. 175, believes Marlow's is the correct view here, and that Powell is exhibiting naivete.

7. Douglas Hewitt, *Conrad: A Reassessment* (Cambridge, Mass.: Bowes and Bowes, 1952), argues that Marlow's many contradictory statements are the result of Conrad's attempt to add an impression of complexity and depth to a rather thin story.

8. Frederick R. Karl. *Joseph Conrad: The Three Lives* (New York: Farrar, Straus and Giroux, 1979), p. 734. Karl also notes that this part of the novel, originally called "Explosives," was begun in 1905, and that Conrad drew to a considerable degree on his own experience for young Powell's account of his examination.

9. Meyer, p. 269.

10. See Jocelyn Baines, *Joseph Conrad: A Critical Biography* (London: Wiedenfeld and Nicolson, 1960), p. 386; Wilfred S. Dowden, *Joseph Conrad: The Imaged Style* (Nashville: Vanderbilt Univ. Press, 1970), p. 151; C.B. Cox, *Joseph Conrad: The Modern Imagination* (London: Dent, 1974), p. 122.

11. Moser, p. 161.
12. In this and other respects, Mrs. Fyne resembles that other "feminist," Peter Ivanovitch.
13. While Tindall argues, p. 281, that "chivalric diminution of women, often attributed to Conrad, is almost peculiar to Marlow," Meyer demonstrates convincingly that misogynism appears with ever greater frequency in the works written after Conrad's mental breakdown in 1910.
14. Moser, p. 162.
15. Roussel, p. 177, also makes this point.
16. For more on the subject see Wolfgang B. Fleishmann, "Conrad's *Chance* and Bergson's *Laughter*," *Renascence*, 14 (1961), 66-71.
17. Meyer, p. 225, describes Flora as "omnipotent," and finds Anthony "merely a tool of a woman's whim and will."
18. Among critics who identify Flora with Conrad are Baines, p. 388n; Karl, p. 52; and Meyer, p. 281, who also feels *Anthony's* history is drawn from Conrad's own experience: both de Barral and Carleon Anthony, Meyer argues, strongly resemble Conrad's father, Apollo Korzeniowski.
19. Although Peter Ivanovitch and Mme de S. (in *Under Western Eyes*) are not married, their relationship, like the Verlocs' and like Anthony and Flora's, is a form of implicit bargain, the terms of which the participants misunderstand. Each partner wishes to make use of the other for his or her own purposes, while the other partner remains unaware of the terms of the transaction.
20. Suicides occur in all the novels under consideration. Furthermore, suicides usually leave a terrible legacy; their deaths affect others' lives profoundly. So Decoud's suicide determines Nostromo's moral delcine; Winnie's causes Ossipon's alcoholism; and Ziemianitch's death leads Razumov to the realization that his own life is unbearable. Meyer, p. 274n, puts the total number of suicides in Conrad's fiction at 15, but he includes Linda Viola, who, as I read *Nostromo,* is still alive at the novel's conclusion. Meyer, Karl, and Jeffrey Berman, *Joseph Conrad: Writing as Rescue* (New York: Astra Books, 1977), emphasize the importance of Conrad's own suicide attempt in 1878.
21. Marlow's assertion here that one's actions and motives are continually being scrutinized by persons known or unknown seems to contradict his earlier statement: "In a general way it's very difficult for one to become remarkable. People won't take sufficient notice of one don't you know" (7,8). But this is only one of many self-contradictions, at least some of which may be the result of simple carelessness on Conrad's part.

Chapter 6

1. Douglas B. Park, "Conrad's *Victory:* The Anatomy of a Pose," *Nineteenth-Century Fiction,* 31 (1976), 167.
2. Donald A. Dike, "The Tempest of Axel Heyst," *Nineteenth-Century Fiction,* 17 (1962), 95.
3. Joseph Conrad, *Victory* (London: J.M. Dent, 1923), p. 3. Subsequent page references follow quotations.
4. For more on Conrad's management of point of view in *Victory,* see Albert Guerard, *Conrad the Novelist* (Cambridge, Mass.: Harvard Univ. Press, 1958), pp. 273, 274.

5. Among critics who have discussed the doubling device in the novel are Park; J.E. Saveson, *Conrad, the Later Moralist* (Amsterdam: Rodopi NV, 1974); and Sharon Kaehele and Howard German, "Conrad's *Victory:* A Reassessment," *Modern Fiction Studies,* 10 (1964), 55-72.

6. Whether Lena's "old" name—Alma—indicates purity of soul or a propensity to sexual license has occasioned critical controversy. For example, Lee M. Whitehead, "Alma Renamed Lena in Conrad's *Victory,*" *English Language Notes,* 3 (1965), 55-57, argues that the name Alma does not indicate "soul" or "spirit," but "is a modern Arabic term for a dancing girl—i.e., a courtesan or entertainer of men."

7. Kaehele and German, p. 57, however, believe that Schomberg proves more capable of action than does Heyst, since he is able to persuade the villains to go to Samburan.

8. There seems to have been a lapse of memory of Conrad's part, for Heyst has laughed earlier, soon after meeting Lena. This laugh, meant (like Lena's smile) to deceive onlookers, outrages Lena, who "nearly choke[s] with indignation at this brutal heartlessness" (80).

9. Dike, p. 110.

10. Ibid., p. 105.

11. Heyst's reflections following his father's death echo the Professor's fears at the end of *The Secret Agent,* when the wizened old walking time-bomb has a moment of hopelessness, as he contemplates the multitude of careless passers-by. Here, after burying his father ("the silenced destroyer of systems, of hopes, of beliefs"), Heyst notes "that the death of that bitter contemner of life did not trouble the flow of life's stream, where men and women go by thick as dust, revolving and jostling one another like figures cut out of cord..." (175).

12. Many critics have noted the phallic symbolism here. See, for example, Bernard C. Meyer, *Joseph Conrad: A Psychoanalytic Biography* (Princeton: Princeton Univ. Press, 1967), especially pp. 231-32, and Thomas Moser, *Joseph Conrad: Achievement and Decline* (Cambridge, Mass.: Harvard Univ. Press, 1957), pp. 117-19.

13. But, as Moser, p. 118 has noted, Ricardo has been unmanned throughout the scene. Ricardo says his heart "has knocked itself dead tired, waiting for this evening, for this very minute. And now it can do no more. Feel how quiet it is" (395)!

14. For a fuller discussion of fetishism in *Victory,* and in other works by Conrad, see Meyer.

15. Kaehele and German have made a detailed comparison of Lena and Ricardo; see, especially pp. 67-69. Their verdict on Lena seems a bit harsh, however.

16. Kaehele and German, p. 62.

17. Park, p. 166.

18. Ibid., p. 168.

Bibliography

I. Published Writings of Joseph Conrad

Works

Conrad, Joseph. *Nostromo.* New York: Modern Library, 1951.
_____. *Works.* Collected Edition. 22 vols. London: J.M. Dent, 1945-55.

Letters

Blackburn, William, ed. *Joseph Conrad: Letters to William Blackwood and David S. Meldrum.* Durham, N.C.: Duke Univ. Press, 1958.
Curle, Richard, ed. *Conrad to a Friend, 150 Selected Letters from Joseph Conrad to Richard Curle.* New York: Crosby Gaige, 1928.
Garnett, Edward, ed. *Letters from Joseph Conrad, 1895-1924.* Indianapolis: Bobbs-Merrill, 1928.
Gee, John A., and Paul J. Sturm, trans. and eds. *Letters of Joseph Conrad to Marguerite Poradowska.* New Haven: Yale Univ. Press, 1940.
Jean-Aubry, Georges. *Joseph Conrad: Life and Letters.* 2 vols. New York: Doubleday, Page, 1927.

II. Biographical and Critical Works Cited

Baines, Jocelyn. *Joseph Conrad: A Critical Biography.* London: Weidenfeld and Nicholson, 1960.
Berman, Jeffrey. *Joseph Conrad: Writing as Rescue.* New York: Astra Books, 1977.
_____ and Donna van Wagenen."*Under Western Eyes:* Conrad's *Diary of a Writer?*" *Conradiana,* 9 (1977), 269-74.
Conrad, Jessie. *Joseph Conrad As I Knew Him.* Freeport, N.Y.: Books for Libraries Press, 1925.
Cox, C.B. *Joseph Conrad: The Modern Imagination.* London: Dent, 1974.
Davidson, Arnold E. "The Open Ending of *The Secret Agent.*" *Ariel,* 7 (1976), 84-100.
Davis, Roderick, "*Under Western Eyes:* 'The Most Deeply Meditated Novel,'" *Conradiana,* 9 (1977), 59-75.
Dike, Donald A. "The Tempest of Axel Heyst." *Nineteenth-Century Fiction,* 17 (1962), 95-113.
Dowden, Wilfred S. *Joseph Conrad: The Imagined Style.* Nashville: Vanderbilt Univ. Press, 1970.
Fleischmann, Wolfgang B. "Conrad's *Chance* and Bergson's *Laughter.*" *Renascence,* 14 (1961), 66-71.
Fleishman, Avrom. *Conrad's Politics: Community and Anarchy in the Fiction of Joseph Conrad.* Baltimore: Johns Hopkins Press, 1967.
Fradin, Joseph I. "Anarchist, Detective and Saint: The Possibilities of Action in *The Secret Agent.*" *PMLA,* 83 (1968), 1414-22.

Fries, Maureen. "Feminism-Antifeminism in *Under Western Eyes.*" *Conradiana,* 5 (1973), 56-65.
Gilliam, Harriet. "The Daemonic in Conrad's *Under Western Eyes.*" *Conradiana,* 9 (1977), 219-36.
Goodin, George. "The Personal and the Political in *Under Western Eyes.*" *Nineteenth-Century Fiction,* 25 (1970), 327-42.
Gose, Eliott B., Jr. "'Cruel Devourer of the World's Light': *The Secret Agent.*" *Nineteenth-Century Fiction,* 16 (1960), 39-51.
Guerard, Albert J. *Conrad the Novelist.* Cambridge, Mass.: Harvard Univ. Press, 1958.
Gurko, Leo. *Joseph Conrad: Giant in Exile.* New York: Macmillan, 1962.
Hagan, John, Jr. "The Design of Conrad's *The Secret Agent.*" *English Literary History,* 22 (1955), 148-64.
Haltresht, M. "The Dread of Space in Conrad's *The Secret Agent.*" *Literature and Psychology,* 22 (1972), 89-97.
Hay, Eloise Knapp. *The Political Novels of Joseph Conrad.* Chicago: Univ. of Chicago Press, 1963.
Hewitt, Douglas. *Conrad: A Reassessment.* Cambridge, Mass.: Bowes and Bowes, 1952.
Howe, Irving. *Politics and the Novel.* New York: Horizon Press, 1957.
Jacobs, Robert G. "Comrade Ossipon's Favorite Saint: Lambroso and Conrad." *Nineteenth-Century Fiction,* 23 (1968), 74-84.
Kaehele, Sharon and Howard German. "Conrad's *Victory:* A Reassessment." *Modern Fiction Studies,* 10 (1964), 55-72.
Karl, Frederick R. *Joseph Conrad: The Three Lives.* New York: Farrar, Straus and Giroux, 1979.
Kirschner, Paul. *Conrad: The Psychologist as Artist.* Edinburgh: Oliver and Boyd, 1968.
Knowles, Owen. "Commentary as Rhetoric: An Aspect of Conrad's Technique." *Conradiana,* 5 (1973), 5-27.
Leavis, F.R. *The Great Tradition.* New York: G.W. Stewart, 1948.
Meyer, Bernard C. *Joseph Conrad: A Psychoanalytic Biography.* Princeton: Princeton Univ. Press, 1967.
Moser, Thomas. *Joseph Conrad: Achievement and Decline.* Cambridge, Mass.: Harvard Univ. Press, 1967.
———. "Ford Madox Hueffer and *Under Western Eyes.*" *Conradiana,* 15 (1983), 163-80.
Nettles, Elsa. The Grotesque in Conrad's Fiction." *Nineteenth-Century Fiction,* 19 (1974), 144-63.
Palmer, John A. *Joseph Conrad's Fiction: A Study in Literary Growth.* Ithaca: Cornell Univ. Press, 1968.
Park, Douglas B. "Conrad's *Victory:* The Anatomy of a Pose." *Nineteenth-Century Fiction,* 31 (1976), 150-69.
Rosenfield, Claire. *Paradise of Snakes.* Chicago: Univ. of Chicago Press, 1967.
Roussel, Royal. *The Metaphysics of Darkness: A Study in the Unity and Development of Conrad's Fiction.* Baltimore: Johns Hopkins Press, 1971.
Saveson, John E. *Conrad, the Later Moralist.* Amsterdam: Rodopi NV, 1974.
Sherry, Norman. *Conrad's Western World.* Cambridge: The Univ. Press, 1971.
Stallman, Robert W. "Time and *The Secret Agent.*" In *The Art of Joseph Conrad: A Critical Symposium.* Ed. R.W. Stallman. East Lansing, Mich.: Michigan State Univ. Press, 1960.
Tindall, W.Y. "Apology for Marlow." In *From Jan Austen to Joseph Conrad.* Ed. R.C. Rathburn and M. Steinmann. Minneapolis: Univ. of Minnesota Press, 1959.
Whitehead, Lee M. "Alma Renamed Lena in Conrad's *Victory.*" *English Language Notes,* 3 (1965), 55-57.
Wilding, Michael. "The Politics of *Nostromo.*" *Essays in Criticism,* 16 (1966), 441-56.
Zabel, Morton. "Introduction." *Under Western Eyes.* New York: New Directions, 1951.

III. Other Significant Critical Works

Allen, Jerry. *The Sea Years of Joseph Conrad.* Garden City, N.Y.: Doubleday, 1965.
_____. *The Thunder and the Sunshine: A Biography of Joseph Conrad.* New York: Putnam, 1958.
Andreach, Robert J. *The Slain and Resurrected God: Conrad, Ford and the Christian Myth.* New York: N.Y. Univ. Press, 1970.
Andreas, Osborn, *Joseph Conrad: A Study in Non-Conformity.* New York: Philosophical Library, 1959.
Bantock, G.H. "Joseph Conrad: Reality and Illusion." *Sewanee Review,* 83 (1975), 502-10.
_____. "Conrad and Politics." *English Literary History,* 25 (1958), 122-36.
_____. "The Two Moralities of Joseph Conrad." *Essays in Criticism,* 3 (1953), 125-42.
Beach, Joseph Warren. "Impressionism: Conrad." In his *The Twentieth Century Novel: Studies in Technique.* New York: Appleton-Century, 1932, pp. 337-65.
Boyle, Ted E. *Symbol and Meaning in the Fiction of Joseph Conrad.* The Hague: Mouton, 1965.
Bradbrook, M.C. *Joseph Conrad: Poland's English Genius.* Cambridge: The Univ. Press, 1941.
Carpenter, R.C. "The Geography of Costaguana: Or, Where is Sulaco?" *Journal of Modern Literature,* 5 (1976), 321-26.
Cheney, Lynne. "Joseph Conrad's *The Secret Agent* and Graham Greene's *It's a Battlefield:* A Study in Structural Meaning." *Modern Fiction Studies,* 16 (1970), 117-31.
Conrad, Jessie. *Joseph Conrad and His Circle.* New York: E.P. Dutton, 1935.
Cooper, Christopher. *Conrad and the Human Dilemma.* London: Chatto and Windus, 1970.
Cox, C.B. "The Two Conrads." *Books and Bookmen,* 19 (1974), 22-23.
Crankshaw, Edward. *Joseph Conrad: Some Aspects of the Art of the Novel.* London: John Lane the Bodley Head, 1936.
Crews, F. "The Power of Darkness." *Partisan Review,* 34 (1967), 507-27.
Curle, Richard. *Joseph Conrad and His Characters.* Fair Lawn, N.J.: Essential Books, 1958.
_____. *The Last Twelve Years of Joseph Conrad.* New York: Doubleday, Doran, 1928.
Daiches, David. "Joseph Conrad." In his *The Novel and the Modern World.* Chicago: Univ. of Chicago Press, 1939, pp. 25-62.
Davis, Harold E. "Conrad's Revisions of *The Secret Agent:* A Study in Literary Impressionism." *Modern Language Quarterly,* 19 (1958), 244-54.
Duncan-Jones, E.E. "Some Sources of *Chance.*" *Review of English Studies,* 20 (1969), 468-71.
Ehrsom, Theodore G. *A Bibliography of Joseph Conrad.* Metuchen, N.J.: Scarecrow Press, 1969.
Evans, Robert O. "Conrad's Underworld." *Modern Fiction Studies,* 2 (1956), 55-62.
Fernando, L. "Conrad's Eastern Expatriates: A New Version of his Outcasts." *PMLA,* 91 (1976), 78-90.
Ford (Hueffer), Ford Madox. *Joseph Conrad: A Personal Remembrace.* Boston: Little, Brown, 1924.
Gillon, Adam. *The Eternal Solitary: A Study of Joseph Conrad.* New York: Bookman Associates, 1960.
_____. "Joseph Conrad and Shakespeare, Part Four: A New Reading of *Victory.*" *Conradiana,* 7 (1973), 263-81.
Gilmore, Thomas B., Jr. "Retributive Irony in Conrad's *The Secret Agent.*" *Conradiana,* 1 (1969), 41-50.
Goens, M.B. "Mysterious and Effective Star: The Mythic World View in Conrad's *Victory.*" *Modern Fiction Studies,* 12 (1967-68), 455-63.
Gordon, John D. *Joseph Conrad: The Making of a Novelist.* Cambridge, Mass.: Harvard Univ. Press, 1940.
Greenberg, Robert A. "The Presence of Mr. Wang." *Boston University Studies in English,* 4 (1960), 129-37.

Gross, Seymour L. "The Devil in Samburan: Jones and Ricardo in Victory." *Nineteenth-Century Fiction,* 16 (1961), 81-85.

Hagan, John, Jr. "Conrad's *Under Western Eyes:* The Question of Razumov's 'Guilt' and 'Remorse.'" *Studies in the Novel,* 1 (1969), 310-22.

Harkness, Bruce. "The Epigraph of Conrad's *Chance.*" *Nineteenth-Century Fiction,* 9 (1954), 209-22.

Haugh, Robert F. *Joseph Conrad: Discovery in Design.* Norman: Univ. of Oklahoma Press, 1957.

Heimer, Jackson W. "Betrayal, Confession, Attempted Redemption, and Punishment in *Nostromo.*" *Texas Studies in Literature and Language,* 8 (1967), 561-79.

Hollahan, Eugene. "Beguiled into Action: Silence and Sound in *Victory.*" *Texas Studies in Literature and Language,* 16 (1974), 351-62.

Holland, Norman N. "Style as Character: *The Secret Agent.*" *Modern Fiction Studies,* 12 (1966), 221-31.

Hudspeth, R.N. "Conrad's Use of Time in *Chance.*" *Nineteenth-Century Fiction,* 21 (1966), 283-89.

Izsak, Emily "*Under Western Eyes* and the Problem of Serial Publication." *Review of English Studies,* 23 (1972), 429-44.

James, Henry. "The New Novel, 1914." In his *Notes on Novelists.* London: J.M. Dent, 1914.

Jean-Aubry, Georges. *The Sea Dreamer: A Definitive Biography of Joseph Conrad.* Trans. Helen Sebba. Garden City: Doubleday, 1957.

Johnson Bruce. *Conrad's Models of Mind.* Minneapolis: Univ. of Minnesota Press, 1971.

Karl, Frederick R. *A Reader's Guide to Joseph Conrad.* New York: Noonday Press, 1960.

Kelley, R.E. "The Chance Glimpse: The Narrator in *Under Western Eyes.*" *University Review,* 6 (1971), 285-90.

Kimpel, Ben and T.C. Duncan-Eaves. "The Geography and History in *Nostromo.*" *Modern Philology,* 56 (1958), 45-54.

Kramer, Dale. "Marlow, Myth, and Structure in *Lord Jim.*" *Criticism,* 8 (1966), 263-79.

Kubal, David L. "The Secret Agent and the Mechanical Chaos." *Bucknell Review,* 15 (1967), 65-77.

Levin, Gerald H. "An Allusion to Tasso in Conrad's *Chance*" *Nineteenth-Century Fiction,* 13 (1958), 145-51.

Lincoln, K.R. "Conrad's Mythic Humor." *Texas Studies in Literature and Language,* 17 (1975), 635-51.

Lodge, David. "Conrad's *Victory* and *The Tempest:* An Amplification." *MLR,* 59 (1964), 195-99.

Lohf, Kenneth A. and Eugene P. Sheehy. *Joseph Conrad at Mid-Century: Editions and Studies, 1895-1955.* Minneapolis: Univ. of Minnesota Press, 1957.

Lordi, R.J. "The Three Emissaries of Evil: Their Psychological Relationship in Conrad's *Victory.*" *College English,* 23 (1961), 136-40.

Luecke, Sister Jane Marie. "Conrad's Secret and Its Agent." *Modern Fiction Studies,* 11 (1964), 37-48.

Malbone, Raymond Gates. "'How to Be': Marlow's Quest in *Lord Jim.*" *Twentieth-Century Literature,* 10 (1965), 172-80.

Marten, Henry. "Conrad's Skeptic Reconsidered: A Study of Martin Decoud." *Nineteenth-Century Fiction,* 17 (1972), 81-94.

———. "Drama and Theme in *Nostromo:* The Relationship of Nostromo, Dr. Monygham and Emilia Gould." *Conradiana,* 8 (1976), 27-36.

Megroz, R.L. *Joseph Conrad's Mind and Method: A Study of Personality in Art.* London: Faber and Faber, 1931.

Meyers, Jeffrey. "The Agamemnon Myth and *The Secret Agent.*" *Conradiana,* 1 (1968), 57-59.

Michel, Lois A. "The Absurd Predicament in Conrad's Political Novels." *College English,* 23 (1961), 131-36.

Miller, J. Hillis. *Poets of Reality: Six Twentieth-Century Writers*. Cambridge, Mass.: Harvard Univ. Press, 1965.
Morf, Gustav. *The Polish Heritage of Joseph Conrad*. London: S. Low, Marston and Co., 1930.
Moser, Thomas. "Conrad, Ford, and the Sources of *Chance*." *Conradiana*, 7 (1973), 207-24.
Mudrick, Marvin, ed. *Conrad: A Collection of Critical Essays*. Englewood Cliffs, N.J.: Prentice-Hall, 1966.
Nash, C. "More Light on *The Secret Agent*." *Review of English Studies*, 20 (1969), 322-27.
Page, Norman. "Dickensian Elements in *Victory*." *Contradiana*, 5 (1973), 37-42.
Perry, John Oliver. "Action, Vision, or Voice: The Moral Dilemmas in Conrad's Tale-telling." *Modern Fiction Studies*, 10, (1964), 3-24.
Pilecki, Gerard A. "Conrad's *Victory*." *Explicator*, 23 (1965), item 36.
Purdy, Dwight H. "Creature and Creator in *Under Western Eyes*." *Conradiana*, 8 (1976), 241-46.
Reinecke, George F. "Conrad's *Victory*: Psychomachy, Christian Symbols, and Theme." In *Explorations of Literature*. Ed. Rima Drell Reck. Baton Rouge: Louisiana State Univ. Press, 1966.
Retinger, J.H. *Conrad and His Contemporaries*. New York: Roy, 1943.
Ryf, Robert S. *Joseph Conrad*. New York: Columbia Univ. Press, 1970.
Said, Edward W. "Conrad: The Presentation of Narrative." *Novel*, 7 (1974), 116-32.
_____. *Joseph Conrad and the Fiction of Autobriography*. Cambridge, Mass.: Harvard Univ. Press, 1974.
Saunders, W.S. "The Unity of *Nostromo*." *Conradiana*, 5 (1973), 27-36.
Saveson, J.E. "The Moral Discovery of *Under Western Eyes*." *Criticism*, 14 (1972), 32-48.
Schleifer, Ronald. "Public and Private Narrative in *Under Western Eyes*." *Conradiana*, 9 (1977), 237-54.
Smith, Curtis C. "Conrad's *Chance*: A Dialectical Novel." *Thoth*, 6 (1965), 16-24.
Smoller, S.J. "A Note of Joseph Conrad's Fall and Abyss." *Modern Fiction Studies*, 15 (1969), 261-64.
Spatt, Hartley S. "*Nostromo*'s Chronology: The Shaping of History." *Conradiana*, 8 (1976), 37-46.
Spiegel, A. "Flaubert to Joyce: The Evolution of a Cinematographic Form." *Novel*, 6 (1973), 229-43.
Stallman, Robert W., ed. *The Art of Joseph Conrad: A Critical Symposium*. East Lansing: Michigan State Univ. Press, 1960.
_____. "The Structure and Symbolism of Conrad's *Victory*." *Western Review*, 13 (1949), 146-57.
Stegmaier, E. "The 'Would-Scene' in Joseph Conrad's *Lord Jim* and *Nostromo*." *Modern Language Review*, 67 (1972), 517-23.
Sullivan, Walter. "The Dark Beyond the Sunrise: Conrad and the Politics of Despair." *Southern Review*, 8 (1972), 507-19.
Tanner, Troy. "Nightmare and Complacency: Razumov and the Western Eye." *Critical Quarterly*, 4 (1962), 197-214.
Teets, Bruce E. *Joseph Conrad: An Annotated Bibliography*. De Kalb: Northern Illinois Univ. Press, 1971.
Tillyard, E.M.W. "*The Secret Agent* Reconsidered." In *From Jane Austen to Joseph Conrad*. Ed. R.C. Rathburn and M. Steinman. Minneapolis: Univ. of Minnesota Press, 1959, 309-18.
Walton, J. "Conrad, Dickens, and the Detective Novel." *Nineteenth-Century Fiction*, 23 (1969), 446-462.
Warren, Robert Penn. "Introduction." *Nostromo*. New York: Modern Library, 1951.
Watt, Ian. *Conrad in the Nineteenth Century*. Berkeley: Univ. of California Press, 1979.
_____. ed. *Conrad: The Secret Agent, A Casebook*. London: Macmillan, 1973.
_____. "Joseph Conrad: Alienation and Commitment." In *The English Mind*. Ed. H.S. Davies and George Watson. Cambridge: The Univ. Press, 1964, pp. 257-78.

Wiley, Paul L. *Conrad's Measure of Man.* Madison: Univ. of Wisconsin Press, 1954.
Wisenfarth, J. "Stevie and the Structure of *The Secret Agent.*" *Modern Fiction Studies,* 12 (1967-68), 513-17.
Wright, W.F. *Romance and Tragedy in Conrad.* Lincoln: Univ. of Nebraska Press, 1949.
Zabel, Morton Dauwen. "Introduction." *The Portable Conrad.* New York: Viking Press, 1954.
———. "Joseph Conrad: Chance and Recognition." *Sewanee Review,* 53 (1945), 1-22.
Zuckermann, Jerome. "Contrapuntal Structure in Conrad's *Chance.*" *Modern Fiction Studies,* 10 (1964), 49-54.

Index

Actions, impact of, 143n21. *See also Nostromo*
Anarchy. *See* politics under individual works

Baines, Jocelyn, 9, 140n14
Bendz, Ernst, 9
Bermen, Jeffrey, 140n14
Betrayal, 59. *See also* listing under individual works

Chance, 1-7, 73, 82, 87-111, 114, 115, 117, 132
  central themes of, 87, 88, 141n24
  confessions in, 107
  cynicism, 88-89
  death, 94, 96, 99, 102-5, 109
  family, 90, 91, 95, 96, 99, 108
  gossip, 65, 107, 141n24
  human nature, views of in, 88
  identity, individual, 88, 107, 111
    influence of others on: judgment of, 89-92, 97, 108, 111
  love, 87, 95, 109
  marriage, 87, 100, 106, 111
  misunderstanding in, 88, 105, 110
  murder, 109
  narrator, 87, 88, 90, 106-7, 111
  samaritanism, 88, 94, 105
  sexuality, 87, 91, 94, 97, 99, 104, 108-11
  suicide, 94, 96, 99, 102-5
  victimization, 92, 98
  women, 88, 91, 93, 94, 98, 100-102
  words, impact of, 87, 98, 106, 107
Conrad, Jessie, 37, 140n12
Conrad, Joseph
  on betrayal, 59
  early works, 1
  family and, 37, 38, 62, 137n5, 141n32, 154n8
  novels, structure of, 6
    motivating forces in, 9
  on politics, 16, 23, 34, 40
  on women, 140n16, 143n13

Davis, Roderick, 140n15

Davidson, Arnold E., 138n18
Death, 21. *See also* listing under individual works
Dike, Donald, 114, 122, 123
Dostoevsky, Fyodor, 139n7

Family relationships, 137n1, 141n32. *See also* listing under individual works
Feminism. *See* women under individual works
Fleishman, Avrom, 141n28
Fradin, J.I., 138nn9,20

German, Howard, 132, 144n15
Gose, Elliott B., Jr., 137n7
Gosse, Edmund, 34
Gossip. *See* listing under individual works
Guerard, Albert, 9, 138n17, 140n9

Hagan, John Jr., 138n21
Hay, Eloise, 137n7, 139n6, 140n14
Heart of Darkness, 7
Hewitt, Douglas, 142n7
Howe, Irving, 137n7

Isolation. *See Chance, Under Western Eyes*

Jacobs, Robert G., 138n15

Kaehele, Sharon, 132, 144n15
Karl, Frederick, 37, 141n26, 142n8

Lord Jim, 1, 7, 61, 80
Love relationships. *See* listing under individual works

Marriage, 100, 106, 111, 143n19. *See also* listing under individual works
Material gain. *See* listing under individual works
Meyer, Bernard, 28, 37, 82, 88
Misunderstanding. *See* listing and silence under individual works
Moser, Thomas, 45, 140nn14,15

Narrator, 7. *See also* listing under individual works
Nostromo, 1, 3-5, 7, 9-35, 37, 41, 56, 59, 82, 85, 88, 90, 105, 114
   actions, effects of in, 9-10, 23, 135n5
   betrayal in, 32
   central themes of, 9, 37
   class distinctions in, 14, 28, 32-33
   death, 12, 14, 16, 23, 28, 29, 32-35
   difficulty of, 9
   family, 14, 15, 17-23, 26, 28
   futility, 23-26
   love, 10, 11, 20, 25, 33, 34
   material gain, evils of, 9, 11-12, 18, 32, 34
   narrator, 10, 11, 15-17, 21, 25
   politics, 9, 10, 37
   relationships, 10-14, 17-18, 34-35
   self-recognition, 27-28
   sexuality, 25, 35
   suicide, 23
   victimization, 23

Parent-child relationships. *See* family under individual works
Park, Douglas, 113-14, 133
Politics/political action
   Conrad on, 16, 23, 34, 40
   See also listing under individual works

Relationships
   breakdown of, 1, 2
   See also family; love; marriage; sexuality under individual works
Roussel, Royal, 142n6
Russia. *See Under Western Eyes*

Samaritanism, 7, 82, 88, 94, 105, 132
The Secret Agent, 1-7, 35, 37-57, 59, 68, 70, 82, 85, 88, 100, 106, 123
   betrayal in, 50-51
   central themes of, 37
   death, 42, 47, 49, 51-55, 61
   family, 37, 38, 49, 50
   marriage, 37, 44, 46, 47, 52
   murder, 42, 47, 49, 51-54, 61
   politics, 37, 39-43, 47
   sexuality, 43-45, 53-55
   silence, 53-54
   women, 38, 42-44, 46
   victimization, 42, 48, 55
Sentiment, destructive potential of. *See The Secret Agent*
Sexuality, 4. *See also* listing under individual works
Silence, 5. *See also* listing under individual works

Suicide, 143n20. *See also* listing under individual works

Typhoon, 13

Under Western Eyes, 1-2, 4-7, 56, 59-85, 87, 88, 109
   betrayal in, 59-60, 65, 72, 77, 80
   central themes of, 59, 81-83
   class distinctions in, 68-69, 78
   Conrad's initial plot, 61, 70, 71, 83
   death, 60, 62, 69, 73
   family, 59-60, 62-66, 72, 75, 82, 84
   isolation, 62, 63, 65, 67, 80
   love, 80, 83-85
   misunderstanding in, 63-65, 73
   murder, 60, 69
   narrator, 56, 60-61, 66, 68, 72, 79-80, 82, 85, 129n2, 141n20
   politics, 68-69, 74, 75, 85
   Russia, 59ff; as mother, 62-65; spirit of, 66-67
   sexuality, 66, 68-71, 75, 76, 85
   silence, 67, 75, 77, 82, 84
   suicide, 73, 78
   victimization, 66, 71, 83
   women, 66, 68, 69, 72, 75, 76, 141nn30,32, 142n35

Van Wagener, Donna, 140n14
Victory, 1-3, 5-7, 62, 82, 100, 113-33
   betrayal in, 113, 117, 128
   central theme of, 141n24
   class distinctions in, 118
   death, 123-32
   escapism, 114-17
   family, 113, 123, 127
   gossip, 6, 114-15, 126
   love, 118, 119, 122, 124, 128
   misunderstanding in, 116, 118, 120, 121, 127, 132
   narrator, 114-16
   reputation, 115
   sexuality, 119, 120, 122, 126, 128-30
   silence, 127
   victimization, 113
   violence, 128, 130
   women, 125, 130-31
Victimization, 4-5. *See also* listing under individual works

Women, 4, 5, 140n16, 141n22, 143n13. *See also* listing under individual works
Words, power of, 5, 6. *See also* listing; gossip; silence under individual works

Zabel, Morton, 139n5

OHIO UNIVERSITY LIBRARY